THE RETREATS
OF RECONSTRUCTION

RECONSTRUCTING AMERICA
Andrew L. Slap, series editor

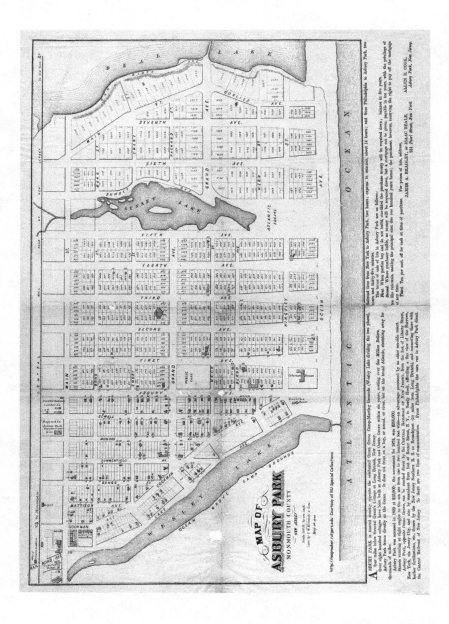

The Retreats
of Reconstruction

*Race, Leisure, and the Politics
of Segregation at the New
Jersey Shore, 1865–1920*

David E. Goldberg

FORDHAM UNIVERSITY PRESS
NEW YORK   2017

Frontispiece: Asbury Park, 1920. Courtesy of the Asbury Park Library.

Copyright © 2017 Fordham University Press

Library of Congress Cataloging-in-Publication Data

Names: Goldberg, David E., author.
Title: The retreats of Reconstruction : race, leisure, and the politics of
   segregation at the New Jersey shore, 1865–1920 / David E. Goldberg.
Description: First edition. | New York : Fordham University Press, 2016. |
   Series: Reconstructing America | Includes bibliographical references and
   index.
Identifiers: LCCN 2016013980 | ISBN 9780823272716 (cloth : alk. paper) | ISBN
   9780823272723 (pbk. : alk. paper)
Subjects: LCSH: Atlantic Coast (N.J.)—Race relations. | African
   Americans—New Jersey—Atlantic Coast—History. | Segregation—New
   Jersey—Atlantic Coast—History. | Racism—New Jersey—Atlantic
   Coast—History. | Atlantic Coast (N.J.)—History.
Classification: LCC F142.J4 G65 2016 | DDC 305.8009749—dc23
LC record available at https://lccn.loc.gov/2016013980

Printed in the United States of America

19 18 17   5 4 3 2 1

First edition

for my mother and father, Carla Hope and Michael Goldberg

Contents

Introduction

On July 23, 1893, an editorial in the *Philadelphia Inquirer* asked frustrated business owners and tourist promoters of Atlantic City "What are we going to do with our colored people?" Noting that "never before" had the resort community seemed "so overrun with the dark skinned race as this season," Atlantic City and other popular northern resort destinations struggled throughout the Reconstruction era to contain the recreational activities and consumer demands of black pleasure seekers. As these struggles reveal, contests over segregation were not restricted to former plantation districts, northern legislatures, the workplace, or public transportation systems. In the late nineteenth century, the popularity of the New Jersey shore coincided with growing concerns over civil rights. On beaches and boardwalks, and inside amusement venues and hotel dining halls, African Americans' claims for integrated leisure were imbedded in political debates over the meaning of race and the rights and health of consumers.[1]

For the northern white tourists who visited the beach resorts of the New Jersey coast, summer vacations were not just valuable moments away from work or idle time to spend with family and friends. In the aftermath of the Civil War, many working-class whites imagined the Jersey shore as a retreat from the sordid politics of the Gilded Age, the regimentation of industrial order, and the turmoil of black civil rights activism. To these aspiring men and women, summer trips to the seashore offered political opportunities to replace the pretentious social boundaries of antebellum-era resorts with an inclusive public sphere that allowed all white wageworkers—regardless of class status—a place to enjoy the "fruits of their labor." Writing for *Harper's New Monthly Magazine* in 1876, Olive Logan explained that the Jersey shore "has equal attraction for rich and poor." There is nothing exclusive," she proudly observed, "about any of the hotel bathing grounds." Stephen Crane, who visited the popular summertime resort of Asbury Park in the 1880s and 1890s, agreed, remarking that it was the "greatest summer resort of America—the vacation abode of the mighty middle class." At the same time, the promotion of the Jersey shore as a free labor utopia was dependent on the subservient labor of African Americans, who in taking care of the recreational needs of white guests reinforced to aspiring white tourists that they had secured their rightful place in a political economy built on the promise of social mobility. By the mid-1880s, however, northern whites increasingly encountered black workers who refused to be props in the popular culture landscape of these vacation fantasylands. Staking out their own claim to an expanding leisure marketplace, black seasonal workers demanded a racially integrated public sphere and their challenges threatened to discredit the social standing, racial identity, and escapist dreams of whites.[2]

Attending to the broader racial and economic dimensions of what one northern newspaper called "the vexatious bathing question," this book examines the political meanings of consumption and racial segregation in northern leisure spaces and the struggle for American Americans' civil rights during the late nineteenth and early twentieth century. Despite a large volume of works that focus on the history of race and the cultural politics of Jim Crow during the nineteenth century, we still have an incomplete understanding about how de facto segregation—as both a practice and an idea—was implemented and functioned in northern society. In his 1955 classic *The Strange Career of Jim Crow*, C. Vann Woodward famously remarked that "one of the strangest things" about the appearance of segregation was that "it was born in the North and reached an advanced age before moving to the South in force." Since then, historians who have written about the making of Jim Crow in the North have generally noted the powerful political vocabulary of "social equality," miscegenation, and the "wages of whiteness" in limiting more progressive civil rights initiatives during the Reconstruction period. Whiteness scholars have touted debates over public memory, cultural discussions of wage labor, and the impact of immigration and industrialization as powerful factors in shaping a dominant white supremacy. Other scholars whose research addresses the history of leisure and tourism have focused their attention on public amusements and other popular culture attractions to emphasize the pervasiveness of racial vigilantism in policing these popular nineteenth-century venues. Yet, despite the remarkable saliency of racism in the implementation and daily realities of segregation, whiteness alone did not make segregation at the Jersey shore. Rather, ideas about race and recreation were bound up in local debates about markets and conflicting interpretations about the rights and health of consumers.[3]

This book tells a different story about the making of segregation in the post–Civil War North by considering how competing notions of political economy, and not an all-encompassing white supremacy, framed racial politics in the postwar

North. In the immediate postwar period, white northerners made the promotion of free labor ideology the cornerstone of their Reconstruction agenda. Made
famous in the preceding decades by northern Republicans, free labor ideology
rested on the belief that under the contract system, all workers were entitled to
receive wages for their labor. Republicans' belief in the contract law reflected the
widely held conception of civil rights as the promotion of legal equality. Sensitive to the critiques of white working-class activists, northern Democrats, and
southern slave owners that the contract system was nothing more than coercive
legal cover to mask growing economic inequalities, northern Republicans vig-
orously championed the idea that both parties—laborers and capitalists—were
equal partners in a mutually beneficial economic arrangement. Thus, in contrast
to southern slavery, where no such relationship existed, Republicans insisted that
the freedom of contract provision of their free labor ideology aided the promise
of social mobility by incentivizing the industrious and frugal worker to one day
transcend his class position and attain property-owning independence.[4]

Throughout the late 1860s, belief in the supremacy of the free labor system
guided northern support for the 1866 Civil Rights Act and the Thirteenth, Fourteenth, and Fifteenth Amendments. With these political and legal rights secured,
white northerners expressed hope that African Americans would humbly accept
the promise of the free labor system and focus their energies toward economic
advancement. Yet, when black activists pushed to desegregate popular amusements in the early 1870s—efforts that eventually culminated in the passage of
the 1875 Civil Rights Act outlawing segregation in public accommodations—
many northern Republicans derided African Americans as enemies of free labor
who wished to escape their responsibilities as workers in order to use the federal
government to grant unmerited social privileges. As Eric Foner, David Quigley,
and Heather Cox Richardson have argued, a commitment to free labor ideology enabled white northerners to discredit the civil rights platform of Radical
Republicans and black political leaders without resorting to political violence or
racist rhetoric. As a result, white northerners derived comfort from their ability
to contain the presence of African Americans in social arenas not already desegregated by wartime emancipation and Reconstruction legislation.[5]

The Retreats of Reconstruction extends the plot of these important works by
analyzing the ways in which white and black northerners debated notions of
freedom and citizenship through the newly problematic meanings of consumption. Beginning in the 1880s, commercialized leisure options challenged long-
standing conceptions of political economy, forcing businessmen, politicians,
and marketing agents at the Jersey shore to confront a unique public setting that

defied common segregationist practices. Thus, while others have insisted that the mere presence of African Americans in public space produced segregation, this book charts how Jim Crow unfolded and operated in the post–Civil War North by emphasizing the importance of consumption and ideas about public health and welfare. The rise of mass consumption as a guiding principle of economic growth, and the debates about political economy that it spurred, intertwined with the ideologies that led to Jim Crow segregation at the Jersey shore.

In a society that had long been organized around production, whites and blacks offered competing definitions of what being a free consumer meant. White working-class tourists argued that the rights of consumers should be determined by a group's aggregate spending power and sought to persuade business owners that the only path toward peace and profits was through segregation. Black workers protested and boycotted whites' segregationist policies because of their own beliefs about consumption. In claiming their rights to integrated leisure, African Americans forced business owners and other public officials to decide whether the right to consume was equal to the right to work and the right to property. Did business have the right to exclude African American consumers on account of race, and if so, was the free labor defense capacious enough to justify the refusal of service without acknowledging racial prejudice?

In recent years, a growing body of literature has examined how nineteenth-century retailers and consumers challenged republican visions of a producer-oriented society. In their coverage of civil rights and suffrage campaigns, Lawrence Glickman, Blair Kelley, Margaret Finnegan, and Nan Enstad explain how consumer issues became central to black and female activists' workplace disputes. Yet, while most of these works champion the role of consumer activism in challenging exclusionary social and economic practices, the politics of mass consumption rarely provided an outlet for permanent racial integration. As Lizabeth Cohen points out in *A Consumers' Republic: The Politics of Mass Consumption in Postwar America*, campaigns for equal access to sites of consumption often limited the northern civil rights movement by preventing "alternatives that challenged more fundamentally the economic and cultural status quo." This outcome, however, was not confined to the twentieth century. Beginning in the late nineteenth century, the various consumer ideologies that emerged in battles over segregation at the Jersey shore proved every bit as powerful in limiting the scope of civil rights activism as free labor ideology and nineteenth-century white supremacy did. While African Americans used the claim of consumer rights and public health to contest Jim Crow, defend black-owned leisure districts, and push for environmental protections and public health, white northerners were able to withstand these political challenges and neutralize discussions about consumer rights by adopting a producer-driven vision of mass consumption that separated the right to consume from the right to integration. By the 1920s, freedom of property and freedom of profits replaced freedom of labor and freedom of contract as market-based correctives against civil rights agitation and institutional guides for promoting economic growth and maintaining Jim Crow.[6]

The New Jersey shore is an ideal setting to examine the consumer origins of Jim Crow because it attracted a variety of northern citizens—white and black— as well as some from the South, who regularly debated the rights and health of consumers and the legality of segregation during the Reconstruction era. As a result, I use the term "Reconstruction era" to signify the ongoing and unresolved civil rights debates between white and black northerners from the end of the Civil War to the formal institutionalization of Jim Crow in the late nineteenth and early twentieth century. The disputes over access to public and commercial leisure space at the Jersey shore—and the wide-ranging discussions about political economy that they provoked—proved that Reconstruction was not simply an event that ended with the political compromises of 1877, but an evolving process by which Americans continued to negotiate critical questions about the rights of consumers and producers in a unique social space where traditional distinctions between work and play were in flux.[7]

As John Sterngrass astutely observes, leisure settings offer rare opportunities to study otherwise repressed changes in society because visitors and local officials often feel "freer to challenge prevailing norms, exercise their fantasies, expand their horizons, and live their aspirations." Like other dominant forms of political economy, the ascendancy of mass consumption during the Reconstruction era altered Americans' sense of freedom and citizenship. For much of the nineteenth century, white northerners used the free labor defense to limit labor activism by appealing to the rights of producers and property owners. Yet, by actively promoting the social and economic merits of individual pleasure and mass consumption, merchants and boosters at the Jersey shore discredited notions of restraint, thrift, and obedience—enduring characteristics that defined Victorian culture and free labor ideology for much of the nineteenth century. In creating a more diversified marketplace, the architects of the Jersey shore helped facilitate the influence of consumer opinion that empowered consumers—regardless of race or class—to challenge the very rights of business to decide marketplace exchanges.[8]

In order to better understand the important role that consumer opinion played in the making of segregation, this book relies heavily on northern newspapers and promotional materials. Unlike other postwar northern communities during the Reconstruction era, the implementation and eradication of Jim Crow boundaries at the Jersey shore were not decided by state legislatures and local judges, or by retaining and enforcing antebellum-era racial customs. Instead, it was a cadre of businessmen, marketing agents, local politicians, white and black tourists, and working-class residents who used the northern press to share, contest, and manipulate local social boundaries. I draw on these sources to emphasize the importance of publicity in framing public debates involving race, space, and economic rights. In contrast to many large-scale industrial enterprises that withstood public scrutiny and ruinous headlines brought about by labor strife and political attacks, local businesses that operated in leisure districts were uniquely vulnerable to slanderous charges since their economic livelihoods depended directly on an appealing public profile that was free of social disorder. Aware of the potential that negative publicity could play in swaying consumer activity and shaping public policy, white and black northerners came to view the press as both an asset and adversary in the fight against segregation. In assessing the political and social impact of these print mediums, I stress the importance of these sources not simply to emphasize events as they actually happened, but to analyze how local merchants, consumers, and workers used them as a political weapon to shape public debates and influence future social boundaries.[9]

The contentious political and social motives of each of these constituencies made it difficult to ensure a uniform segregation policy while also maintaining the peaceful profile of a summer resort. Under pressure from white tourists to respond to their appeals for segregation, and from black workers who pressed for unlimited consumer rights, local authorities initially adopted a variety of temporary and informal measures to maintain the legitimacy of free labor principles and to forestall more drastic racial policies. Some, like Asbury Park mayor and founding father James Bradley, attempted to contain racial tensions and avoid interruptions to business by instituting "clock-time segregation," a move that asked black workers to postpone their leisure time on area boardwalks until after 10:30 p.m. Others responded to appeals to harden segregation laws by asking black tourists to accept "seasonal segregation," inviting them to visit popular resorts like Atlantic City at the end of the summer season when other working-class northerners vacationed. To defend these requests, local merchants and public officials brushed off racial tensions as rare incidents in an otherwise resplendent free labor vacation setting, recreational sites where middle-class whites could retreat from the monotony of everyday work and black workers happily served them.

African Americans challenged these moves by arguing that the right to consume was equal to the right to labor. In calling for a free consumer society, they
remarked that efforts by whites to shroud their segregation policies in market-
based language only reified the hierarchy of race in the late nineteenth century. In a political rally held in Asbury Park in 1887, the Reverend John Frances
Robinson exclaimed, "The Colored man now has the same consumer rights as
the white man, including the right to walk on the beach of Asbury Park." To those
who joined Reverend Robinson in protesting segregation, such pronouncements
spearheaded their attempts to reframe the economic rights of consumers and to
protect the common law tradition. For much of the nation's early history, Americans subscribed to the common law belief that the right of business to earn a
profit did not absolve it from engaging in behavior that threatened the conduct
or welfare of the public. As such, many local statutes and public accommodations
laws restricted the rights of property owners in order to protect travelers, lodgers,
and patrons from being exploited by unscrupulous and greedy proprietors. While
previous common law statutes applied only to white patrons, African Americans
successfully employed the common law defense throughout the Civil War era to
desegregate public transportations systems in Philadelphia, Washington, D.C.,
and New York City. During the 1880s, black protestors at the Jersey shore fought
to extend the common law to recreational venues as well. Exploiting class divisions between white tourists and white business owners, black protesters staged
a series of consumer protests on boardwalks, inside hotel dining rooms, and in
front of amusement venues that denied them entry, actions that helped to secure
them readmission to public space and access to a world of goods.[10]

Black workers successfully integrated these spaces because they circumvented
the segregation debate, trading a hostile political vocabulary—"social equality"—
for one focused on consumer rights. In doing so, they exploited the political
anxieties northern politicians and business owners held regarding race and free
labor ideology after the Civil War. As the early struggle to define segregation at
the Jersey shore proved, the postwar politics of Jim Crow required that white
officials honor and protect the emancipationist legacy of Union victory and the
accompanying triumph of free labor ideology by regionalizing race as a southern
problem. The unwillingness of many white tourists to enjoy their leisure alongside African Americans forced business owners and politicians to adopt an un-
popular and unsuccessful middle ground when it came to segregation notices.
Yet, in acknowledging the consumer-based complaints of black protestors, they
exposed their inability to control the postwar marketplace by appealing to free
labor principles. As merchants and boosters touted Jersey shore beach towns as

bastions of middle-class social mobility, black workers and patrons who sought
entry to the array of amusement venues and public leisure spaces highlighted the
racist regulations that restricted opportunities to enjoy the "fruits of their labor."
Highly adept at reading the hidden transcripts of Jim Crow, African Americans
cleverly ignored and evaded unofficial public notices that they believed lacked au-
thoritative consent. In adopting an informal tone of polite appeals and respectful
pleas, local white authorities advertised the illegitimacy of their requests. Their
guarded hesitancy to adopt more stringent polices and the boldness of African
American protests remind us that an emphasis on white supremacy and official
public notices often obscure more intricate maneuverings of a color line that was
rarely so black and white.[11]

Beginning in 1893, however, a variety of factors worked to limit and contain
future desegregation efforts. In particular, the local business class abandoned
free labor ideology in their defense of segregation and instead appealed to a
producer-driven vision of mass consumption that sought to tie future economic
growth to Jim Crow. As a policy referendum on consumer rights and market
principles, Jersey shore segregationists argued that Jim Crow boundaries were
permissible in a service economy because they protected the property rights of
business owners and defended the public welfare against disruptive consumer
protesters who threatened to undermine the economic prosperity and social
preferences of others. Defenders of Asbury Park's recently segregated bathing
facilities proclaimed that segregation was implemented not to harass black patrons, but to protect instead the financial welfare of business owners from "colored people who are doing their utmost to ring the projector and patrons of
that resort into odium contempt." Justifying James Bradley's policies later that
summer, correspondents for the *New York Times* echoed the town's sentiments,
explaining that "Mr. Bradley has had so much to do with the growth of Asbury
Park" that his "interests in it and his stake in its prosperity are at all events much
larger than those of anybody else."[12]

The philosophical consensus that emerged from these Jim Crow contests
highlights the origins of a subtler—yet no less enduring—strand of racism that
grew out of the everyday concerns of business owners and local boosters. During
the 1880s and 1890s, an increased faith in the consumer marketplace replaced a
waning faith in racist rhetoric and free labor ideology to police black behavior.
In rebranding Jim Crow as a product of market forces, commentators and local
officials embraced this change as a contrast to an older racism that was direct,
visceral, and easily recognizable. To sanction these changes within an existing
market order, local business owners reworked nineteenth-century ideas about

the common law that historically subordinated the property rights and profit motives of businessmen to the public's welfare. As consumer growth became synonymous with economic freedom in the late nineteenth century, the need to protect citizens and travelers from profit-seeking schemers became less important. Instead, Jersey shore segregationists marketed a reworked common law tradition as a pro-business and race-neutral solution to the complicated web of interests groups that composed a mass consumer society. The adoption of this new strategy gave them confidence that in future segregation debates, the need to protect the profitability of popular leisure spaces from black consumer activists would be equal to ensuring the common good. This story is familiar to scholars of the post–World War II civil rights era, when consumer protests moved to the center of America's political economy. Yet, as early as the 1890s, northern whites were working hard to disassociate business decisions from personal opinions in a leisure industry that embraced a consumer-based model of economic growth far sooner than the rest of the nation.[13]

In response to these changes, many black civic leaders, entrepreneurs, and investors raised doubts about the practicality and sustainability of civil disobedience. Between 1900 and 1920, they called on black workers and tourists to protect their right to consume by boycotting the region's white-owned leisure marketplaces. In boycotting Jim Crow, black capitalists helped build a thoroughfare of hotels, shops, and cheap amusements to meet the housing, labor, and social demands of black consumers. Yet, by adopting the producer-driven vision of mass consumption championed by white segregationists, many African American leaders moved away from the formal claim of integrated leisure that an earlier coalition of black workers employed to successfully contest Jim Crow. After subsequent vice raids and congressional hearings touted the immorality of black leisure and consumption and threatened the profits of black entrepreneurs, black business owners and community leaders often retreated from white beaches and consumer districts in order to defend their own recreational venues from the intrusions of law enforcement and other local saboteurs.

By redirecting their formal complaints against segregated leisure toward intraracial leisure-based ventures, local black business interests displayed the importance of class and the powerful appeal of consumer growth and property ownership to the evolving formation and maintenance of Jim Crow. Within the white and black community, class tensions both confounded and assisted segregationist practices. In the 1880s and early 1890s, black working-class activists successfully contested segregated leisure by exploiting class divisions between whites business owners and white tourists. Their insistence that the right to consume was equal to the right to integrate recast free labor notions of political economy and helped facilitate an expanding vision of economic freedom that delayed the retreat from the nation's controversial 1875 Civil Rights Act. However, later decisions by black entrepreneurs to boycott white marketplaces and protect black-owned consumer districts prevented many black workers—the leading participants in earlier civil rights demonstrations—from mounting formal attacks against Jim Crow.

The Retreats of Reconstruction thus joins a growing number of civil rights histories that emphasize the ways in which a shared commitment among black and white elites to property ownership and consumer-based capital acquisition forestalled desegregation efforts and prolonged Jim Crow. For many black capitalists, claiming their rights as citizens meant not only gaining equal access to sites of consumption—as many black workers during the 1880s claimed—but also transforming leisure space into real estate. The historian Nathan Connolly points out that "as personally edifying as everyday forms of resistance could be . . . the exigencies of property ownership created an equally quotidian and arguably more potent power that many colored people were up against and after: infrastructural power." For many black northerners who were regularly relegated to domestic-style work within the Jersey shore's service economy, the right to attain and to maintain coastal real estate property provided those with the financial means with an alternative vision of civil rights in the face of a constantly evolving Jim Crow system.[14]

In the years that followed, efforts by black capitalists to hold their property became increasingly tied to new discussions about the moral and physical health of consumer districts. As the definitions and uses of consumption took on new forms at the turn of the century, the local black business community worked to secure their commercial enterprises against white moral reformers intent on indicting black consumer culture, and against environmental threats and municipal deficiencies that threatened the value and health of their properties. To maintain legal claim over their businesses and to enhance the environmental health of their commercial spaces, black capitalists and local residents lobbied for and against government intervention. In Atlantic City, black business owners cooperated with white Republican Party officials to thwart efforts by state investigators and local Democrats to regulate business activity. Elsewhere, black community leaders lobbied on behalf of government intervention to relieve black property owners from the environmental inequalities and municipal deficiencies that plagued their consumer districts. Confronted with the environmental and economic consequences of a separate but *unequal* color line that threatened the health of black residents and white consumers, and forestalled commercial growth for white developers, white and black property holders in Asbury Park lobbied local authorities to "clean up" Jim Crow by annexing and regulating black homes and businesses. Yet, like so many other mixed outcomes during the Jim Crow era, the effort by local blacks to straddle the line between black autonomy and interracial cooperation hindered long-range efforts to desegregate public and private leisure space. Instead, the incorporation and increased surveillance of black consumer and residential districts ensured the potency of a new consumer movement that narrowed the definition of civil rights as the white and black propertied classes linked the public health of consumers and consumer districts to political stability and future commercial growth.[15]

By the 1920s, the solidification of consumption as a political goal marked not the triumph of civil rights agitation and racial integration, but instead the institutionalization of consumer protection, public health, and economic independence, as white developers, politicians, and business leaders retreated from plans to control black marketplaces and conceded to demands for municipal improvements and environmental reform, in exchange for an end to civil disobedience, consumer activism, and party loyalty. In the years that followed, the African American business class increasingly gravitated toward the position that protecting their right to consume was more important than fighting for integrated leisure. While many African Americans still claimed the right to leisure and free consumption, the vision they constructed to obtain and protect these rights was recast within the developing political vocabulary of "separate but equal" that assumed national prominence in America's segregation debate following the Supreme Court's 1896 *Plessy v. Ferguson* decision.

More than simply a struggle for leisure, the making of segregation at the New Jersey shore reveals the promise and limits of consumption as an economic philosophy for deep-seated social change. Jim Crow survived because, just as free labor ideology once had, the idea of mass consumption became a universal language that justified a range of conflicting public policy choices, social practices, and cultural meanings. The ideas and practices that resulted from these debates became an important part of the larger story of how segregated leisure was implemented and retained as white and black northerners fought to shape new competing consumer-based approaches to political economy after the Civil War.

1   Reconstructing Jim Crow

In the summer of 1890, a reporter for the *Philadelphia Times* dispatched to Atlantic City interviewed white tourists about ongoing racial tensions publicized in the local press. Describing the insistence of many working-class blacks to demand admission to commercial leisure spaces, one white visitor echoed the sentiments of many in the beach town when he explained that while black workers often responded, "Alright, boss," when told "you can't sit here," when it came to removing themselves from amusement rides and other consumer venues "they draw the line at the flying horses . . . If the flying horse goes they go on it, much to the disgust of the would-be exclusive patron." With this statement, the white tourist expressed a common political complaint about the ambiguities of social space and economic rights in Reconstruction-era leisure settings. For much of the nineteenth century, racial disputes over access to public accommodations were often solved through violence, popular minstrelsy, and the politics of free labor, strategies and tactics that by 1877 had enabled white northerners to successfully contain the recreational and consumer behavior of African Americans. But beginning in the 1880s, the decision by black workers to demand access to public and commercial leisure spaces, and disputes among whites over how to stop them, unsettled long-standing northern segregation practices and exposed the fragility of racial solidarity and the limits of free labor ideology in a consumer-driven economy.[1]

The development of the Jersey shore for commercial and recreational use in the late nineteenth century paralleled the rise of mass consumption and the implementation of Jim Crow. Yet, as the early battles between white tourists, black workers, and business owners would prove, the politics of segregation in these vacation settings went beyond simple racism. The increased racial hostility also pointed to the changing social demographics of white crowds, the political and economic insecurities of white business owners, and the advent of consumer opinion in challenging free labor principles. Throughout the Reconstruction era, campaigns for "eight hours for what we will," improvements in modern travel, and the promotion of beach resorts as middle-class retreats brought a new wave of white tourists to northern vacation settings. In response to the appearances and actions of black workers, white tourists attempted to evoke their power as consumers to shape public policy by calling on local authorities to officially institute segregation. Yet, to their surprise, the local business class often ignored their demands for segregation by refusing to engage white tourists and black workers in their disputes, a decision they believed would protect traditional social boundaries, retain the faithful services of black workers, and maintain the appearance of a free labor retreat.

Despite their desire to remain neutral, business could not ignore the increasingly problematic political power of consumer opinion in shaping segregation in the post–Civil War North. Unsure of how to employ the new racial language of the Reconstruction era in their promotional literature, in editorials, or on early segregation signs, local merchants and tourist promoters often ignored the charges of black impropriety and tolerated a limited African American presence on area boardwalks and beaches and inside amusement venues. Yet, to both black and white consumers, their refusal to promote either full integration or official segregation was viewed as sign of political weakness and came to reflect a postwar period where enforcement of the color line often appeared confused and unmanageable. In response, white and black consumers battled with one another and with local authorities in promotional brochures, pamphlets, and editorials to define the ideological and spatial boundaries of public and consumer leisure space. By failing to offer a coherent and consistent segregation strategy, business owners let local public policies fall victim to the volatile and shape-shifting whims of consumer opinion. It was against this unstable political backdrop that competing consumer and leisure discourses emerged and a new segregation debate took shape at the Jersey shore after the Civil War.[2]

In the summer of 1848, Rebecca Sharp accompanied her friend Henrietta Roberts for a weeklong excursion to Cape May, New Jersey, a popular beach town frequented by Philadelphia's cultural elite. Like many antebellum-era contemporaries, Sharp and Roberts were part of a Victorian class of northern Americans— socialites, financiers, and merchants—who sought to escape the North's raucous urban recreational spaces frequented by working-class patrons. Writing in her diary as they waited to depart, Sharp noted that the two of them would use their time at the shore to "stroll on the beach with a congenial spirit" and to "drink the sublimities of nature." Come nighttime, they would "call on a social visitor for a midnight walk" or take a carriage ride to one of the many outdoor cottage parties. Sharp's itinerary was a common one for well-to-do northerners, who used summer vacations to commune and relax with Victorian contemporaries in dining halls, outdoor verandas and hotel parlors and along promenades. In this noncommercial world of coastal bathing and public recreation, tourists and observers used summertime visits to beach resorts to remark on and bask in the free labor promise of social mobility, while scorning frivolous consumption and crude behavior.[3]

In contrast to other social arenas in the pre–Civil War North, patrons and onlookers marveled at the coastline's remarkable ability to dissolve class boundaries. In the presence of the Atlantic Ocean, one observer explained, "human beings do not appear great" as "the garments in which they are attired are not designed to set off beauty." Instead, as Frederika Bremer remarked upon visiting Cape May in 1850, "carriages and horses drive out into the waves, gentleman rise into them, dogs swim about, white and black people, horses and carriages, and ladies—all are there, one among another." Such an idyllic scene she concluded, created a uniquely northern "republic among the billows, more equal and more fraternized than any upon dry land." Olive Logan, who visited the popular beach resort of Long Branch, New Jersey, also admired the striving spirit and entrepreneurial vitality of the Jersey shore's supposedly free labor utopia. Marveling at

"The Beach at Long Branch." *Appleton's Journal*, 1869.

the foresight of businessmen to harness the powers of the sea for public recreation and economic gain, Logan exclaimed, "Long Branch illustrates a side of the American character that is a direct result of business energy, enterprise, shrewdness, and push."[4]

Despite the testimonials of Bremer and Logan, antebellum resorts were notorious for their social exclusivity, keeping out unwanted and unseemly working-class excursionists, new immigrants, and free black workers. Thus, while the untamed waters of the seashore enforced a rough equality, off the beach, social status and class distinctions prevailed. *Frank Leslie's Illustrated Newspaper* described the scene on a crowded promenade in Long Branch as one littered with "portly merchants, fresh from Wall Street and Broadway," accompanied by "pretty girls in a halo of French rosebloods and kid gloves," basking in the comforts of the "old fashion social style." During the dinner hour, these gentleman and ladies would dine together in grand hotel ballrooms as a "regiment of forty negroes" marched in and out in perfect syncopation. As black waiters filled glasses, delivered meals, and cleared dishes, white patrons joked about innkeepers rubbing the dirt off the faces of white guests to "see whether they were serving Negroes by mistake," utterances which reinforced the commonly held racial exclusions that defined Victorian leisure in the years before the Civil War.[5]

"Steamboat Landing." *Frank Leslie's Illustrated Newspaper*, August 23, 1879.

Yet, while northern elites sought to limit access for working-class whites and black seasonal laborers, businessmen and merchants increasingly sought to extend the public sphere to an evolving white middle-class clientele during the 1850s. Saloons, ice cream parlors, dancing halls, billiard rooms, and horse-drawn racing competitions enticed summer guests who were no longer "interested in taking in waters" as their preferred recreational outlet. By the eve of the Civil War, these commercial changes to the seashore's built environment spurred new conversations about access to public leisure spaces. As northern citizens coped with disruptions to the economy and the family, and struggled to understand draft riots and civil rights protests brought about by the Civil War, local commentators also debated who should use, control, work, and enjoy popular tourist sites. Following a financially sluggish tourist season in 1861, the *New York Herald* noted that "war like time, tries all things, and it has tried the watering places pretty severely." While some observers optimistically reassured resort owners and businesses that "even civil war admits the possibility of people enjoying themselves," others were less hopeful. "We are afraid," some declared in June 1861, "this season will not be a very extensive or profitable one."[6]

Shapers of northern popular opinion used the economic disruption of the early war years to transform the social profile and business practices of summer resort communities. "This war of ours," the *Herald* declared, "is to revolutionize politics and politicians, to make the government stronger, to make the nation greater; to make business better and better conducted; to make us all more economical, prudent and steady—why may it not revolutionize fashion also?" For conservative northern critics, the specter of civil war provided an opportunity to correct the abuses by landlords that, according to one editorialist, ran "riot at watering place hotels." Throughout the mid-nineteenth century, cultural critics complained that many popular vacation sites had increasingly abandoned the democratic spirit of the times by surrendering the "people's welfare" to profit, charging exorbitant rates that failed to correspond to the increasing income inequality of the Jacksonian age. In particular, critics complained about the social climate of northern watering places that linked higher admission rates to the growing and pretentious "scepter of fashion" that forced "Jones to go because Smith went, and not because he liked it." In its wake, many northerners hoped that the "rule of as your neighbors do" would be replaced with the "rule of as you like."[7]

Efforts by cultural critics to strip northern beach resorts of antebellum-era social pretensions underscored efforts to remake the relationship between producers and consumers. Many hoped that consumer opinion, rather than the rules of free labor ideology and Victorian culture, would dictate personal enjoyment, social behavior, and rights of entry. Indeed, as unique social spaces, beach resorts challenged the critical principles of the free labor system. Throughout the early nineteenth century, northern intellectuals and Republican Party officials championed the regimentation of the industrial system and the promise of the wage labor contract as requirements for economic growth and personal freedom. In this producer-driven political economy, capitalists argued that great wealth derived from increased production, rather than the promotion of mass consumption. A holdover from an earlier republican ideal that scorned a political economy built on consumer luxuries, seaside resorts challenged these principles by equating mobility with pleasure, entertainment, and a "release from the conventional city life."[8]

From the outset, Victorian skeptics warned northern travelers and politicians that the freewheeling spirit of watering places undercut free labor's insistence on social restraint and frugality. Jersey shore promotional agents challenged these warnings by insisting that public recreation was necessary "for the man who has been caged for months in an office, reduced to a mere machine run for the purpose of churning out so many dollars per diem." Yet, for conservative social critics, it was not just that vacations threatened to undermine the free labor work ethic, but that they also enticed normally responsible men and women to relinquish hard-earned savings on cheap amusements that they might of otherwise saved for future entrepreneurial endeavors. For a time, some critics were pleased that the Civil War unleashed a growing public distain toward fashionable resorts like Saratoga Springs and Cape May, which seemed deserted as northern vacationers chose "retired spots along the coast" or in rustic outdoor retreats. "Fashion has succumbed to mars. The War has revolutionized the watering places," the *Herald* gleefully declared on August 23, 1863. "The war, which is reforming the manners, the dress, the society, the commerce, and the manufacturers, has reformed the fashionable also," elevating the "healthful retreat" to a place of cultural prominence, while downgrading the preference for "artificial, enervating, corrupting" influences of northern watering places.[9]

By August 1863, the optimism of the previous summer faded as northern conservatives began to blame displays of fashionable elitism on abolitionists and black domestic workers. As northern whites confronted the national ramifications of emancipation, debates about class shifted to questions about the place of African Americans in leisure spaces. According to several white patrons, black domestic workers were beginning to use wartime emancipation as a pretext to harass white tourists, negotiate larger gratuities from summer guests, and enjoy their leisure time alongside white patrons. While many northerners came to accept leisure time as necessary for the physical and mental health of white wageworkers, they scoffed at the notion of extending such luxuries to black workers. As a result, conflicts over race and leisure in Civil War–era vacation settings contributed to the evolving historical debate about how to characterize black recreational behavior in northern popular culture. In marking black leisure workers as objects of fear and social disruption rather than amusement and comic relief, white northerners reconfigured the racial dynamics of public amusements during the Civil War. During the revolutionary era, theatrical depictions of the master-slave relationship were often violent and antagonistic. By the 1830s and 1840s, public depictions of African Americans' recreational behavior and consumer habits shifted as promoters of mass culture and working-class audiences dealt with changes wrought by gradual emancipation, industrialization, and immigration. Minstrel shows, carnivalesque comedies, and traveling exhibits portrayed free blacks on stage, as well as in political cartoons and artistic essays, as social inferiors, whose bodies, movements, dialect, and cultural expressions represented a juvenile race that was to be mimicked, parodied, and pitied. These theatrical representations provided a retreat from the partisan politics of the Jacksonian age and the exploitation of wage labor, enabling a divided working-class community to unite around the cultural authority of "whiteness" by lampooning "blackness."[10]

In their everyday encounters with whites, African Americans who participated in recreational outings received a much more hostile reception than black performers did inside minstrel theaters. In many antebellum northern cities, African Americans were routinely the victims of savage attacks from white gangs who viewed black leisure activities as a political reminder of the future of race relations during the era of gradual emancipation. More than perhaps other northern public venues, leisure spaces became violent battlegrounds where whites and blacks routinely squared off, proving that while popular culture representations of blackness promoted a narrative of subservience, the politics of the marketplace signaled that whites viewed black intrusions into entertainment districts as a serious public danger to be solved by violent force.

Such was the case in Philadelphia in 1828 when black couples emerged from coaches to a mob of angry whites who attacked a handful of the black women, stabbing their dresses with knives and shoving their dates into nearby gutters, while others frantically attempted to make their way into the night's feature event—a subscription ball for the city's black elite. Six years later, white gangs attacked local black residents attempting to ride a city carousel. Throwing stones at black riders and demolishing the "flying horses," local whites expanded their assaults to surrounding black communities, marching down city streets with clubs, stoning black couples out for an evening walk, and attacking the homes and churches of other black property owners with clubs and "brickbats" in a campaign one rioter described as "hunting nigs." Before city officials could contain the assaults, many black residents fought back, defending their properties and their right to enjoy area leisure venues in a three-day riot that exposed the seriousness with which many ordinary whites approached black recreation. In an era in which the fate of whiteness was tied to the defense of slavery in the South, whites also viewed black leisure as a growing affront to the widening economic divisions within the burgeoning free labor society. Relating the events of the era, Philadelphia's popular press cautioned northern whites to be vigilant in maintaining clear divisions between workers and consumers. "How long will it be," the *Pennsylvania Gazette and Democratic Press* asked, before "masters and servants change places?"[11]

Whites' violent punishment of blacks' leisure activities during the antebellum era shifted as popular culture representations of African Americans evolved during the Civil War. Northern periodicals, political cartoons, and short stories each attempted to depict the anxieties of the northern mind toward the changing status of black Americans. While a variety of antebellum-era racial stereotypes permeated these artistic depictions, the war years also witnessed profound adjustments in the ways many northern whites viewed African Americans. Ideas on racial injustice were transformed as Union soldiers infiltrated the southern interior and black soldiers were proven to be capable and courageous defenders of their freedom. And for the first time, wartime literature moderated the popular image of "Sambo" by highlighting the courage of black soldiers.[12]

Yet, to many whites, acknowledging the accomplishments of black soldiers was much different from relaxing social standards and racial restrictions at leisure sites. After emancipation, whites used racial imagery not to amuse white audiences, but to warn them about the dangers of black civil rights intruding into spaces of leisure and consumption. As many northern critics charged, wartime emancipation allowed black waiters to preside over "ill-kept tables," while allowing others access to "gun contracts, ship charters, and government jobs." An editorialist at Saratoga Springs angrily noted that the "black waiters, who levy black mail upon all guests, must be taught to do their duty without the stimulus of extra postage," unless white business owners desire to see their watering places succumb to the "perpetual swindle" of black domestics. Threatening landlords to either "make a reform in these matters" or face public scrutiny, northern critics observed that the "carelessness of their blackamoors is one of the many pernicious results of the emancipation proclamation." To preserve the "future welfare and conduct of the nation—to say nothing of the comfort of ladies and success" of the summer vacation season—many white tourists lectured northern proprietors to instill harsher discipline on their black waitstaff and to initiate a more "thorough reform in the management of the watering place hotels." If prices were to remain high, many white northern critics promised that "the public will not be satisfied" unless black workers were to be reassigned to their "proper place" in leisure districts.[13]

In making the link between economic prosperity and the campaign for integrated leisure, editorialists reassured the northern public that the "abolitionists and shoddy contractors" who presided over the degradation of leisure by promoting the hubris of black domestic workers would soon find themselves in the "deluge" of 1865, when the summer season would be "far more delightful than that of 1864." However, by the end of the Civil War, neither the desired egalitarianism of 1861 and 1862 nor the promise of retribution and Jim Crow came to the leisure destinations of Saratoga, Sharon Springs, Niagara, or Newport. Although each of these resorts resumed their popularity after the Civil War, the developing beach communities of the New Jersey shore quickly outpaced them.

Like another popular creation of the American imagination, the "Wild West," the Jersey shore appealed to fatigued Victorians and striving white middle-class wage earners as a refuge from the physical and political congestion of the urban metropolis. Offering sunny beaches, cheap amusements, and an endless array of boardwalk shops, the beach communities of the Jersey shore became an ideal distraction for a war-weary nation eager to retreat to a futuristic and pleasurable realm where time seemed to be suspended after decades of sectional conflict, political struggles over black civil rights, and unending labor strife. The attraction of towns like Asbury Park and Atlantic City as futuristic fantasylands allowed local merchants and officials the luxury of historical distance, freeing these "founders" from the contentious racial politics and class stigmas attached to older northern vacation spots. By the time the creators of the Jersey shore began envisioning places like Asbury Park and Atlantic City in the 1870s and 1880s, they were free to explore and create from barren beaches and untapped shorelines social visions of their own, spaces which sought to blend the environmental with the cosmopolitan, the egalitarian with the hierarchical, revivalism with consumerism.[14]

Few businessmen shared the relentless social vision of Asbury Park's founding father, James A. Bradley, a brush manufacturer from New York City who saw potential in the untapped land along the Monmouth County coast in the late

1860s. Seeking a spiritual and rehabilitative escape from his urban environment, James Bradley arrived in the small Methodist shore community of Ocean Grove in 1869 with his black servant, John A. Baker. After consulting with the town's treasurer, David H. Brown, who pointed Bradley toward an unsettled section of land, Bradley and Baker proceeded to travel through a wilderness of shore brush that grew on the uninhabited beaches. Reaching the water's edge and "desiring a bath," Bradley stripped off his clothes and eagerly advised his reluctant companion to do the same and join him in the sand of the cool evening surf. A devout Methodist, Bradley explained that he found the cool waters of the Jersey surf to be "the best nervine for a man who is not absolutely past repair," and who "desires to break away from his calling or greed and camp out in the sea shore." After Baker eventually joined him by his side, Bradley recounted in a later local history of Asbury Park that he found the exercise reminiscent of "Robinson Crusoe by his man Friday," a place he intimated where both whites and blacks could peacefully seek refuge together.[15]

Bradley's local history of Asbury Park reflected the desire of northern business leaders and tourist promoters to fashion a postwar resort industry that shielded tourists from the civil rights agitation and social disorder of Reconstruction. Concluding his personal story with the description of co-racial bathing enabled Bradley and other white northerners to retain the humanitarian legacy of the Civil War while containing potential complaints from northern black tourists for greater access to leisure time and space. Bradley's local history also revealed the cultural strategies business leaders and tourist promoters increasingly undertook to appeal to a greater variety of summer guests. By the late nineteenth century, northern businessmen could no longer rely on the natural beauty and physical landscape of the seashore to sell itself to striving middle-class tourists and consumers eager to spend their leisure time in places that provided entertainment and cheap amusements.[16]

Over the next two decades, merchants and local officials set about transforming the physical and social geography of the Jersey shore. In the process, they discredited the free labor political economy and accompanying Victorian culture that prized economic restraint as requirements for social mobility. Instead, they directed patrons to the endless array of shops, penny arcades, thrill rides, peep shows, and vaudeville acts that littered the beachfront promenades. Whereas antebellum-era tourists used the promenades for noncommercial socializing, postwar merchants remade the public platforms into the marquee arena for purchasing pleasure. During his first visit to Atlantic City, James Hannay recorded in his diary that "a pier makes an irresistible appeal to the pleasure-seeker." Outside the normal rhythms of home life, "the impulse to buy things is irresistible." Beachgoers would "eat ice cream on a pier," Hannay remarked, "than in an ordinary shop, though he has to pay more for it." No impulse was more alluring, though, than the draw of the postcards. "I found it very hard to pass any of them without buying," Hannay shamelessly noted, and even though "they would probably be no use whatsoever when we got them home, if we had enough money, we bought them."[17]

In Asbury Park, James Bradley initially attempted to curb rampant consumerism and illicit amusements by restricting the sale of boardwalk property. Unlike many resort communities that were littered with private mansions and stately cottages, lots along the boardwalk and on Asbury Park's main thoroughfare, Ocean Avenue, were leased rather than sold. By refusing to sell these territories, Bradley attempted to maintain his rule over those tenants who might be prone to oppose the founder's temperance policies. Yet, rather than restrain consumption, by excluding the sale of residential property on Asbury's beachfront and by setting the city's hotels, boardinghouses, and cottages back off the beach, the area's ensuing development as a commercial thoroughfare of recreational attractions— replicated on an even grander scale in Atlantic City—helped reimagine northern beach resorts as a place to purchase pleasure.

Up and down the beach piers, tourists in Bradley's thriving resort and elsewhere were lured by an array of cheap amusements and knickknacks. Some of the wilder attractions were even arranged and constructed by Bradley himself. Animal cages, old boats, and oversized household items like stoves and marble tubs were placed along the edge of the sand. However, as "queer and extraordinary" as these sights were to the curious tourist, it was the exotic items being sold by the region's "foreign" merchants that often attracted his guests. "Hindu Fakirs" peddled Indian goods, silk handkerchiefs, and embroidered petticoats. Elsewhere, cinematograph shows, marionette theaters, conjuring booths, and Ferris wheels enticed thrill seekers and those seeking exotic entertainment.[18]

However, as merchants and boosters peddled an increasingly consumer-driven political economy, they retained faith in the promise of free labor principles to control and mediate social behavior. As with their antebellum-era predecessors, the stories that proprietors, boosters, and politicians told and sold in their promotional literature reflected the class divisions many resort owners sought to close and the racial history they sought to forget as they attempted to shape and mold consumer opinion and control public policy. By seeking to attract a diverse pool of northern citizens through the allure of both rehabilitative and consumer enticements, the local business community crafted an array of historical narratives designed to sell as well as mediate the social performances and consumer habits they sought to cultivate from summer travelers.[19]

In designing and selling their resorts to prospective tourists, local boosters reached out to a variety of important print culture markets. Asbury Park and Atlantic City each published multiple periodicals and pamphlets that sought to advise and council visitors on the cultural experience they were to expect and the social rules they were to follow while on vacation. Northern newspapers such as the *New York Times*, the *New York Herald*, the *Philadelphia Inquirer*, and the *Baltimore Sun* assisted the marketing strategies of the business community by listing the region's elite citizens who spent their summer at the seashore. In addition, marketing agents adopted promotional tactics initiated by many New England communities, who published local histories that announced a physical and social environment dedicated to overcoming the confusing social world and racial history of their own recent past. These Reconstruction-era retreats spoke of a racial past that was to be forgotten, while also insisting on a future in which social behavior, rather than race, would set the markers of citizenship rights in leisure spaces.[20]

Atlantic City's proprietors narrated these visions in a variety of tourist litera-ture disseminated to the northern public during the Reconstruction period. Un-like the traditionally elite communities of Saratoga Springs or Cape May, Atlantic City's business class hoped to cater to a variety of white northern tourists during the summer months. Describing the South Jersey resort as the "City of Homes by the Seaside" in hopes of luring in the region's "better elements," the Camden and Railroad *Annual Report* of 1873 also boasted that the region hoped to convince aspiring "subordinates in their shirtsleeves" to enjoy the "quiet home-like atmo-sphere of the place." The success created by these marketing campaigns enabled Atlantic City to proclaim in 1885 that its resort town created the only community of its kind whose success depended "mainly to the unacknowledged distinctions of class in society." Its official guidebook boasted that in comparison to other rival communities, Atlantic City's residents, "the rich and the poor, the healthy and the invalid[,] are equally well received." Indeed, "such a conglomeration of all classes," Atlantic City's proponents argued, "cannot be seen in any other sea-side resort in the world. The rich banker does not look down upon the shop boy he meets," and with equal certainty, the literature proclaimed, "the boy thinks himself equally as good as the banker for he feels the few dollars in his pocket that he has been for so long scraping by" will prove him worthy of leisure time to his social superiors.[21]

In marketing the Jersey shore to the common man, businessmen and civic boosters benefited from a developing culture of commonality that gripped Gilded Age advice literature. Listing the "Don'ts of Hotel Life," the *New York Recorder* cautioned northern tourists, "Don't think because you're important in your own town, you're somebody in a hotel." For first-time visitors to the Jersey shore, William Bishop instructed potential summer tourists that such spaces were "not a place to be permanent in." Indeed, throughout the Reconstruction period, many northern resorts fulfilled the egalitarian promises and common law tenets that cultural critics fought for during the early years of the Civil War. While Gilded Age literature promoted Horatio Alger rags-to-riches feats, advertising agents, litigators, and civic boosters undermined those narratives by promoting a common law culture dedicated to the public's welfare over the profit motive of enterprising elites. Thus, contrary to laissez-faire dogmas popularized by nineteenth-century contemporaries, the Gilded Age marketplace was never wholly surrendered to the impartial devices of an "invisible hand." Amid the onslaught of industrialization and privatization, many leading legal scholars justified the importance of preserving the social nature of man. "It is not fit," James Wilson pronounced, "that man should be alone." As a social creature bound by a common identity with other travelers and consumers, Nathaniel Chipman argued, "man, sociable by the laws of his nature, has no right to pursue his own interest or happiness, to the exclusion of that of his fellow man." For legal theorists as well as Jersey shore merchants and boosters, the "common" reaffirmed a recommitment to the "public" that many northerners believed was abandoned in the later years of the Jacksonian era by greedy landlords and scheming socialites. These commitments were reinstituted in a host of public amusements and leisure venues throughout the Reconstruction era. Factory workers in Pittsburgh and Massachusetts enjoyed interacting with one another in saloons and baseball fields, while working-class women sought out social connection in dancing halls, dime novels, and street-corner boutiques.[22]

The architectural considerations of New Jersey's many beach towns reaffirmed these social priorities by stripping away the physical barriers that often divided classes of tourists at other northern vacation destinations. Businessmen and social engineers designed arcades, carousels, and restaurants with entrances that spilled out onto open-air boardwalks, leading tourists and summer bathers into endless stretches of sand and ocean waves. At Long Branch and Atlantic City, resort owners accommodated the voyeurism of beach life by building "swimming tanks" that provided hotel guests and paying customers with viewing rooms and "comfortable chairs" that allowed spectators to take in the latest summer fashions and amuse themselves with the daytime theatrics of bathers and flirtatious couples seeking relaxation, cheap thrills, and romance in the summer sun. Yet, by the 1880s, white vacationers clashed with increasing numbers of black tourists and seasonal workers who appeared on the same beaches and boardwalks and in the same restaurants, bars, and dancing halls as whites, threatening with their presence to upset the idyllic fantasies that white tourists had fashioned for summer vacation spaces. As they sought to persuade local authorities to adopt segregationist measures, white patrons raised the question of whether their power as consumers was influential enough to dictate public policy and exclude black patrons. In the years that followed, the debate over segregation would become a larger contest about who could properly control, manage, and shape consumer opinion as free labor principles became harder to employ in a service industry where traditional distinctions between work and play were no longer clear.[23]

"On the Beach." Atlantic City bathing pavilions, 1904. Courtesy of the Heston Collection.

For a northern black laborer in the late nineteenth century, few workplaces were as exciting as the beach towns of the Jersey shore. Throughout the Reconstruction era, Asbury Park and Atlantic City became summertime meccas for black college students and southern laborers who struggled to find lucrative employment opportunities elsewhere. Laboring often as dishwashers, cooks, hotel attendants, and other service-oriented positions in Philadelphia, New York City, and Baltimore during the winter months, many blacks often left their posts for the summer to take up similar work in Atlantic City, Asbury Park, and Cape May. Although the competition for these jobs left many to accept positions and wages beneath those they occupied back home, service work at the shore offered economic and social advancement beyond the opportunities available in many northern cities. Indeed, the availability of such positions allowed many African Americans to accept job opportunities as headwaiters, managers, desk clerks, and entertainers that accorded them middle- and upper-class status, which would have been nearly impossible in other northern communities. On the other hand, black seasonal laborers who took work as busboys, dishwashers, or boardwalk rolling-chair attendants faced harsh work schedules and degrading workplace encounters, and they were often susceptible to economic downturns, bad weather, and dismal living conditions that affected their pay and leisure opportunities. As one local historian of Atlantic City has noted, for many seasonal laborers, working at the Jersey shore often meant "three months to hurry" and "nine months to worry."[24]

Despite these restrictions, many northern blacks wasted little time in seeking out area beaches, boardwalk shops, and the throng of cheap amusements. Like white tourists, black workers insisted that they be defined not solely by their place of employment and saw admission to recreational spaces as proof of their acceptance as citizens. Because of the proximity of these vacation spots to northern black communities in New York City, Philadelphia, and Baltimore, Atlantic City and Asbury Park quickly became a convenient and cheap recreational outlet for local black workers and a popular leisure destination for out-of-town black fraternal and church organizations that planned annual excursions to the seashore. In contrast to local amusement venues in other northern cities, articles in the northern black press highlighted the Jersey shore's desirable summer conditions, tolerable Jim Crow standards, and growing commercial enticements for black men and women with time to spare and money to spend. Over time these and other middle-class black northerners established businesses for white and black tourists and operated black schools, churches, and fraternal organizations for the area's year-round residents.[25]

The desire of many African Americans to enjoy their leisure time in areas for-
merly reserved for whites threatened to undermine the cultural meanings white
tourists and businesses crafted for leisure space after the Civil War. Beginning
in the 1880s, editorials in northern newspapers soon appeared with headlines
proclaiming the dilemma of the "Negro by the Sea," increasing "Race Problems,"
and prompting many business owners and boosters to ask, "What are we going
to do with our colored people?" For white consumers, the tourist attractions of
the Jersey shore held value beyond their immediate ability to entertain and thrill.
They spoke to one's economic station and social status, ideas that transcended
the rights of citizenship and portended levels of privilege that existed outside the
realm of democracy.[26]

These attitudes conformed to the prevailing Victorian ideas that governed
nineteenth-century leisure activities. According to the advice literature that instructed and regulated social life for many middle- and upper-class northern
citizens, American men and women were expected to appear restrained and dignified when socializing in public. In particular, they were expected to refrain
from participating in rowdy recreational acts and controversial political specta-
cles that defied the formulaic and decidedly conservative social customs of more
refined leisure activities. Yet, while antebellum-era Victorians focused attention
toward private leisure endeavors and away from less refined public amusements,
postwar northern travelers began to frequent the public and consumer-minded
spaces of the Jersey shore with the expressed goal of escaping the regulated confines of their Victorian home life. Upon arriving at the shore, this new generation
of middle-class whites—as well as a great number of working-class patrons—
expected to find a resort space where they could leave behind their personal
histories, the regimentation of industrial life, and the stoicism of Victorian culture. Outside these boundaries they would dine in luxury, try out new fashions,
and dance with strangers. These experiences were rewards for a year of hard
work, careful savings, and negotiations with employers for time off. At the same
time, black workers who seemed to occupy such spaces without the prerequisite
planning and hard work discredited the cultural values they assigned to leisure
venues and the legitimacy of free labor ideology. To free labor proponents who
believed in a harmony of interests between workers and employers, black workers who engaged in social behavior and defiant political protests that threatened
the financial interests of their employers' enterprises endangered the very cooperation between capital and labor on which the northern free labor system
depended. Moreover, by ignoring social customs and making public demands
for integrated leisure, black activists transformed once racially segregated public

amusements into dystopian reminders of the white middle class's own changing social position in new recreational spaces dedicated to mass entertainment
and consumption.

The ambitious expectations that white tourists brought with them to the shore
clashed with the promise of an inclusive social space peddled by area boosters
and exposed the tenuous power of business to control consumer opinion by appealing to the values of free labor. From the very beginning, local leaders like
James Bradley feared potential uprisings from summer guests and sought to control social behavior by regulating the power of business and consumers alike. Yet,
Bradley often struggled to peddle a political economy built around consumption with his commitment to a fading Victorian code of ethics that prized social
restraint over mass entertainment. While he promised a vacation setting free
from the political disorder and class structures of everyday life, he balanced such
liberties with a host of social and economic regulations that were in keeping with
a quickly vanishing free labor culture. Anti-liquor decrees were written into all
residential properties, and only a limited number of commercial establishments
were permitted to sell alcohol. Strict rules on bathing, along with appropriate
clothing and social behavior, were posted on pamphlets along the boardwalk.
In order to honor the Sabbath, all businesses, trains, and beaches were ordered
closed on Sunday. While some tourists and businesses followed Bradley's auto-
cratic rule, most resisted the imposition on their leisure time, consumer rights,
and attempts to secure a profit. In defiance of Bradley's ordinances, boisterous
summer parties danced to the beats of the Salvation Army Marching Band, summer lovers snuck onto area beaches after dark, an illicit black market of booze
and gambling survived in backrooms and abandoned alleys, and local merchants
entertained customers on Sundays.[27]

To Bradley and other local officials, such rebellion seemed trivial compared to
the potential economic disaster wrought by persistent racial conflict. Fearing that
segregation would initiate a public backlash from black workers that would in
turn drive away white tourists, local officials and shore correspondents worked to
calm the fears of white vacationers by reminding them of the marginalized space
black workers occupied at the shore and the important economic and cultural
function they served in maintaining a service industry. A local merchant interviewed by the *Atlantic City Daily Union* declared, "He found no serious 'problem'
agitating the public." Black workers were visible, but by and large they came,
he reassured, "because they were needed and had been sent for as servants." In
contrast to many urban tourist locations, in which the "servant problem" created
animosities between guests and proprietors, Atlantic City's hired help, the *Daily*

Union insisted, "kept in their place becomingly, and did not intrude to offend those who were over-sensitive as to race prejudice."[28]

Reluctant to control the flow and behavior of black workers at their beach resorts, local officials attempted to point out the ways in which their presence was necessary to staff the jobs that whites refused. A shore reporter at Atlantic City declared that "the colored people" who make their living within the resort community "are natural born servants, taking bossing more meekly and gracefully than white help, and are for these and other good reasons generally preferred." An article published in the *New York Times* on the role and personality of black waiters reiterated these sentiments. Reversing the wartime feelings that cast black workers as labor radicals, the article sought to educate whites on why "the negro waiters always say, 'Yes Sir.'" Explaining that waiters in northern resorts were "the best colored waiters I have every seen," the article continued by noting, "They grin whenever they move, go about as softly as many kittens and speak even more quietly than they move." Although black waiters remained "theatrical of course," those interviewed for the article acknowledged that such deferential "gesticulations" were important to "cultivate a degree and a kind of servility" that played up the artistic qualities whites were told to expect from black waiters. These cultural explanations allowed whites to promote a racially restrictive marketplace in which blacks' labor was at the service of white consumers. As another frequent visitor to popular northern leisure spots noted, "No Sir does not sound very well to a man that's come to get whatever he wants. Whatever a gues' wants, the waiter must respond, 'Yes Sir.' That's what the guests are here for, and that's what the waiters must give them."[29]

The postwar desire to staff domestic service jobs with black men and women reflected a growing concern over labor and leisure in the Reconstruction period as emerging consumer economies threatened traditional conceptions of free labor ideology. In hotel journals, travel manuals, and etiquette guides, white northerners routinely debated the ideal worker for service employment. In the end, the demand from white tourists to be served only by blacks compelled local businesses to reject employment applications from other job seekers, pointing the way toward the emerging power of consumer opinion and consumer choice in shaping new debates over segregation. Defining blacks as workers and minstrels was also critical to a broader developing strategy of containment that white business owners and local officials adopted in the face of white hostility to black leisure and incessant consumer complaints. This strategy allowed business owners to appease the two most important racial sensibilities of white tourists: that only whites were deserving of recreation and consumption and that blacks were more than happy to serve. More important, these linguistic strategies enabled businessmen, local officials, and advertising agents to postpone the implementation of potentially disruptive segregation laws that antagonized black workers and interrupted business.[30]

Despite these assurances, many white tourists were not convinced that local officials were doing all they could to isolate blacks from the beaches and other public amusement venues. In the summer of 1885, a vocal group of white visitors to James Bradley's resort called on Bradley and other local officials to remove black workers and patrons from Asbury Park's public sphere. In an attempt to purge the assembly of working-class and "average" persons who mingled about freely after working hours, white guests in Asbury Park began calling for permanently enforced social and racial boundaries for their public sphere and sought to use their influence as valuable consumers as economic leverage. In the town's *Daily Journal* on July 7, 1885, an editorial pointed out that the "average man is easily distinguishable," and insisted that the mass of "curiosities that have taken their position under the pavilion (white as well as black) be removed."[31]

For many white northern tourists, the Jersey shore's eclectic mix of wealthy guests, working-class laborers, middle-class patrons, and black tourists and domestic workers made the area's social landscape into a melting pot of cultural and political conflicts rather than a place of leisure. To solve the problem, a follow-up article appeared in the *Daily Journal* ten days later narrowing the list of objections to the black workers and tourists of Asbury Park, who, according to the complaint, "hang, intruding themselves in places designed only for guests, monopolizing the promenade, pavilion, and seats, and not content with that they come on excursions by the train load, and some days the whole beach is given up to them." The cultural and economic liability posed by the presence of black tourists and domestic workers revealed the fragile nature of racial identity for many ordinary white northerners after the Civil War. Throughout the Reconstruction period, white northern citizens found themselves renegotiating racial hierarchies in a variety of new daily encounters, while politicians and litigators worked to solidify old social and racial categories upset from emancipation and postwar civil rights debates. The inability of Reconstruction-era politics to effectively solve these disputes led to a variety of uncomfortable social encounters and political protests throughout the North's amusement and consumer districts.[32]

By the mid-1880s, Asbury Park was not alone in feeling the effects of these lingering political conflicts. In Gloucester City, New Jersey, a small beach resort that dubbed itself the "The Poor Man's Cape May," residents used a similar coded vocabulary to isolate black consumers, blaming "sporting" and "rough behavior" on black excursionists who frequented area taverns. The choice of the words "sporting" and "rough" were not accidental or insignificant. Instead, they were intended to remind whites about the broader cultural implications of integrated leisure. Throughout the nineteenth century, white northerners worked hard to typecast black leisure as dangerous, juvenile, and unruly, associating even the most innocent of recreational activities with the nation's most ruthless outlaws. Such stigmas, many insisted, were not a result of racial animosities, but reflected long-standing commitments to regulate the consumer behavior of individuals who threatened the rights of business by engaging in behavior that drove away more valuable guests. At Lakeside Park, a modest resort in southwest New Jersey, white patrons singled out supposedly "unruly" black excursions and entertainment as justification for segregated leisure. For years, black organizations from Philadelphia frequently leased out days at Lakeside Park for working-class men and women who could not afford extended vacations to Atlantic City or Asbury Park. A frequent form of entertainment at these excursions was the presence of marching bands that paraded behind excursionists in their way in and out of Lakeside Park. On June 26, 1885, however, Leon Davis, the bandleader of the West End Colored Fife and Drum Corp, led his unit beyond the confines of Lakeside Park. Followed by a "hooting and yelling mob of several hundred people, of all ages and colors," Davis was arrested and black excursionists came under increased attack for betraying the decorum of leisure spaces and inciting social disorder by "creating a nuisance on the street."[33]

The racial incidents at Asbury Park, Gloucester City, and Lakeside Park exposed broader political tensions over the meaning of the public in postwar leisure spaces. As many whites claimed, the everyday sociability of the workaday public was a much different social space from the pleasure-seeking settings of the Jersey shore. The workday public reaffirmed a society committed to free labor ideology, in which common artisans, mechanics, clerks, and factory workers met as equals, each laboring in a burgeoning democratic society dedicated to the promise of social mobility. Although this everyday public witnessed heated political debates concerning job discrimination, interracial contact seemed less likely to overturn the nation's political economy. In contrast, the interracial public of beaches, boardwalks, and amusement parks elicited fears of social equality and consumer rights that threatened to radicalize the economic and social order of Reconstruction-era America.

Throughout the late 1880s, white tourists increasingly pressured tourism promoters and business owners to rebrand their beach towns as segregated leisure destinations. To do so, several northern whites sought to ignore the emancipationist narrative constructed by Radical Republicans and black political figures during Reconstruction. Writing in the *Daily Journal*, one patron of Asbury Park lectured the town's local officials and northern blacks that the effort to provide political and legal aid to African Americans during Reconstruction was a paternal and "generous aid" provided by the "Christian spirit of right-minded white men." The constitutional amendments which followed Emancipation and the Civil Rights Act extended by the Republican Congress were soon replaced, the individual explained, by the ungrateful attitude of African Americans who clamored for social equality.[34]

Although many scholars have addressed the multiple ways that Civil War memory was created and contested through monuments, parades, pageants, and southern plantation tours, white middle-class tourists who took to the boardwalks and beaches of resort communities and the editorial pages of the northern press created their own narratives of emancipation in the postwar period. Indeed, the recent inclination of scholars to emphasize northerners' southern tourism as a cultural marker of national reunion has obscured the postwar realities of leisure and the distinct regional interests and political meanings that white middle-class tourists placed on leisure time and space during the Reconstruction era. Most northern citizens lacked both the time and money for extended southern trips. Leisure time was limited and often included weekend getaways to the seashore, rather than lengthy vacations to southern tourist sites. Working-class whites who visited the Jersey shore offered their own views on the legacy of Reconstruction that had less to do with reuniting with the South than they did with exercising their newfound status as consumers to protect their privileged access to leisure marketplaces through the execution of segregation laws. Moreover, those who visited the Jersey shore sought to create rules for public leisure spaces by clinging to prewar notions of racial and class separation that rejected the justifications of white proprietors and black pleasure seekers alike. Uncomfortable with the way the postwar political and social climate had led many business owners to appease black workers and tourists, many white tourists who visited the seashore reminisced fondly of a time when racial tension had been muted by slavery and more oppressive forms of class subordination.[35]

In seeking to strip the towns of Asbury Park and Atlantic City of their former spiritual and rehabilitative identity, summer guests pressured the proprietors and town councils of the Jersey shore to create segregation laws that mirrored their own northern neighborhoods, while rewriting the history of the Civil War and Reconstruction to justify the policies. As whites in Asbury Park explained to business owners and local officials, "There were those among the colored race who were not satisfied with what had already been done, but wanted more. It was not enough to possess all the rights and privileges as white citizens, but those rights must be insolently demanded." To black activists they explained, "Respect and equality can never be gained." Instead, they argued that only through passive acceptance of the current social standing could the cultural stereotypes accompanying black grievances be eliminated.[36]

These competing historical narratives between white business owners and white tourists reveal the public relations dilemma marketing agents faced in promoting beach resorts as free labor utopias at a time when white middle-class opinion sought to regulate the rights of "unwanted" black consumers. Yet, rather than appease the policy proposals of white tourists, marketing agents and northern journalists responded to their complaints by downplaying the racial tension to a few agitators and by highlighting the racial progress exhibited at many northern beach towns. A local business owner in Atlantic City observed that on its famous boardwalk "all nations and races" mingled freely during the bathing hours without the slightest hint of Jim Crow tensions. "Sit on the beach for an hour and you see the widest diversity of human types" the man declared. "The Saleswoman brushes her best all-wool against the silk of the millionaire's wife, and the millionaire" is forced to interact with the "waiter who just handed him his bill of faire." A correspondent dispatched to Long Branch observed similar sights and sounds. "Up and down the beach," the reporter observed that "bathers of all sizes" mingled "happily in the water without reference to age, sex, or previous condition of servitude."[37]

To many members of the northern press and the local business class, the integrated atmosphere of the Jersey shore seemed to reaffirm broader changes in northern race relations after the Civil War that were brought about by the triumph of Union victory and free labor ideology. The editor of the *Atlantic City Review* explained, "While the colored people have never attempted to secure accommodations at a hotel, they have in perhaps all cases been supplied with refreshments at the bar." Covering the racial tension in Asbury Park, the *New York Times* similarly observed that the region's leisure destinations witnessed "greater social mobility than at Long Branch or at any other place along the coast." When these observations were not enough to appease blacks who insisted on unregulated access to public amusements, white citizens occasionally called on Bradley to erect public spaces and establishments that would cater solely to the interests of its black workers and tourists. Criticizing the "colored invasion" of its space, one objector in the *Daily Journal* asked whether "Mr. Bradley could be persuaded to build a pavilion for their use and locate it in the immediate neighborhood."[38]

To defuse the racial tension, white business owners and local political figures sought a variety of temporary compromises. In Asbury Park, Mayor Bradley instituted clock-time segregation by temporarily yielding the boardwalks and beaches to working-class blacks after regular business hours. As one local official explained, "Everybody turns out upon the promenade after 6 o'clock, and fill the pavilions and all the seats and gaze upon the majority." This "keeps in motion," the individual exclaimed, "until 10 and 10:30, when the colored population turns out, as if at a pre-concerted signal, and swarms over the boardwalk." Uncomfortable with allowing African Americans access to its public sphere after dark, Atlantic City and Lakeside Park divided up the summer vacation season, reserving the months of August and September for African American vacationers. This form of seasonal segregation served as an intermediate move between integration and full segregation. In doing so, northern whites believed they could appease both constituents. White tourists could enjoy summer outings during the prime summer months without having to interact with seasonal laborers or black tourists, and African Americans would be granted unrestricted access to leisure accommodations during the latter part of the summer when other working-class tourists usually took their vacations. To market the proposal to African Americans, the northern press touted the measure as the extension of a working-class holiday season to black workers, rather than a Jim Crow policy aimed to shield civil rights protests. When African Americans criticized the measure during the 1890 summer season, the *Philadelphia Times* explained that black workers were not the only ones restricted to the late summer months. "The last two weeks of August," the *Times* instructed, was also the "popular holiday time for the great company of Philadelphia store girls, and for the respectable working-classes generally."[39]

Highlighting the late summer excursions of other marginalized working-class groups allowed segregationists to offer a Jim Crow policy based on class difference rather than race prejudice, forestalling more permanent solutions to the escalating problem. During the summer of 1887, Bradley appointed a beach superintendent to enforce "modest bathing suits," which allowed law enforcement to "prevent the colored people from monopolizing the beach to the exclusion of visiting white people." However, Bradley's ad hoc approach to segregation allowed blacks to consistently ignore his "polite requests" and informal policing tactics. In the years that followed, many black workers and tourists continued to refuse the requests to enjoy their leisure elsewhere or restrict their excursions to August and September. Unable to prevent black workers from holding all-night parties in defiance of permit laws or from accessing the beaches without purchasing the required passes, James Bradley relocated the black population to facilities set up exclusively for their own recreation.[40]

In a last-ditch effort to appease local black workers in the spring of 1889, Bradley commissioned the construction of three Jim Crow bathing facilities set conspicuously apart from those used by whites. However, during that summer racial tensions once again arose as many black workers ignored the requests to stay off the beaches and boardwalks during the day and continued to use the old bathing pavilions. The *New York Times* explained in June 1889 that despite requests to keep away from whites during prime bathing hours, the "teeming negro settlements in West Asbury Park shows no decrease." In response, Bradley posted an official notice asking area blacks again to "please refrain from using the beach during the fashionable hours of the day."[41]

To defend the new Jim Crow boundaries, business owners and the northern press compared the irrationality of black behavior to the racial liberalism of local white business owners. A defender of Bradley's notices explained to the northern press that ordinances were adopted as a final reaction to the "swarthy African" who has become "bolder year by year." Documenting the preference of whites to police leisure spaces through informal means, the town's segregationist defenders insisted that bolder plans were initiated only after "the other side responded with mass meetings," and "zealous pastors" called on area blacks to "maintain their rights at any cost." In its coverage of the escalating racial tension, the *New York Times* declared that Bradley consistently expressed his public support for the town's black community by explaining that his request was in the best interest of all black workers who wished to retain summer employment in a profitable service industry.[42]

The following summer, Bradley's gradual approach to enforcing segregation introduced new problems when whites attempted to use the Jim Crow beach facilities during hours reserved for blacks. The *Asbury Park Press* noted on July 19, 1890, that "now whites have to be watched to keep from trespassing on the colored people" since "white people do not seem to understand" that the cordoned-off area at Second Avenue is "not for their use, and the authorities are having a considerable trouble in causing the rule to be understood." Before the start of the 1893 summer season, Bradley moved to officially restrict all African Americans, both those who worked as well as those who sought to vacation in Asbury Park, from the beaches and other shore facilities. Posting signs throughout the community and stationing officers at pertinent shore locations, Bradley prohibited all black citizens from entering the beaches, bathing houses, pavilions, and local boardwalk amusements.[43]

Reluctant at first to embrace Jim Crow, Bradley and local business owners subtly crafted segregation notices and adopted gradual social boundaries to avoid interruptions to business. The sporadic and impromptu nature of these strategies reflected the instability of racial imagery and the limits of free labor ideology to peacefully police the public sphere. As the democratization of wage labor provided workers with greater wealth, and contentious legislation proposed to decrease their working hours, free labor ideology was no longer a reliable defense to regulate a leisure marketplace where public policy was increasingly beholden to consumer opinion and consumer choice. To separate themselves from the mass of white racists, they used phrases like "Please refrain" and "We ask that you" in their public notices, language that hinted at the unique political space that black workers occupied in public leisure spaces and the limits of producers to control their consumer behavior. As the passive phrasing of these decisions indicate, the years between the start of Reconstruction and formal Jim Crow required new methods of marketing and enforcing segregation from those deployed before the Civil War. Yet business owners and local officials struggled to define what message and tactic would replace older strategies, consistently failing to manage the public behavior of black consumer activists or the public sentiments of white tourists through informal requests and ad hoc policing tactics. Their inability to manage consumer opinion opened the door to a wave of black civil rights demonstrations and public protests that delayed the nation's retreat from the 1875 Civil Rights Act and allowed African Americans to contest and sometimes defeat segregation during the late 1880s and early 1890s.

2

Occupying Jim Crow

On the night of June 28, 1889, William Nelson, a black employee of an ice cream parlor, stood watching a carousel ride inside the Palace, an indoor amusement arcade located on the boardwalk of Asbury Park. When a white security guard attempted to remove him from the facility, Nelson resisted the imposition, prompting a fistfight with the officer, John A. Krause, outside the Palace premises. After both men were arrested and fined for the incident, the Palace owner Ernie Schnitzler responded by restricting entrance into the pavilion to season ticket holders, which, according to an account published in the town's *Shore Press*, were sold and distributed only to the Palace's white patrons. In the days that followed, local black workers protested the denial of their consumer rights in a series of public acts that eventually forced Schnitzler to reverse his decision and readmit black customers. Concluding its coverage of the altercation a few days later, the *Shore Press* predicted, "It is probable that no future trouble will result."[1]

The preference of local whites to disregard black protests did little to halt additional claims to integrated leisure and free consumption. After four black waiters completed their shift at the Plaza Hotel in Asbury Park on the night of August 4, 1893, they attempted to access the hotel bar. Barred from entering the establishment by the hotel's manager, John H. Quinn, the men pushed their way through the door. In response to the brazen political move, Quinn struck one of the waiters, initiating a full-scale brawl on the barroom floor. The next day, the hotel proprietors ejected all black members of the waitstaff and replaced them with white men and women. When the white replacements arrived, the black workers refused to leave their posts; area police were finally dispatched and arrested the ousted employees. In the days that followed, black workers picketed on the boardwalk outside the hotel, demanding both their jobs back and access to the hotel bar during their free time. In response to the disruption of business that the protests incited, the Plaza Hotel owner, James Bly—like Ernie Schnitzler before him—readmitted the black workers to their posts the following week.[2]

"Black Women Bathers in Asbury
Park," 1908. Courtesy of the Library of
Congress.

The successful integration of the Palace arcade and the Plaza Hotel demonstrated the potential of black consumer activism as a successful weapon in the
fight against segregation. To achieve these victories, black activists used violent
and nonviolent resistance to manipulate class divisions among whites and fight
against discrimination by claiming full rights as citizens and free choice as consumers. With money to spend and expanded leisure hours, they took seats on
boardwalk benches, spent their free time riding cheap amusements, changed
alongside whites in bathhouses, sunbathed on area beaches in the afternoon, and
defiantly sought entry to the array of restaurants, saloons, dancing halls, and
other assorted amusement venues that lined local boardwalks. Despite public
notices asking them to "please refrain" from such activities, many openly defied
these requests by evoking the common law tradition and their rights as consumers, confronting white northerners in public and in print in an attempt to dispute
and disrupt the cultural hierarchies of race that placed disproportionate marketplace regulations on black consumers.

Over time these protests became part of a broader strategy by black workers
to promote a free consumer society, one where the right to consume was equal to
the right to work and the right to property. To black workers, the goal of free consumption was necessary not simply to spare African Americans from the indignities of social exclusion, or to force unwanted social alliances with whites, but to
sanction a market order free from the visible hand of race. The absence of such
freedoms, they maintained, threatened not only the economic rights of black
consumers, but called into question the legitimacy of the entire capitalist system.

The successful implementation of this message and vision ultimately helped African Americans refute free labor ideology as the basis of economic freedom and, in the process, enabled scores of black workers to defeat segregation throughout the 1880s and early 1890s.[3]

Throughout much of the nineteenth century, northern black activists, litigators, and political leaders routinely contested the legality of segregation by drawing on the common law. Although white segregationists attempted to absolve their obligations and duties under the common law by evoking the emerging discourse of individual rights and social propriety, by the end of the 1860s African Americans used common law legal precedent to access a host of public conveyances and facilities that attempted to refuse them admission. Having successfully integrated public transportation systems in New York, Philadelphia, and Washington D.C. during the Civil War era, leading black figures attempted to apply the common law defense to popular amusements as well. In a speech delivered at Oberlin College in 1874, John Mercer Langston explained that the fate of the common law lay in its ability to protect the rights of northern blacks to access popular amusements and other public accommodations. Explaining that common law rules are "explicit and rigid," Langston went on to argue that such complaints by northern blacks for integrated leisure were "indispensable to rational and useful enjoyment of life that without them citizenship itself loses much of its value and liberty seems little more than a crime." After the Supreme Court ruled in favor of segregationists in 1883, John P. Green, the first black state senator in Ohio, defended the rights of African Americans to regain access to popular amusements. In a speech delivered in May 1884, Senator Green explained that blacks would continue to fight for integrated access under the common law as the "means necessary to the enjoyment of our civil rights."[4]

Along the New Jersey shore, local black workers employed the common law defense espoused by Langston and Mercer in their push to contest local segregation ordinances and promote free consumption. Guided in their efforts by the political and religious leadership of the African Methodist Episcopal Church, civil rights demonstrators and organizers in Asbury Park and Atlantic City reminded northern proprietors and tourists about the common law's long-standing oath to allow unregulated access. At a large meeting held at the African Methodist Episcopal Church of West Asbury Park in the summer of 1887, the Reverend J. Francis Robinson called on his congregation to attack "all class legislation and race distinction where the statutes of citizenship and of good behavior introduce the common right." Robinson declared that the "man who advocates the separa-tion of whites and blacks from the equal enjoyment of civil prerogatives solely on the grounds of color places himself in a position to be questioned as to his patriotic proclivities and the genuineness of a Republic form of government." Explaining the need to maintain the common law tradition, the Reverend J. H. Morgan asked whether the moral and civic lapses by a few people of a given class could be held against an entire race:

> It does seem strange that so many of our friends on the other side do not seem able to distinguish any difference between colored people as regards to moral, religion or the right of manhood; and those of them who admit it seem to view it in the same light as the boy who visited the country fair and saw a cow that looked for all the world like his father's cow. You could not tell them apart, only one was white and [the] other black. "All colored people are alike" seems to be the maxim (especially if there is finance to be considered) either by action against us or indifference for us.[5]

To black activists pushing for free consumption, a marketplace that failed to reward good behavior violated critical principles that had sustained the common law for generations and called into question the legitimacy of the capitalist sys-tem. As G. W. Johnson, a waiter in Asbury Park's Sheldon House, instructed, "If a white man acts boisterous, rude, or ungentlemanly, he is arrested and/or fined." Yet, Johnson attested, "the white people as a class are not blamed for the actions of one man." A black protestor who penned an editorial in *The Sun* echoed John-son's sentiments in his defense of integration. "It seems that the white visitors are not averse to employing them as servants," but "are outraged when they find the privileges of the beach largely enjoyed by the colored visitors." To promote a marketplace regulated by conduct instead of race, local black workers and lead-ers took to the press to catalogue and report instances of orderly black behavior. A frequent visitor to Asbury Park recalled that the majority of black tourists and workers are "very fine-looking men and women, and generally they are remark-able for the dignity of their behavior." Indeed, most blacks displayed, he noted, "more taste than the run of white people of same circumstances." A. J. Chambers similarly instructed the *New York Times* that he had "never seen anything in the conduct of the colored people here that would cause me to feel ashamed," not-ing that three thousand black tourists visited the Jersey shore annually during the summer months. After each visit, Chambers pointed out that Dr. Stokes, president of the region's Jubilee association, invited the excursion party to return the following summer. In the event that black excursions did become unruly, Reverend Chambers made it clear that local black leaders would not hesitate to discipline such persons. "Once this year, when some colored people were a little noisy in seeing some friends off at a station," Chambers recounted, "I spoke from the pulpit about the propriety of good behavior in the street." After the public denunciation, Chambers noted that he had visited the beach every day and "never saw the colored people misbehave themselves there."[6]

To discredit the cultural stigma of black criminality, local black residents contrasted Chambers's defense of black morality with incidents of white unruliness. While white tourists and business leaders complained about late-night black entertainments, a "white haired negro" recounted to the New York Times an incident involving the boisterous public performances of the Salvation Army Band. Observing the "noisy dwarf and some young women with tambourines," he noted that "one of the women said that she 'couldn't sing, but she could holler,' and holler she did, like a drunken woman." Standing up, other interested observers recalled that the man "raised his cane and said very impressively, "Now will anybody in this crowd tell me whether Asbury Park's colored would disgrace God or man in such a manner as this?"[7]

When Asbury Park mayor James Bradley moved to officially enforce segregation in the summer of 1893, northern black lawyers drew on the common law defense to urge local blacks to verbally and physically contest the measure. Speaking to an Asbury Park audience on July 20, 1893, Alfred C. Cowan, a black New York lawyer, explained that James Bradley's ordinances violated Reconstruction-era federal statutes along with the laws of New Jersey. Noting that both white or black citizens would have a "good case of action against Mr. Bradley," he called on area blacks to justify integrated leisure by claiming their rights under the "Fourteenth and Fifteenth Amendments to the Constitution and the civil rights law of New Jersey." Speaking after Cowan, T. McCants Stewart, a black member of the Brooklyn Board of Education and a frequent visitor to Asbury Park, defended Cowan's legal judgment. "He has drawn a distinct color line that the law will not support," Stewart explained, instructing his "good friends, professional and business men in all walks of life," to call the mayor's bluff. If he insisted on following through on his threat to impose segregation in leisure venues, Steward instructed all area blacks to "call on every provision of the law to ensure that 'justice' is restored." Such demonstrations, he insisted, would prove the seriousness with which African Americans approached their consumer rights and "would make a large hole in his finances" if Bradley continued to refuse service.[8]

Even after the Supreme Court ruled the 1875 Civil Rights Act unconstitutional in 1883, northern blacks found refuge in local civil rights laws. In Asbury Park, one African American patron was able to successfully contest segregation by evoking New Jersey's own civil rights law. Passed in 1884, the law was one of the few throughout the nation to prohibit hotels, theaters, restaurants, and graveyards from discriminating against any person based on race. In 1895, Robert Holland brought restaurant owner James F. Angel to court after Angel refused to serve him a meal. Ruling in favor of Holland, the court ordered Angel to pay Holland $1,000 in damages. Elsewhere, African Americans found that local civil rights laws could protect them against hotelkeepers that denied them accommodations. On December 23, 1893, the Worcester Central District Court in Boston ordered Mrs. Mary Place, the owner of the Colenade Hotel, to pay a $100 fine for refusing to accommodate the Fisk Jubilee Singers. Although such decisions were rare, they confirmed the legal legitimacy of the common law in matters pertaining to the question of integrated leisure and helped push others to protest for consumer rights through acts of civil disobedience.[9]

To ensure that the common law retained public support, African Americans often stopped short of promoting social equality in their claim for free consumption. While white segregationists at the Jersey shore and elsewhere used the threat of social equality to limit civil rights initiatives, black activists appealed to the rights of all citizens to gain access to consumer spaces. Yet, in making those claims, they were careful to reiterate that such rights did not intimate a preference for social intimacy. A citizen identified as the "Negro Menard" by the *Minnesotan-Herald*, summarized the position of many black protesters when he claimed, "A black man can ride squeezed up by the side of a finely dressed white lady in the street car, and nobody can think anything of it. Is that social equality? Of course not. Street cars are public, not private conveyances. Are theatres public places? Yes." Menard, went on, however, to distinguish between public amusements and private social clubs, noting that "we do not demand admission into the private social circles of whites, but we do demand and intend to gain admission to any seat in the theatre, steamboat, steamcar, hotel, saloon, omnibus, or any other place designed for public amusement, provided that we pay the common fare."[10]

African Americans at the Jersey shore evoked the sentiments of Menard by drawing a distinction between public rights and social privacy. In an interview with the *New York Times*, Alfred Cowan explained that despite white claims to the contrary, the boardwalks, beaches, and bathing facilities were not protected by private property claims. "By opening up the beach and the board walk to the public," Cowan pointed out that Bradley "gave an easement to the lessees and owners of cottages and hotels which they had the right to enjoy and which their guests and servants had the same right to enjoy." Yet, in pointing out the public functions of such establishments, Cowan stopped short of calling for social equality. As the sentiments of Menard and Cowen demonstrate, the use of the common law defense provided African Americans political leverage against individual hotel proprietors. In Asbury Park and other northern resort communities, African Americans were granted favorable settlements or allowed integrated access under the common law defense that theaters, hotels, and restaurants served public functions. Yet, the area's leading black legal scholars and civic leaders were hesitant to push for broader social rights. Since the 1830s, African Americans who lobbied for social equality were routinely denied access to public amusements by public officials and private businesses, while courtrooms rolled back civil rights laws that sought to endorse the controversial idea. Ohio state senator John P. Green acknowledged this political reality in May 1884, when he explained that African Americans did not look to the government to regulate "matters of a strictly social nature." Every citizen, Senator Green explained, "has a right to select his own company, no gentlemen or lady of color demands or expects any legislation on this behalf, for to do so would be superlative nonsense."[11]

Lawyers for the Hyer sisters traveling singing troupe established precedence for this strategy in 1877 when they declared that the right of the group to gain admittance to northern hotels was not a call for social equality, but a claim made in defense of consumer rights. On September 1, 1877, the Hyer sisters were in Indianapolis to perform at the Grand Opera House when they attempted to secure lodging at the accompanying Grand Hotel. When the front desk clerk refused to tender them accommodations, the members of the singing company attempted to enter the hotel's dining room facilities but were turned away by a police officer. Charging the hotel with violating section 5.510 of the Civil Rights Act, police arrested members of the hotel's management staff, with bail set at $400 each.[12]

In taking the Grand Hotel to court, the Hyer sisters and their legal team declared that their protests reflected the "right to occupy the same places as other freemen in hotels, traveling conveyances and places of amusement." Yet, in bringing their suit, the group's manager declared that the Hyer sisters were only "insisting upon its constitutional right. Being placed upon an equality with white men in his privileges at public houses does not place the negro upon social equality with anyone." Differentiating between the dignified behavior and appearance of the Hyer sisters and the area's working-class blacks, the group's manager noted that whites had nothing to fear from the entrance of respectable black entertainers. The "depraved and ignorant," he instructed, would "never be acknowledged the social equals of the virtuous and the intelligent." On September 3, 1877, the judge ruled in favor of the traveling musical troupe. By noon the next day, the sisters "marched into the dining room and were served a square meal."[13]

The attempts by northern blacks to move the conversation away from social equality was not just a clever political strategy. Unlike white northerners, who saw any admission of equality as an invitation for political corruption and miscegenation, many black activists failed to equate integration and consumer rights with social intimacy. Instead, they pressed to partake in these activities without the fear of social pressure or racial exclusion. To many black men and women who lobbied for consumer rights at the Jersey shore, the freedom of leisure was an economic right and not a intrusive claim to social privilege—rights they argued were sanctioned under the common law and promoted by the free market system.

By the late 1880s, black workers at the Jersey shore recognized that the barriers blocking their path to integration were not just legal, but cultural as well. The focus on free consumption in debates over segregation required that black workers and consumers remain vigilant against market forces and cultural ideas that worked to undercut and delegitimize their right to access leisure venues. Thus, while journalists, cartoonists, and tourists helped popularize white supremacist imagery in their efforts to solidify Jim Crow, black workers, reformers, and tourists regularly contested such cultural stigmas as barriers to free consumption. On August 24, 1888, black tourists ended a prolonged struggle to close down an "African dodger" booth in the beachfront community of Gloucester City in order to rid local amusements of degrading market stigmas. A standard carnival game at northern amusement parks, the African dodger challenged whites to test their accuracy by throwing a series of balls at the live head of a black attendant. For those who protested the use of the racist "bull's-eye" contest, the African dodger was a familiar visible reminder of the many damaging popular culture images that whites created to degrade black leisure habits and manipulate market behavior after the Civil War. In their efforts to eliminate these racist public displays, activists argued that the presence of such games was not only a personal affront to the dignity and social status of respectable black consumers, but also a visible political reminder that the cultural authority of Jim Crow rested on its ability to use fraudulent market forces to restrict the entertainment and consumption habits of African Americans.[14]

Since the antebellum period, northern black intellectuals and political leaders utilized the ideologies of the market revolution to protest economic inequality and racial prejudice. In a speech given in 1847, leading black abolitionists called on blacks to challenge the cultural power of Jim Crow and become a "ruler of opinions." Noting that all African Americans "struggled against opinions," the signers of the document exclaimed that "our warfare lies in thought." As abolitionists and later black civil rights demonstrators knew all too well, an "invisible hand" did not dictate the ability of black northerners to access consumer districts. Instead, blacks routinely informed the public that it was the racially coded visible hand of the white business community that created and enforced the rules of the marketplace—regulations that rested on white supremacist images and rhetoric that restricted black recreation and free consumption. Yet, despite these challenges, antebellum black protestors retained faith in the market to self-correct if regulatory features like racial prejudice could be eradicated. In pamphlets and public speeches, leading black intellectuals routinely embraced the logic of market principles to contest the corrosive regulations that inhibited upward mobility and denied black wage earners from competing in a meritocratic economic order. As Charles Remond explained to the Massachusetts House of Representatives in 1842, segregation enabled the market economy to become corrupted under a system in which "the most vicious is treated as well as the most respectable." In the emerging postwar civil rights debates at the Jersey shore, black tourists and seasonal workers called on white segregationists to confront a similar contradiction in the way the free market operated at local beach resorts. They asked whites to make a choice between the prejudicial market of Jim Crow and the free market of mass consumption. Were the rights of consumers only reserved for white tourists, and if so, how could black workers embrace a capitalist system that restricted their ability to enjoy the fruits of their labor?[15]

To combat an economic and social order that denied African Americans a place in a meritocratic system, local black activists used the popular press and public political stages to denounce and correct the regulatory prejudices of northern marketplaces. In particular, they refuted the promotional narratives of the Civil War and Reconstruction that white marketing agents and boosters drafted to appease white tourists, and called into question the sincerity of the Republican Party's support of black civil rights. In recounting the unofficial means by which skating parlors were segregated in Asbury Park in 1885, W. H. Dickerson insisted that blacks should look cautiously toward their allegiance with northern Republican leaders. "When we are called on as 'our colored friends,'" Dickerson explained, "there is always a purpose to serve as tools or instruments." "We would ask those who for many years have been using us to further their plans and fill their coffers," he continued, "if they think we will always remain docile subjects to their dictation and the plain minions of their selfish interests."[16]

Like many white residents had done, African Americans used these incidents and others to give the Civil War and Reconstruction alternative meanings. While white citizens increasingly viewed wartime emancipation as the benevolent gift of white Union soldiers and moderate Republican leaders, black activists at the Jersey shore articulated a more radical history of those years. Mirroring the complaints expressed by black civil rights protesters throughout the nation after emancipation, Reverend Robinson reminded Asbury Park's white audience of the achievements and struggles of black men who fought to preserve the Union. "We are here," he exclaimed, "to defend our citizenship and our manhood." He reiterated to the white members of the audience that "we colored people fought for our liberty some years ago, and we do not propose to be denied it at this late date. We will not be dictated to in this manner by Mr. Bradley or any other man. The colored man contributes largely to the wealth of this country, including the town of Asbury Park, and we are here to stay. We fought to save the Union as the white man did. This country is for the whites and blacks alike, including even the beach of Asbury Park."[17]

After James Bradley ordered local police to remove black tourists and workers from Asbury Park's public and commercial spaces in 1893, Joseph Francis Smith, a wholesale druggist, protested that the move violated the "spirit" of emancipation and the Reconstruction period. "It is pretty late in the day," Smith complained, "for a white man in this part of the country, where the color question has been so freely discussed and so literally agreed upon, to attempt to draw the color line so sharply as Founder Bradley has drawn it." A spokesman for the Fisk Jubilee Singers offered a similar complaint against white hotel owners who refused admittance to the popular traveling black singing troupe in 1877. "It is not only in violation of the law," the spokesman announced, "but of the spirit of the age, which recognizes no distinction among men based on color or nationality." Appealing to the better elements of the northern white public to vote down the sentiments, he chastised those who persisted in popularizing "a relic of the race prejudice engendered by slavery," which "all right-minded people should assist in frowning down."[18]

When the Fisk Jubilee Singers were refused admission to the Troy Hotel in Chautauqua, New York, in December 1885, their manager, Henry Cushing, reiterated that the move was "an old story" that did not belong in a post–Civil War world. Charting the troupe's northern touring stops throughout the year,

Cushing outlined the racial discrimination they encountered in their travels. In Springfield, Illinois, "the home of Abraham Lincoln," Cushing recounted that the troupe was "refused accommodations in two hotels," and "obtained shelter in the third only on condition that we should hide ourselves from the other guests." While performing at resorts in New Jersey, he acknowledged, "we have been treated more shamefully than we ever were in a southern state." In contrast, he reminisced fondly over touring stops in Great Britain and "on the continent," where the "slave songs have been sung before nearly every throne" and the troupe were treated as proper guests "at the tables of the noblest houses in England, Ireland, Scotland, France, Germany, and Austria." Demanding that northern establishments acknowledge integrated access to public amusements overseas, Cushing justified the complaints for integrated leisure. "With such remembrances to look back upon," he declared, "we can well afford to treat with contempt, the petty indignities by northern hotel proprietors."[19]

By evoking the claim of consumer rights, African Americans were often able to attain significant concessions from white businesses and politicians. The Reverend J. Francis Robinson informed a congregation of black protesters in 1887 that, despite the presence of signs prohibiting their access, they should continue to resist their exclusion by visiting the beaches after hours. In the days and nights that followed, Robinson led a group of black workers in a series of "wade-ins," a new form of civil disobedience in which black demonstrators would stage marches on the beaches in order to bring public attention to the emerging segregation notices that denied them the ability to purchase the passes required to access Bradley's beaches. In a meeting held the night before the first wade-in, Reverend Robinson called out to the participants that "they may put up signs telling us to keep off . . . they may put up notices to keep us off the beach," but, he warned, "we will go there just the same. If there were notices tacked up to the doors of hell, telling them not to go there, some of them would because they have a right to go there." In the days and weeks that followed, black workers staged a series of late-night wade-ins in open defiance of local notices that required them to purchase passes before using the beaches.[20]

After many black residents heeded his calls, Robinson found that African Americans mingled freely with one another and other white working-class residents on Asbury Park's beaches. As Robinson informed the *Daily Journal*, "The fact is that neither the paper nor Mr. Bradley can keep us off the beach. I went down there last night and saw some elegant colored ladies. There were Chinamen there too, and Italians." Two weeks later, black tourists again mobilized to fight Bradley's ordinances. On July 20, 1887, three large excursions of black protestors arrived from Newark, Jersey City, and Orange, New Jersey, as well as from New York City and Philadelphia to partake in in an annual "Jubilee day." Ignoring the signs restricting them from the beaches and bathing houses, the black patrons visited the beaches at Ocean Grove and Asbury Park in "droves and sat for several hours on the sand." In addition, "a dozen or so" applied for bathing suits at the bathhouses but were refused. Covering the demonstrations, the *New York Times* reported that in each instance the patrons took the refusal of service in "good spirits," though they remained nonetheless.[21]

A few miles inland at the popular town of Red Bank, black protestors organized to fight the implementation of segregation ordinances drafted to reassign seating arrangements in local theaters. Noting the influence of Jim Crow laws instituted at Asbury Park, local race leaders organized an indignation meeting to instruct local blacks how to refuse instructions to sit in the balconies and upper corners of the area's assorted entertainment venues. Led by Lewis Sommerset, editor of Monmouth County's leading black newspaper, *The Mail and Express*, members of the meeting expressed outrage that they could no longer "sit where we could pay to sit." Pointing out that the new proprietor of the venue, H. J. Garrity, hailed from Asbury Park, "where race prejudice in amusement places is almost as thick to cut with a knife," Sommerset declared that local blacks would not allow similar Jim Crow policies to restrict their consumer rights. Before Garrity's appointment, the *Mail and Express* declared, "There were not many white people who were afraid to sit alongside a decent, self-respecting colored in the opera house or any other place." For those reasons, Lewis Sommerset noted that he would mobilize a series of mass meetings and sit-ins to challenge any policy that refused to acknowledge past interracial precedent. "Colored people have always sat where they wanted to in the opera," Sommerset explained, and "Mr. Garrity's color line will not prevent them for fighting for those rights in the future."[22]

The successful application of both violent resistance and peaceful protest allowed African Americans to confidently challenge many of the Jersey shore's Jim Crow boundaries. In the summer of 1891, the *New York Times* remarked that "the colored waiters are in hot water" after they refused to put an end to all-night dance parties held in the Convention Hall pavilion. According to local ordinances, individuals or groups had to obtain a pass to host a party or small gathering in the pavilion. Black patrons, however, found that their requests to reserve the space were increasingly rejected as Mayor James Bradley attempted to rein in the consumer demands of black individuals. Yet, despite these restrictions, African Americans ignored repeated threats by Mayor Bradley to raid the pavilion if the dancing continued. Indeed, the *Times* admitted that the "colored people will resist any interference from the authorities," and "there is likely to be a lively time" if African Americans wanted one.²³

White citizens also quickly discovered their limitations in enforcing segregation ordinances in Atlantic City. During the summer of 1890, the *Washington Post* complained that "local blacks by the hundreds were invading the bathing districts heretofore patronized by the best visitors." Off the beach, the article noted, the situation was "similarly lax." "After the colored waiter serves his master's supper," the columnist explained, "he can go out and elbow him on the boardwalk, crowd him in cars, or drink at the very next table in almost any café." Responding to the *Philadelphia Inquirer*'s plea to "keep blacks in their place," the *Atlantic City Daily Union* admitted that only the "collaboration of all the beachfront proprietors could keep the blacks in their place, a collaboration which (one suspects) was unlikely."²⁴

As these incidents make clear, the refusal by black northerners to abide by the segregation statutes not only spoke to their desire to maintain their moral dignity and assert their rights as citizens and workers for leisure time, but also reflected their claims to consumer rights. For black and white citizens in the post–Civil War North, the right to consume became a new proving ground for citizenship and social affirmation of individual rights. While white citizens sought to group all African Americans within a subaltern racial class, black workers and tourists insisted that they were autonomous individuals capable of competing in a free labor system and enjoying their rights as consumers in a responsible manner. By staging public protests against white business owners, black workers at the New Jersey shore transformed the segregation debate by destabilizing the cultural symbols and texts that shaped the region's legal and social rules. Whereas whites sought to legitimate segregation as a system that the invisible hand of the market—and not the personal prejudice of northern citizens—sanctioned, African Americans argued that the postwar northern marketplace carried specific racial values that often trumped its supposedly neutral ones. They reiterated to those who sought to deny them their right to leisure space that race had an economic value in the postwar North that prevented citizens—even those with the financial means—from taking part in a rapidly expanding mass consumer society.

In a short speech protesting the emerging segregation laws in Asbury Park, Robinson spoke of the discriminatory language of Asbury Park's *Daily Journal*, whose resentment and prejudice encouraged "one to think it was edited in Georgia." Robinson explained that "at a place set apart for temperance and religion we witness a spectacle that should shame the boasted civilization of the North. Let us devote ourselves to stripping off false religious sentiment and hypocritical philanthropy, that we may expose before the people just how far race hatred can go in New Jersey." Fellow Methodist minister Rev. H. H. Monroe of St. Mark's Church similarly remarked that talk of exclusion and separation "would be bull-dozing if it was reported from Texas," and pointed out that in many northern public spaces devoted to leisure and consumption the same "ante-war spirit of race distinction still prevailed."[25]

By nationalizing the problem of segregated leisure, black northerners contrib-uted to the postwar tradition that white industrial workers in the 1860s and 1870s initiated in arguing for "eight hours for what we will." Yet, while many white industrial laborers rejected the consumption habits and amusement venues of New England's leisure class, black workers and tourists who traveled to the New Jersey shore claimed those consumer spaces as their own. "Let the necessity of labor," W. M Dickerson instructed, "never take away a person's claim to respect-ability. One's ability to board at a hotel and dress well is no criterion of one's moral worth." Reverend Robinson of the African Methodist Episcopal Church in Asbury Park instructed the town's white boosters that the "poor colored people did as much for the prosperity of the park as the poor whites, and yet the poor whites wanted protection from them." Andrew Chambers, writing in the *Christian Recorder*, mirrored Reverend Robinson's complaints. Chambers challenged Bradley and others to answer, "To whom are we a source of annoyance? To whom are we an offense and an eyesore?" Noting the interracial contact between black domestic workers and white tourists throughout the town's business establish-ments, Chambers answered that "it surely cannot be those whom we pass the butter dish in hotels and boarding houses," since, he pointed out, "if it were, then they would seek other resorts, if it be possible for them to find anywhere they will not find some of us."[26]

The debate between segregationists and northern blacks reflected broader nineteenth-century struggles over the category of the "social" in deciding the rights of consumers and shaping the political vocabulary of segregation. Throughout the nineteenth century, legal rulings evoked the defense of the social to justify the exclusion of blacks and other outsiders—especially those who lob-bied for rights that the marketplace had supposedly denied. According to James Bradley and other local Jersey shore business owners, such measures were le-gitimate regulations not because they were motivated by racial prejudice, but because they were sanctioned by the economic realities of leisure enterprises—a special circumstance that allowed all public and commercial space to fall under the realm of the social, thereby officially eliminating the "public" sphere until it was permanently privatized.[27]

Black workers and tourists, on the other hand, argued for a limited definition of the "social," one that reflected the public and democratic nature of the
common law tradition, while also allowing them freedom of movement and the
right of "choice" they had come to believe was inherent in a consumer-oriented
market economy that northerner merchants began to champion in the 1880s.
Writing in the *Christian Recorder* on August 3, 1893, J. H. Morgan offered an
alternative solution to the values northern whites attached to the common law
and the postwar marketplace. "We think Mr. Bradley's position is better illustrated," Morgan instructed, "by a party who owns a house and turns it into a
public inn for the accommodation of the public," with the exception, Morgan
acknowledged, "of ejecting all disorderly and obnoxious persons, but not simply
on the ground of color."[28]

In calling for a free consumer society, black activists pushed to make the right
of consumer choice the new proving ground in deciding economic freedom. In
redefining the legal and ideological parameters of public and private in a free market system, blacks and whites reached opposing definitions of choice. Northern
whites believed that the market permitted segregation because economic sanc-
tions and regulations were based on social tastes and public opinion, a feature
of the market, which if deregulated would erode the moral foundations of civil
society. Black protestors, however, believed that the right of consumer choice was
absolute, and if struck down would allow other industries to promote racially
restrictive covenants. In an editorial to *The Sun*, a black visitor to Asbury Park
remarked that the right of consumers to make unregulated choices was a basic
civil right. "If seats are provided for the public," the unnamed visitor to Bradley's
resort noted, "the colored people have as much right to them as the white people.
First come first served must be the rule, and whoever finds an empty seat is at
liberty to take it, whatever his complexion." Noting the insistence by many whites
that property rights precluded demands for integration, the editorial forcefully
declared that the religious origins of towns like Asbury Park disallowed such
harsh measures. "Nor even if they are private property," the visitor exclaimed,
"is it possible to make any reasonable discrimination against their use by decent
colored people."[29]

To counter the Jim Crow sentiments and segregation laws, many black workers resorted to a variety of hidden tactics and strategies to desegregate the region's
public sphere. Occupying spaces white citizens had deemed off-limits to black
visitors, African Americans stripped those spaces of their cultural value and, as a
result, their economic value. In 1893, the *Atlantic City Daily Union* reported that
after a black waiter became disgruntled with the food options available to him

during his shift he decided to order a meal from the main menu. Upon being refused his request because the menu was off-limits to black workers, the waiter rounded up the waitstaff and walked out. A similar demonstration took place when black workers at the Albion Hotel in Atlantic City walked off the job to help secure better wages and integrated access to the hotel's leisure accommodations during their free time. In even less visible ways, many black service workers sought out revenge outside the watchful eye of white consumers. As one Atlantic City black worker explained, a waiter might act the role of a dutiful servant in front of white patrons, but back in the kitchen he or she often resorted to more subversive and rebellious behavior. A black college student who waited on white guests in Atlantic City recounted, "We suffered from rude or half drunk guests who called us degrading names because of our color. We could in a way always get back at them. We could spit in their soup or in their beer . . . Rebellion caused us to think of ways to get even the very minute we stepped on the floor."[30]

For these and other black domestic workers, consumer culture offered a way to reject the ideologies of the marketplace that white, middle-class northerners assigned to the northern public sphere in defense of segregation. As producers of a popular culture landscape dedicated to amusement and mass consumption, as well as consumers whose spending and social habits threatened the tastes and customs of a northern Jim Crow culture, black workers found themselves in a unique position to challenge and undermine the cultural hierarchies and legal boundaries of segregation that often restricted the consumption habits of many northern black workers. By relying solely on black seasonal labor, civil rights protests from black northerners made the project of Jim Crow in the North—particularly in places along the New Jersey shore—as difficult for northern business owners as it did for those in the South. Thus, while many white northerners might have viewed black industrial laborers as a threat to white wages and free labor ideology, the demands of a service economy placed greater restraints on the marketing agents and proprietors of leisure venues than they sometimes did for other northern capitalists. James Bradley, for example, acknowledged that many families left his resort because they could not "endure the crowds of Africans infesting every promenade and public space, day and evening with their presence." After the barroom brawl at Asbury Park's Plaza Hotel in 1893, the hotel's proprietor remarked that his decision to readmit the black waiters came after he was unable to persuade whites to dine in the hotel. Many families, proprietor James Bly noted, "have been compelled to get their meals elsewhere, as the waiters would not allow any one to enter the dining room to serve the families."[31]

As a result of these protests, James Bradley was forced to assemble Asbury Park's black workers and civic leaders in town hall meetings throughout the 1880s and 1890s to reiterate that such decisions were not made to appease his personal prejudices, but enacted as a last resort to protect area businessmen who relied as much on seasonal white tourists as he did on black service workers. Speaking to local audiences in Asbury Park, Red Bank, and Long Branch, Bradley attempted to win local black support by hosting elaborate galas and allowing black audiences a chance to voice their concerns. The move backfired, however, when many northern black voters believed Bradley was resorting to bribery to retain black support. Members of the black press criticized the events as an attempt to "draw the wool over their eyes" with music and refreshments. Criticizing "Founder Bradley's case" in *The Sun* on October 3, 1893, New York civil rights leaders challenged black voters at the Jersey shore to protest the events and defeat him at the polls. "They ought to vote against him, and knock him out at the polls," the editorial declared, not only because of his segregation policies, but also "because of his conduct since he became a candidate for political office." At a campaign stop in Long Branch on November 2, 1893, soon after Bradley began speaking a black voter sprang to the podium. Rattling off a list of offenses enacted against local black citizens, the individual was soon accompanied by several black preachers and lawyers who used the public platform to call on the black voters in attendance to refuse Bradley's appeals for support and to reject his candidacy.[32]

Despite Bradley's eventual electoral victory, the consumer politics of segregation in leisure settings offered black seasonal laborers and community leaders an opportunity to engage in political issues of regional and national significance that were often denied to them by mainstream northern politics. While black intellectuals and national civil rights leaders struggled to overturn Jim Crow laws throughout the country, black workers at the Jersey shore employed an array of successful strategies and tactics to upset the social and legal boundaries that many white northerners fought to maintain throughout the late nineteenth century. Indeed, black occupations of consumer venues and commercial spaces left them virtually alone among Reconstruction-era consumer activists in lobbying for an unregulated marketplace. Unlike traditional boycotts, which were often waged to enact workplace changes or secure product safety, acts of civil disobedience on the Jersey shore attempted to fundamentally alter ideas about political economy. Black protestors who organized "wade-ins" on local beaches and refused to leave amusement venues were not lobbying for wage increases, more humane workplace treatment, or regulations on food and drugs (although they participated in these campaigns as well). Instead, in both their strategic objectives and their tactical maneuvers, public occupations of consumer venues aimed to transform the legal boundaries and social accessibility of the postwar marketplace by threatening the financial solvency and political legitimacy of local business owners.[33]

By lobbying local Republican officeholders, engaging in infrapolitical protests, and challenging the rhetorical cover of white supremacy, black workers helped make issues of leisure, entertainment, and consumption indispensable from other educational, electoral, and economic concerns that preoccupied the nation's more famous black political figures. In doing so, they made sure that free labor ideology could not be reinterpreted to exclude black recreation or to forestall political decisions on the rights of consumers. Instead, by occupying the Jim Crow spaces of the region, they actively fought to reshape segregation policy—and won—by consistently calling on white segregationists to institute a more democratic form of market capitalism that defended the rights of all consumers.

3

Marketing and Managing Jim Crow

On October 24, 1893, Asbury Park mayor James Bradley strode to the podium inside the Red Bank Opera House convinced that in order to manage the segregation debate more effectively, he and other local business owners would need to reaffirm the rights of property owners to regulate marketplace exchanges. Throughout the 1880s and early 1890s, local authorities had often tolerated black consumers, responded favorably to their demonstrations, and sought quiet calls for stricter social policies. Such actions, however, raised fundamental questions about whether business or consumers would control the marketplace. Addressing the 350 local black residents and workers in attendance, Bradley informed the polite but skeptical crowd that the notices outlawing them from the town's public and commercial spaces were posted not because he was "opposed to the colored man," but instead because "boarders refused to mingle with the servants." Reminding those assembled that he was a "Republican from head to foot," Bradley reiterated time and again that he "did not post the notices to offend the Negroes," but rather to protect the economic interests and property rights of area businesses that employed many blacks.[1]

By 1893, Bradley and other business owners awakened to the threat that civil rights activists posed to their power, profit margins, and traditional ideals of political economy. In addition, they sought a way around the complicated web of national and state legal decisions that further compromised their ability to control and regulate public and private leisure space. While federal court decisions overturned the more radical civil rights laws of the Reconstruction era, subsequent laws were quickly implemented in states like New Jersey during the mid-1880s to corroborate the decisions of the Fourteenth Amendment and the defunct 1875 Civil Rights Act. As Bradley's remarks to those inside the Red Bank Opera House made clear, more than the loyalty of white consumers was at stake. New Jersey's new civil rights laws, as well as the ability of local black workers to defy local segregation notices, not only antagonized the social preferences of white tourists, but also called into question the legitimacy of business to decide marketplace exchanges, protect their property, and shape the social profile of northern resort towns. In response, local business owners and political figures mobilized to protect these interests by selling segregation as an unfortunate but necessary solution to maintaining the free enterprise system.

Throughout the 1890s, business publicized a producer-driven vision of the marketplace that regulated the rights of all consumers and instead promoted respect for property, profits, and propriety. In response to local black workers who argued for unlimited consumer access, local authorities insisted that only proprietors could grant such rights. To accomplish this task, they adopted an informal Jim Crow legal strategy built around social precedent and a revised common law, a policy they claimed was legitimate because it operated outside the formal restrictions of federal and state jurisdiction and overrode the buying power of consumers. In doing so, they hoped to recast the segregation debate as being about political economy instead of race, castigating black consumer activism as a disruptive act that threatened not just the reputation, financial solvency, and property rights of the local resort industry, but the entire future of the American economy.

When Reconstruction ended in 1877, many white northerners marked the event as a retreat from the civil rights debates of the Civil War era. Yet, for local business owners, the years that followed yielded only increasing frustrations over how to interpret an ambiguous legal period in which laws no longer controlled social interaction or racial customs. As states like New Jersey signed into law new public accommodations restrictions against segregation, local authorities not only struggled to control the "place" of African Americans in public life, but also expressed broader concerns about the legitimacy of business to use long-standing social customs to police public space. For local proprietors and tourist promoters, such customs were critical requirements for protecting Victorian notions of etiquette and decorum and maintaining social order, ideas that were built into the mission statements and bylaws of many northern beach towns. Such restrictions, however, had been routinely ignored as tourists began insisting on an economy built for pleasure, rather than one traditionally built around restraint.

Protecting Victorianism was also critical for controlling the consumer marketplace. While an open and unregulated marketplace was often viewed as a threat to the social tastes and preferences of fashionable white tourists, local business owners saw a more insidious economic problem at hand. Without proper restraints and regulations, they argued that local producers would be left exposed to an insurgent minority faction of consumers who could disrupt the flow of goods and threaten the profits of local enterprises by driving away valuable business. In response to these fears, the local business community turned away from the courtroom to control social and racial boundaries. In particular, they hoped to make themselves immune from state laws by classifying beach resorts as private property and thus outside the purview of public accommodations. Such decisions did not mean that the law did not play a leading role in mediating political and physical boundaries. Throughout the nation, a host of legal statutes segregated schools, limited employment options, restricted interracial marriage, and denied the vote to countless numbers of African Americans. At the same time, in many public and commercial spaces, northerners turned to the cultural laws of the period to manage the marketplace, protect their property, and justify and enforce segregation.[2]

The proliferation of etiquette manuals and advice literature provided one of the many intellectual networks that whites deployed to justify segregation without admitting racial preferences. Public complaints from white tourists throughout the postwar period revealed that they took this advice as serious guidelines for dealing with "unruly" blacks who refused to comply with local segregation notices. Explaining the utility of etiquette, Timothy Howard instructed northerners that "a nation is a number of people associated together for common purposes, and no one can question the right of those people to make laws for themselves." To those black northerners who felt themselves wronged by the emergence of segregation, white tourists seemed to agree with Howard's explanations that "no one, however fine his education, or however great his wealth, power, or fame, should feel himself wronged in the least if this society refused him admission until he has made himself fully acquainted with the laws."[3]

Mirroring the sentiments of these advice guidelines, northern business owners and local civic leaders rejected the notion that segregation violated the spirit of emancipation. Instead, they argued that Reconstruction-era etiquette laws helped police social arenas that neither legislation nor legal rulings could effectively govern. Those who agreed with Asbury Park's Jim Crow ordinances routinely pointed out that black workers were not the only ones who were forced to abide by Bradley's rules. In defending Bradley, the *New York Times* explained, "after getting to the beach," all visitors "found that they could remain there only by doing precisely as Mr. Bradley wanted them to." If one combed the town, the *Times* instructed that both blacks and whites would find "numerous printed cards with specific rules and regulations," informing visitors "that they must not peddle anything, must not use profane language, must not wear bathing suits open to a suspicion of immodesty, must not pose in attitudes that might be considered questionable, must bathe within certain hours, and on Sundays not after 8am."[4]

Aside from these formal declarations, local officials pointed out that the public was also informed that "most respectable people would wish to be off the promenade by 10:30 p.m." This last point was an instructive one when it came to justifying segregation. In order to be incorporated into polite society, postwar Victorians believed that citizens needed to have a familiarity with society's discourse and customs, an informal set of guidelines that instructed decent and respectable people in the appropriate social rules to follow besides the formal laws of a given place. In taking stock of Bradley's rules, the *Times* reported, "the majority of white people observe them, so that Mr. Bradley has little cause for complaint." Yet, "not so it is claimed with the colored folks." Frequent visitors recounted to the *Times* that too many blacks "do not read the rules, and consequently do not obey them." In permitting African Americans to congregate in Asbury Park's public venues after 10:30 p.m., Bradley avoided civil rights complaints from most local blacks. Yet, in choosing 10:30 p.m. as the designated Jim Crow time, he conveniently placed African Americans in a precarious predicament. If they followed Bradley's stated rules and isolated themselves from the beaches and boardwalks until after 10:30 p.m., they would remain in compliance with the law and not risk further restrictions. Yet, by socializing in public after 10:30 p.m., they risked the cultural stigma of violating the informal laws and customs that marked late-night recreation as unruly, dangerous, and immoral.[5]

Bradley's clever manipulation of law and custom was part of a broader effort on the part of northern whites to deflect charges of racism that emanated from black protests, and instead to justify stricter social regulations as consistent with market principles. To accomplish this task, Bradley and other white segregationists rewrote the origins of Jim Crow. Eager to paint themselves as victims of economic warfare, they took to the press to castigate black political activists as the perpetrators of unwarranted and socially unacceptable hostility who destroyed the prospect of future interracial cooperation in leisure resorts. "It has always been custom," many whites admitted in recounting the offenses of blacks, "to allow them considerable liberty." Indeed, few white business owners remembered a time when black workers and tourists had not "mingled freely on the beach, disported in the surf, skated in the rinks, and rolled baby carriages in the avenues." The purpose behind these reshaped narratives was to tell a story of racial discontinuity, in which, as Bradley explained, a period of peaceful interracial cooperation in public leisure spaces was interrupted when a new coalition of African American activists proved themselves unfit for unregulated social interaction. "The result has been," the *New York Times* noted in 1885, "that white guests have complained to hotel keepers that colored persons were overstepping their bounds, intruding themselves in places where common sense should tell them not to go, and monopolizing public privileges to the exclusion of whites." In 1890, the *Times* again noted that debates over integration came down to the "presumption of some of the colored people who offensively assert themselves where they are not wanted."[6]

For many whites, the inability of African Americans to abide by what they termed "common sense" reaffirmed their belief that most black consumers were incapable of understanding the social prerequisites for admission into public leisure space. In observing the inability of black civil rights demonstrators to conform to the social standards of northern advice literature, whites came to see black behavior as strange, grotesque, and politically dangerous, requiring the permanent implementation of segregation until blacks could prove themselves worthy of integration. Just as the recreational activities of African Americans after 10:30 p.m. reaffirmed whites' attitudes toward black's social habits, the large excursions of black tourists in September also served to exacerbate racial feelings toward black leisure and further justify segregation. "One of the harbingers of fall," the *Philadelphia Inquirer* exclaimed in September 1896, is the "annual excursion of colored citizens from Philadelphia, Delaware, and New Jersey to the seashore." Regional coverage of these excursions emphasized the comical "antics" of African American tourists whose behavior was "excruciatingly funny and furnished a fund of amusement to the whites who visited the vicinity out of curiosity." Covering the excursions of black tourists in September 1898, the *Philadelphia Record* spoke to one observer who noted that "their white brethren enjoy the antics of the naturally care-free colored folks . . . their dark faces smiling all the time and the picturesque costumes of women with their great love of color and sensuality interested and amused the spectators."[7]

Reports of black leisure were also often undercut with a foreboding sense of danger, criminality, and lewdness. A visitor who came to amuse himself with the sights of black vacationers pointed out that one particular beach in Atlantic City was littered with black women in "grotesque" costumes. However, he acknowledged that he was disappointed he did not get to witness the gangs of unruly blacks he was promised. "There were very few arrests made," he admitted, and "the race weapon, the 'razor,' was conspicuously absent." One of the revealing observations made in these reports was the characterizations of black women as "picturesque" and "grotesque," whose "sensuality" displayed for many whites unfamiliarity with—and perhaps worse, neglect of—Victorian notions of respectability among blacks in general. This stood in contrast to the evolving perception of white women throughout the late nineteenth century. In unprecedented numbers, white working-class women demanded greater access to recreational venues, frequenting dance halls, amusement parks, beach towns, and eventually movie theaters throughout the Gilded Age. These new women—independent, promiscuous, and decidedly modern—recast leisure spaces and codes of etiquette once reserved for men. Labeled "rowdy girls" by Progressive reformers, working-class women told risqué jokes, swapped stories about their sexual experiences, and courted male companions in open defiance of conventional protocol.[8]

Despite the success working-class women achieved in popularizing and legitimizing leisure time for themselves, Victorian stigmas on unoccupied and unchaperoned women still prevailed, attaching themselves to a growing public concern about the proliferation of commercial sex. Such stigmas made it increasingly difficult for working-class black women to enjoy their leisure time without offensive or degrading remarks accompanying their public outings. When white women "stepped out" alone to participate in leisure activities, it only hurt them as individuals, and usually only when they behaved poorly. In contrast, black women were rarely represented as individuals. Instead, their actions, conversations, and style were held up as representative features of the entire race. For these reasons, the leisure activities by black women and their demands for integrated leisure and free consumption aided the complaints whites publicized to defend segregation. Segregationists in Asbury Park recounted that as soon as the day's work was done, "colored women flocked by the hundreds to Bradley's beach, jostled for room on the plank walk, and said impudent things to persons who resented any effort at familiarity." The situation became worse, the individual noted, after "9 o'clock every evening," when "the negro waiters from the hotels would join them, and by giving full play to the spirits natural to the race, drive white persons back to the cottages and hotels long before Mr. Bradley's" curfew kicked in. Another white woman recounted to her husband an incident involving four black women who "jostled her off her seat." After protesting, she reported that one of the women exclaimed, "Oh, sho! 'Ts time fo' de white folks to moobe around when we gits hyar." Reporting these incidents allowed whites to use social behavior and racial reputations to shape and enforce public policy.[9]

It was not just the replaying of black criminality that whites used, but also the goodwill gestures from local white officials that segregationists deployed to control the political debate. Correspondents to the *Asbury Park Press* defended Bradley as a "friend to the negro," who unlike many southern segregationists went "to the trouble and expense of fitting up grounds and bathing houses especially for them," and through generous financial contributions gave "$1 per week to the supper of every" black church in the town. Echoing the sentiments of the *Asbury Park Press*, the *New York Times* reminded Asbury Park's black population that "Mr. Bradley has earnestly endeavored to solve the light and dark problem without giving offense to either shade of it," yet continues to face "a large amount of vituperation because, as was aptly said, he undertook to separate the sheep from the goats at the bathing pavilions and on the boardwalks."[10]

In framing segregation in the emerging slogan of "separate but equal," claims of white generosity served to limit and confine the charges of racism that black protesters used to condemn segregation. Through public reprisals, the laws of etiquette helped local authorities police public space without the interference of law enforcement personnel or courtroom legal judgments that white northerners believed were destructive to the social harmony many had come to expect in leisure and recreational venues. Instead, many officials relied on the physical stages and platforms themselves; they expected beaches, boardwalks, and viewing rooms to compel obedience. In tandem with the discursive boundaries outlined in the era's advice literature, these physical spaces contributed to the Victorian spectacle of public surveillance and self-reflection, allowing ordinary white citizens by themselves to maintain and manage self-constraint, mediate disputes, and ensure the coherence of social boundaries.

Alongside appeals to individual propriety and traditional social customs, white northerners advanced an aggressive defense of the rights of businessmen to deny African American access to recreational spaces and to control how they managed their time. In an editorial to the *New York Times*, a frequent visitor to Asbury Park complained that the "colored servant" who calls on Bradley to maintain "God's beach, depopulates it of every paying Caucasian," forcing Bradley "into the abyss of bankruptcy" and dooming his "hotels to tumble into a ruinous wreck of live slapboards and Indian red shingles." Another white visitor to Bradley's community, in what could have been adopted as the resort's unofficial slogan, declared, "This is a white people's resort and it derives it support from white people."[11]

As a "white people's resort," white middle-class tourists marked black citizens who sat beside them in streetcars or mingled with them on the beaches and boardwalks as "evil." A white visitor from New York lamented to the *Journal* that in his excursion into Asbury Park, he confronted firsthand the "evils" of black servants who served as waiters, cooks, and dishwashers in Bradley's resort community. The unidentified "Hotel Man" observed that on trains from New York and Philadelphia, as well as on the benches and seats at train depots, a sizable black faction seemed to "regard themselves as owners of all below the sky and are offensive and indecent." A reporter for the *Philadelphia Inquirer* similarly noted during the summer of 1893 that "never before" has the town "seem so overrun with the dark skinned race . . . It is easy to see," the reporter continued, "what an evil it is that hangs over Atlantic City." The widespread use of the term "evil" by white citizens demonstrates the ways in which political contests over postwar social boundaries forced segregationist defenders to defend the moral economy of consumption, a critical component to the integrity and preservation of free labor ideology. Indeed, for many whites, the market itself had become a dangerous threat to property and propriety because of its occasional tendency to homogenize social relations and equalize access. In response, local authorities attempted to promote a version of the market that defended the interests of property owners above the claims and actions of consumer groups.[12]

Alongside the routine use of the word "evil," white citizens also used more explicit economic language in their efforts to control the social behavior and consumption habits of black northerners. In editorials calling for the end of interracial space on the trains that carried tourists to the shore, whites insisted that blacks were "monopolists," "intruders," and "idle" paupers who sought to disguise their racial features for economic and social gain. Atlantic City's *Daily Journal* complained, "Both the boardwalk and Atlantic Avenue fairly swarm with them during bathing hours, like the fruit in a huckleberry pudding." Similarly, an Asbury Park visitor described to Stephen Crane the black "monopolists" who had become a "nuisance" to the resort's white tourists by demanding that unless "the number of black monopolists becomes smaller, we shall urge the proprietor of the beach to assert his right as owner and exclude them out."[13]

Such statements reflected the tendency of many segregationists to frame black consumer activity as fraudulent and politically disruptive. Throughout the Civil War and Reconstruction period, words like "contraband," "occupiers," and "intruders" entered the public's vocabulary to reveal the undefined place of African Americans in the public sphere and to mark them as saboteurs and social counterfeits whose ability to access consumer districts could only be assigned by whites. These practices were familiar strategies employed by antebellum white northerners, who during the 1840s and 1850s took pride in their ability to observe the workplace and personal habits of slaves and other industrial black workers. The practice of taking in the "spectacle" of black work during leisure hours allowed whites to delineate the divisions between work and play among racial groups, while highlighting the role that race and class played in constructing the economic boundaries of consumer culture. The unique environment of leisure venues recast notions of work and play that had traditionally maintained industrial order and solidified free labor ideology. By playing where they worked, African Americans asked whether workers' rights extended to spaces that doubled as sites of consumption and leisure. Was it possible, in other words, for an African American to be both a worker and a consumer in the same recreational space? As a result of these disruptive changes in political economy, many white business owners and cultural tastemakers were less concerned with preserving white supremacy than they were in defending their rights as merchants. To white authorities confronting a new political coalition of consumer activists, ideas about free labor became less a defense of workers' rights to labor, than it did a convenient expansion of property rights to aid consumer growth. In tightening social restrictions on area boardwalks and beaches, local authorities embraced and marketed Jim Crow policies as the rational outcome of a market that was publicly sanctioned, voluntary, and consistent with a capitalist culture dedicated to the sanctity and preservation of private property.[14]

To honor these new commitments, many business owners and resort promoters began to revise their previous motives for advertising the region's beach communities as progressive retreats. Mayor John Gardner of Atlantic City reflected that "in the early days, experiments had to be resorted to which nobody desired, because they were necessary to life." He noted further that "when the cheap excursions had to come, when questions about who came on them could not be raised" or when "other desperate expedients to raise the cash" were explored, all "deplored it." As Gardner and others who promoted Atlantic City in its "early days" noted, the delicate balance between giving "the people what they wanted" and the "hard business reality" of maintaining a profitable and popular summer resort exposed the public relations dilemma many resort owners faced under the regulations of the old common law tradition.[15]

Throughout the Civil War era, African Americans used the common law defense to pursue integration and gain legal admission to popular amusement venues. In hotels especially, proprietors faced a litany of requirements instructing them how to treat and care for paying customers. Local ordinances prohibited hotel proprietors from refusing service to paying customers who behaved themselves, and also held them responsible for providing meals and looking after the belongings of their guests. Legislators justified these restrictive measures by arguing that in taking care of the public welfare of travelers, proprietors were maintaining the peace of local communities and ensuring that confidence men and other illegitimate swindlers would not cheat decent, well-paying customers. Yet, by the 1880s, a new generation of white and black tourists flooded northern beach towns for the first time, violating—in the minds of white elites—conventional social tastes and respectable etiquette. For these reasons white business owners maintained their suspicions of national and state courts' willingness to defend social customs and justify segregation. Unable to defend their property rights against black protestors in particular, proprietors of public accommodations became increasingly subjected to local fines, disruptions of service, and jail time for refusing to obey common law rulings. As a result, African Americans successfully desegregated streetcars and other common carriers in New York City, Philadelphia, and Washington, D.C.[16]

The segregation debate at the Jersey shore, however, allowed whites to reconfigure local understandings of the common law. In Asbury Park, James Bradley's position as both proprietor and mayor blurred the lines between public and private on which the common law defense rested. John Coffin, one of Bradley's advisers, explained Bradley's unique position in defending segregation. "To reach the bathing pavilions or the bath houses or to walk on the wide stretch of hard sand where the billow came tumbling in," Coffin instructed, "visitors must encroach on the territory of James A. Bradley, who bought property here when it was a barren waste." Yet Coffin noted that Bradley did not restrict his property to his own private affairs. Instead, he "built clusters of little houses, pushed poles beneath the sand, made comfortable pavilions for people to sit and enjoy the salt breezes, and laid down a solid plank walk wider than the average street pavement." Coffin's narrative of Asbury Park's humble origins was intended to dispel the complaints of local blacks that beach towns were the public's domain. In advertising Asbury Park to prospective tourists, Bradley consistently remarked that his town was "his property to do as he pleased." As in other northern resorts that sought to relinquish the public's demands on its proprietors, Bradley called on northern "guests" to "come make yourself at home." The words "guests" and "home" by Bradley were chosen in order to remind civil rights protestors that Asbury Park was an apolitical sphere that responded only to the desires and tastes of its proprietor, a place where tourists were expected to act as if they had entered someone's home.[17]

Asbury Park was not alone in circumnavigating the common law. Many cities during the late nineteenth century found creative ways to violate state civil rights statutes by passing restrictive ordinances that permitted proprietors to eject any person found to be creating "disturbances" in hotels, theaters, or restaurants. To defend the restrictions, whites defined "disturbances" in expansive ways. This could include a drunk or thieving patron, or it could include anyone whose actions violated publicly sanctioned decorum or social tastes. Part of the laws of etiquette on which "respectable people" agreed was the idea that politics should be kept out of polite conversation and leisure spaces. African Americans who publicly demonstrated in favor of integration were cast as illegitimate social guests who ruined the vacation experience for others and threatened the public's welfare by violating standardized rules of etiquette. As a result, white proprietors declared that they were within their rights as arbiters of the public's welfare to refuse admission and uphold segregation.[18]

To defend the restrictions against those who pressed for their rights as consumers, segregationists maintained that similar impediments to consumer rights were already established in theaters, which long held to the established practice of denying ticket-goers admission to shows with tickets purchased by someone else. However, most segregationists maintained that a blanket complaint of consumers' rights was beside the point of the Civil Rights Act. "Educated colored men will not force an offensive interpretation," one innkeeper noted, and "coarse ones will not be sustained by the sentiment of the people, save to protect them against discrimination in public conveyances." Thus, while many whites agreed that the rights of consumers should be respected, they also insisted that these rights did not trump those of proprietors. As one advice book advised, northern black citizens needed to understand that true respectability was "contained in the homely maxim, 'Mind Your Own Business,' which means by a pretty evident implication, that you are to let your neighbor's business alone."[19]

Benjamin Butler, a vigorous champion of black civil rights throughout the Civil War era, exemplified this view when he upheld the common law's oath to defend the rights of African Americans, but stopped short of promoting full integration and free consumption. Interviewed shortly after the passage of the 1875 Civil Rights Act, Butler reiterated that the laws of etiquette trumped traditional interpretations of the common law and modern notions of consumer rights. Asked about the rights of black consumers to enjoy popular amusements alongside whites, Butler noted that while he was "willing to concede" that he was a "friend to the negro," he was also committed in his belief that "the white race may have at least this one superior privilege to the colored man." Like those who justified segregated leisure elsewhere by noting that respectable blacks would never place civil rights above the laws of etiquette, Butler argued that whites who ejected blacks from saloons and other leisure venues would be doing the "colored man no greater kindness."[20]

With respect to the common law, Butler refused to acknowledge that any civil rights act was a promotion of unregulated liberty. "All ideas that the civil rights bill," Butler explained, "allows the colored man to force himself into any man's hop, or into any man's private house, or into any eating house or establishment other than those I have named," is not supported by the law. Indeed, he justified the rights of "private business and private parties" to eject any African American consumer attempting to interfere with the rights of proprietors, since "it is beneath the dignity of any colored man to do so." Like the expansive definition of "disturbances" that whites created to justify segregation, politicians like Butler, and local officials at the Jersey shore, used a liberal understanding of "force" to deny African Americans admission to leisure venues. When whites talked about "force" they were not only talking about maintaining the peace from the illegal activities of conventional criminals, but were also conjuring up an implied threat to property, privacy, and propriety from individuals and consumer groups whose political activism reminded them of other social deviants.[21]

Part of the difficulty both whites and blacks faced in defending the common law was the tenuous case it presented for both sides. While many African Americans successfully applied the common law in protesting segregation, white northerners in the 1890s also began to retain faith in the common law tradition by evoking its private property qualifications. For example, while proprietors were held responsible for the well-being of travelers, the same rights did not apply to local residents. Community officials were routinely notified of out-of-town guests so that appropriate steps could be taken to remove unwanted or unsightly locals. In *State v. Wilby*, the Delaware Supreme Court upheld these decisions by allowing proprietors flexibility in defining "disturbances" and "force." Although the court reaffirmed the right of admission to "all persons," it offered one important caveat. Any guest, the court declared, "has a right to remain there so long as he behaves himself peaceably and properly, he paying for the entertainment." These exceptions aided segregationists by legitimizing two of the most important components that Jersey shore proprietors drafted in justifying Jim Crow laws. By permitting the refusal of service based on behavior, whites were free to invoke the laws of etiquette that universally marked African Americans as unfit for social life. In addition, the court ruled that integration was only absolute for paying customers, a condition that excluded a good number of black workers whose acts of civil disobedience were undertaken without obtaining necessary passes and permits.[22]

In most northern settings, the right to access beaches, boardwalks, and other leisure venues would have allowed African Americans legal options since the common law denoted differences between public and private dwellings. Yet as James Bradley's defense indicated, the unique makeup of many Jersey shore beach towns complicated the definition of public space. Bradley and his supporters routinely pointed out that the borough of Asbury Park stopped short of the boardwalks and beaches, allowing him to charge admission to such spaces and regulate them as any property owner was free to do. Indeed, the flexibility that beaches, boardwalks, and bathing pavilions provided segregationists highlighted the problematic functions of the common law defense for integrationists. Even the most ardent common law proponents and advocates of integration believed that social space could not be regulated by the state or infringed on by activist courts. Many leading legal advocates had made this clear throughout the nineteenth century. Charles Goorich, for example, explained that any legal statute had to conform to the "habits of the people." Horace Wood echoed these sentiments in *A Practical Treatise on the Law of Nuisances*. Of importance for Jersey shore segregationists were Wood's ideas about the limits of liberty and the sanctity of property. "No man is at liberty," Wood declared, "to use his own without any reference to the health, comfort, or reasonable enjoyment to like public or private rights by others." By defining personal liberty in relationship to the preservation and health of the community, Wood reassured officials at the Jersey shore that local notices and practices did not conflict with the state's antisegregation laws. Because the common law rested on a restrained notion of liberty and individual rights, segregationists remained committed to the common law since it allowed them to counter the civil rights appeals of black protesters.[23]

Wood's interpretation of the common law also offered segregationists a way around African Americans' claims for consumer rights. By arguing that a person's liberty could not endanger or sacrifice the health and welfare of the community, he reaffirmed key components of a service industry's responsibilities. As many officials were quick to explain, Asbury Park and Atlantic City were not typical communities. White business owners were obligated, they argued, to provide a service to high-paying customers, which required that they sometimes pander to the interests and opinions of more valued guests. Activities by African American consumers, which endangered the financial solvency of that enterprise by dissuading white tourists to frequent their resorts, justified the enactment of certain regulations.

As segregationist defenders at the Jersey shore articulated, a defense of privacy and property denoted that African Americans could not rush public sentiment or speed up the pace of racial feelings. To do so would violate the core philosophy of late nineteenth-century liberalism, which emphasized the primacy of the individual as the sole arbiter of his thoughts and actions. The widespread acceptance of beach towns as antipolitical spaces exacerbated and complicated these beliefs. Because the leading political and legal figures were also the region's primary property owners, the entire notion of individual rights was highly fluid. While Reconstruction politics enshrined individual rights in a host of political and legal documents throughout the postwar period, northern whites retained a contradictory approach to maintaining the peace in northern beach resorts. Indeed, the great irony of Jim Crow at the Jersey shore was that the same language used to legitimize individualism was the same one used to stifle it. In the end, this became the double bind of the common law and the postwar marketplace. African Americans could look to each as appropriate templates for integration, while segregationists could manipulate and re-create certain features of both to justify Jim Crow.[24]

Throughout the late 1880s and early 1890s, white officials in Asbury Park and Atlantic City would apply the common law to justify segregation. After officially barring African Americans from the region's beaches, boardwalks, and bathing facilities, white property owners and local officials appealed to a reconfigured common law tradition that linked the public welfare with a defense of private property and economic prosperity. James Bradley explained that African Americans were denied the same rights accorded to white tourists, because as both "colored citizens" and as "servants" their presence decreased the attraction to white visitors and threatened the economic value of the community. In a personal letter to the *Daily Journal*, Bradley explained that although racial prejudice had declined in the years since the Civil War, the presence of black tourists still provoked anxieties that would need to be worked out through public opinion, rather than through legal rulings. "There are undoubtedly many whites," Bradley explained, "who object to the mere presence even of well behaved and well conducted colored people" desiring the same leisure and commercial spaces as white tourists. A frequent visitor to Asbury Park explained in an editorial for the *Daily Journal* that "we allow them to vote, to have full standing of the law, but when it comes to social intermingling then we object most seriously and emphatically."[25]

When Atlantic City proprietors began posting segregation ordinances in their hotels, restaurants, and other venues throughout the late nineteenth century, local officials explained the need to revise the common law. "Until recently," one proprietor declared, "hotel men were disinclined to force the issue, which to them would look like discrimination." Yet "when it reached the issue of dollars, the hotel men acted." Signs posted in the employee sections of restaurants and hotels notified black workers that "we therefore require that you, our colored employees, and your family and friends, not to bathe or lounge in front of our respective properties." In an attempt to preempt claims from black workers that the new statutes violated their rights or reflected the growing racist sentiments of white northerners, the notice concluded its instructions by reiterating, "Feeling sure that you will appreciate the appeal in the good spirit in which it is made and that its observance will benefit both yourselves and ourselves."[26]

The segregationist appeals to the public's welfare revealed the defensive state of free labor ideology in an age of mass entertainment and the new discourse of consumer rights. While white elites heralded the independent worker "on the make" as the embodiment of the free labor ethic, they also sought to use the market to restrain those undesirable citizens whose personal ambitions and consumption habits threatened to undermine the social profile and profits of northern beach resorts. As James Bradley explained, "in order that those people may earn their living it is necessary" that only citizens of the "Caucasian race shall find Asbury Park attractive." "The question of color or rights," he informed, was not "to enter into consideration." John Coffin, who edited Asbury Park's *Daily Journal*, responded to those who criticized the paper for inflaming racial tension by insisting, "Perhaps people who have not been troubled with such a disagreeable monopolization of both private and public places by Negroes will think our action harsh and unjustifiable." Yet Coffin warned that "something must be done or we cannot induce visitors to come here."[27]

Mirroring Coffin's justifications, the northern press often defended Bradley's policies, explaining that economic realities, and not personal prejudice, justified Asbury Park's new segregation laws. "When he forms the opinion that a particular line of conduct on the part of a particular class of people is injuring the place," the *New York Times* declared, "it must be supposed that this is his opinion as a man of business, and has nothing to do with his personal sentiments." During the 1880s and 1890s, white northerners thus came to see two types of African Americans in places of leisure: those who worked diligently for wages without laying claim to consumer rights, and those who threatened the integral relationship between the social order and the market economy by refusing to yield to the judgments of the market. Indeed, the comments by Bradley and his supporters reveal key distinctions between how blacks and whites interpreted the role that consumer opinion played in regulating market behavior. While many officials tried to ignore the racial comments posted on the editorial pages of Asbury Park's periodicals, they could not always prevent members of the northern press and ordinary citizens from admitting that racism was the primary catalyst for the appearance of Jim Crow laws in the region. The *New York Times* confessed that the "majority of the white people" in Asbury Park "do not conceal the fact that they are pleased" with the new laws. Yet, for the most part, white northerners reaffirmed a discontinuous white supremacy. "There is no doubt," a visitor remarked to a reporter, that the calls for segregation "only reached its present outspoken vehemence after much forbearance and long suffering. Matters have simply gotten to a pitch," the individual insisted, "where the white people must sit quietly down and let the negroes run the place," or act decisively in enforcing stricter segregation ordinances.[28]

Other segregationist defenders, however, denied that public sentiment and consumer opinion were against black recreation. A group of defensive white patrons resented the claims by Bradley and other local officials that the racism of white tourists ensured the justification for segregation, a notion they believed sidetracked the debate from matters of economic philosophy. Drafting a letter to *The Sun*, the individuals exclaimed that "we protest to those portions of the article which declare that Mr. Bradley does not care to draw the color line, but public sentiment insists in drawing it for him, and that hotel keepers might almost as well admit a small-pox patient as a negro, and that white people refuse to go where they will be brought into contact with large numbers of negroes." Instead, the individuals noted that the liberal spirit of Reconstruction had ensured just the opposite sentiments. "Was it not a public sentiment," the group asked, "which was brought about by the very general feeling that the Negro was justly and honestly entitled to his citizenship and all that it entailed, and should have it?" To this question they answered, "If the color line was then drawn, it was drawn in the interest of justice and in consonance with what I would believe was an American idea of fair play."[29]

Like the racially coded language of "common sense," "disturbances," "force," and "nuisance," whites often resorted to the term "fair play" to denote segregation's market-based origins and outcomes. "It is not a race war," an editorial in New York's *The Sun* declared. Instead, it was "purely a matter of business policy," conducted for the "practical purpose of making money." Another individual interviewed for the article agreed, exclaiming that if "Mr. Bradley could make Asbury Park more profitable by turning it into a negro resort exclusively, we have no doubt he would make the change. The color of his patrons' money, not the color of their faces, is what he is interested in." To white business owners tired of explaining themselves to white liberals and black activists, discussions of race were irrelevant to the segregation debate. As a matter of sound business policy, segregation was legal, legitimate, and necessary to ensure basic market principles, without which the system would cease to remain solvent.[30]

The arguments over the uses and role of consumer opinion illustrate conflicting versions of the market's social responsibilities. African Americans insisted

that social—and not just political—equality was a precondition for an unregulated marketplace. Whites, however, insisted that political constraints like equality
imposed their own set of regulations on the market that denied white consumers
and producers free choice. "Social relations," one Jersey shore business owner
maintained, "are entirely voluntary. They cannot be controlled by force." In denouncing the claims of African Americans that equality must predate an invisible hand, the businessman instructed that "the negroes are free politically. They
have the same legal rights as the rest of the people, and the same social rights.
Social equality, on the other hand, is an impractical request in a democratic and
market-based society. Neither a white man nor a Negro can compel people to
like and associate with him." Segregation was thus legitimate, others noted, because it was not a function of the law, but rather a function of social tastes that
resided outside the realm of government or the courts. "If white people at Asbury
Park objected to the association of the negroes with them in the pavilions," another white visitor to the beach town remarked, "no law can prevent them from
expressing the objection."[31]

In defending segregation as a policy that promoted free expression and social
choice, local authorities argued that the market was still "free" since it allowed
black citizens the opportunity to pursue alternative leisure and consumer options. African Americans could accept the free expression of opinions by following the rules of a given social environment, or they could choose to frequent
a more hospitable public or commercial area. If neither of these choices were
acceptable, whites informed African Americans that if they desired integrated
and interracial leisure options they could do so only by preparing themselves to
better meet the tastes and preferences of those environments. A frequent visitor
to Asbury Park explained, "The best advice their preachers can give them is to
keep quiet and improve himself or herself individually, so that they will be more
valuable to industry." Yet, rather than follow this advice, the individual noted
that African Americans were letting their "restlessness under social discrimination interfere with their practical prosperity. . . . They cannot change the feeling
by fighting against it any more than they can change the color of their skin by
washing it."[32]

Justifying segregation as a defense of political economy entailed a careful manipulation of cultural and legal ideologies. By making the choice of integration
and segregation entirely one for blacks, whites challenged African Americans to
violate both the laws of etiquette and the laws of the marketplace—a tactic that
allowed segregationist defenders to justify their policies as just, rational, and in-
offensive. For white business owners and local officials, this narrative was a cru-

cial prerequisite for maintaining the appearance of a color-blind public sphere. If black workers and consumers conformed to the standardized modes of behavior drafted by whites, the public language of Jim Crow signs could be less offensive and perhaps nonexistent, allowing future policy makers to manage racial change by defending market-based solutions. While this strategy still left white business owners exposed to charges of discrimination from African Americans, it prevented local officials from having to correct these flaws through formal legal or political means.

4   Boycotting Jim Crow

In July 1911, *The Crisis* marked the arrival of summer with a full-page advertisement announcing to black tourists the opening of the Dale Hotel in Cape May, New Jersey. Constructed with the financial backing of prominent businessman and popular community leader Edward Dale, the Jersey shore's newest hotel symbolized the long-fought efforts of local blacks to counter the disparaging attacks on black leisure and to fill the void of respectable tourist accommodations for out-of-town guests. Acknowledging that black consumers were often turned away from many of the region's respectable hotels and confined to ill-kept and cramped accommodations, *The Crisis* proudly exclaimed that the Dale Hotel was the "finest and most complete hostelry in the United States for the accommodation of our race." Boasting magnificent views, modern amenities, and convenient access to the seashore, the Dale Hotel—and similar capitalist ventures—became proud symbols for African American tourists and political models for entrepreneurial skill, property ownership, and free consumption during the early Jim Crow era.[1]

During the 1880s and early 1890s, the preference for civil rights activism and the lack of capital prevented many African Americans from developing an entertainment and consumer district of their own. Yet, despite early civil rights victories, by the late 1890s northern black workers faced mounting obstacles in their quest for integrated leisure and free consumption as the white business community consolidated its power over the public sphere. In response, local black leaders reconfigured their approach to civil disobedience and consumer protests by calling on black workers and tourists to boycott white establishments and public venues that denied them entry and instead to "spend your money among your own people."[2]

The decision to boycott the Jersey shore's white marketplaces signaled an important departure in the political ambitions and economic goals of black activists in the face of mounting Jim Crow restrictions. Recognizing the urgent need for economic expansion and social autonomy, many black ministers and entrepreneurs argued that the right to consume was now greater than the right to integrate. The public image and financial solvency of the black community rested, they argued, not on their ability to enjoy area beaches, boardwalks, and amusement venues alongside whites, but instead with the ability of African American entrepreneurs to build lucrative leisure ventures that provided black consumers with affordable, safe, and popular recreational options.[3]

To promote and sustain a black leisure industry, black business owners negotiated land deals with skeptical developers, sought out fund-raising dollars to promote their ventures, fought against prevailing cultural norms that denied the prospect of black entrepreneurial skill, and strove to keep away the long arm of law enforcement and scheming whites who sought to belittle, shut down, and regulate their enterprises. This philosophical change differed significantly from earlier intraracial debates, in which a culturally influential black elite had historically scorned consumer culture as an economic impediment that blocked upward mobility for African Americans and incited white backlash. In contrast, black entrepreneurs articulated a path toward free consumption and economic autonomy that looked to promote intraracial production and consumption from within. By boycotting the white boardwalk economy, they hoped this new strategy would permanently shield black workers and patrons from the damaging moral and financial effects of Jim Crow's expanding reach, while also protecting their own ability to profit from the burgeoning U.S. leisure industry.[4]

Throughout the late nineteenth century, northern black leaders seldom agreed on how African Americans should enjoy their free time and spend their money. In 1897, W. E. B. Du Bois declared that the "manner, method, and extent of a people's recreation is of vast importance to their welfare." Yet even Du Bois offered few specific plans regarding how blacks should promote entertainment and consumption without sacrificing traditional ideas about racial uplift and political economy. To many black political thinkers, the traditional notion that consumption of even "cheap amusements" led to the long-term impoverishment of the race prevented many from developing a comprehensive and modern civil rights plan for meeting the challenge of segregated leisure and regulated consumption. In the antebellum North, the black press spoke openly about the "cruelty of idleness" and the lack of respectable outlets for spending one's leisure time. In 1837, the *Colored American* admonished its readers for "always finding some excuse for killing that precious time," which could be better spent, in the "cultivation of our minds," building libraries, frequenting reading rooms, and attending "useful lectures." For conservative black leaders concerned with how the examples of black workers affected racial progress, the "pernicious example of idleness" presented a "national burden to others" interested in discrediting racist imagery and Jim Crow policies that denied African Americans equal access to civic and consumer life.[5]

After the Civil War, Booker T. Washington advanced these ideas most famously in his acclaimed autobiography *Up from Slavery*. In an effort to persuade white northerners that African Americans were the true champions of the free labor legacy, Washington offered scathing rebukes against workers—black or white—who championed leisure and consumption over labor. Using his own history as a domestic servant to extol the virtues of industry, thrift, and sobriety, Washington admonished those who sought to achieve equality through political and social agitation, exclaiming it foolish to pursue integration by means other than "perfecting" oneself in the "industries at their doors and in securing property." Although his promotion of industrial education brought him into contentious debates with more liberal critics like Du Bois, and his accomodationist rhetoric drew the scorn of militant integrationists like T. Thomas Fortune, Washington's emphasis on economic self-help mirrored his contemporaries who subscribed to a similar racial uplift philosophy for working-class blacks.[6]

To set an appropriate example for working-class black northerners, leading political figures like Washington and Du Bois, along with many other members of the northern black elite, retreated from public leisure venues. They spent their summers in peripheral and secluded spots at Saratoga Springs and Newport. In the "off-season," many families and well-to-do individuals entertained guests in private residences, turning parlors, verandas, and gardens into inclusive leisure outings. These class-based enclaves, which originated in the pre–Civil War era, continued to dominate black leisure life during the immediate postwar period. Indeed, even after the war, many black consumers who desired to participate in the Reconstruction-era marketplace chose to do so through the anonymity of mail-order catalogs. Yet the growing popularity of commercial leisure during the late nineteenth century compounded the moral and economic dilemma that race leaders believed impeded national progress. Throughout the Reconstruction era, regional journalists, community pastors, and civic activists frequently admonished working-class blacks for their reckless behavior in area resorts, at amusement parks, and on street corners. Challenging black workers to "think well of yourself," they called for a national referendum on "good manners" and the eradication of the "noisy and dirty negro." By the turn of the century, scores of advice literature publications outlined appropriate public decorum and scrutinized attendance at interracial social clubs, gambling dens, and prostitution houses.[7]

Despite the proliferation of advice manuals, members of the black elite never completely surrendered their claim to public leisure or purchasable entertainment. Throughout the postwar period, evolving attitudes toward mass consumption motivated many to reclaim a space in public life. Joining other well-to-do black vacationers for extended summer stays at the Jersey shore, they found themselves in competition for public space with members of the black working class, whose own class ambitions conflicted with the standard protocol of their social superiors. Compounding these long-standing class tensions was the advent of the excursion trip. A product of modern transportation, such voyages were often financed and popularized by church groups and other fraternal affiliations. A truly democratic creation, the excursions placed well-to-do black professionals on board with the North's working-class tourists. Yet, once the trains and boats that ferried blacks to their destinations docked, the travelers quickly separated. Well-to-do blacks took up residence in cottages and sought out peaceful refuge on secluded stretches of sand. Many working-class excursionists, on the other hand, spent time in the more public sections of town. To the disappointment of black elites and white tourists, they demanded entrance to crowded boardwalks and other cheap amusement venues.

The popular appeal of the excursions made it increasingly difficult for conservative black leaders to contain the activities of black working-class consumers. Throughout the 1880s and 1890s, more and more black laborers left behind the folk traditions and local leisure districts of Philadelphia, New York City, and Baltimore for the diversified marketplaces of the Jersey shore. Out of the watchful eye of moral guardians, and unrestrained by local politics, black tourists adopted the language, behavior, and political sensibilities of free consumers. Worried that unrestrained consumption would bankrupt black laborers and incite white backlash, elite blacks kept a close watch over the behavior of excursionists and pressured promoters and religious groups to curtail their activities.

To the North's more conservative black reformers, the appeal of commercial leisure posed a direct challenge to traditional conceptions of race, gender, sexual morality, and political economy. To these elite black leaders, excursions gave license to immoral and indecent behavior that discredited careful savings, humble living, and public propriety, capitalistic prerequisites that those like Booker T. Washington believed secured their own financial success and good character. In turn, they pressured churches and fraternal bodies to eliminate the excursions altogether. The Reverend R. R. Downs of Philadelphia lobbied area organizations to disallow the practice, noting that they "are a curse to the people of the Negro race, an injury to them financially and morally, destructive to both religion and society." Highlighting the example of the excursionist who "with barely a decent chair in the house spends nearly ten dollars fixing for the excursions," Downs reiterated the sentiments of many conservative northern blacks who questioned the day-to-day decisions of working-class residents. He pointed out that too many participants were "too poor, children too barefooted and ragged," and their "homes too scantily furnished" to spend extra money on day trips to the seashore.[8]

The economic relationships that formed between churches and excursion outings also prompted many critics to question whether black ministers should be involved in coordinating and funding such trips. Noting that it causes "too many people to lose faith in the financial institutions of the church," Downs exclaimed that the inability to separate faith and finance from such activities left working-class blacks at the mercy of swindlers and susceptible to fraud from potentially corrupt religious leaders. For traditional religious figures like Downs, churches were to serve black parishioners and congregations in moral matters. While social welfare operations were encouraged, Downs wondered whether the promotion of consumption-oriented activities and profit-making schemes—however well intentioned—disrupted the appropriate ecclesiastical distance necessary to attain moral authority and uphold traditional ideas of political economy. "Loss of respect for the pulpit," Downs lectured, is inevitable when religious figures become immersed in the profit-making schemes of entertainment. "The Preacher is looked upon as a railroad agent, a huckster of tickets, both manager and flunkey on the train." Becoming part of the hustle itself, Downs argued that excursions placed preachers and other religious leaders into the raucous and deviant fray of the "bowery," embedded in the hisses, catcalls, and jive talk of such scandalous spaces. In "attempting to play the gallant in providing the comfort of ladies," Downs noted that instead, moral figures found themselves "jested, hinted at," and returned home "assailed by scandalous rumors." No one placed in such a precarious environment, he reasoned, could "maintain his dignity and run an excursion at the same time."

The vulgar language, coarse behavior, and sexual tension of the excursion train was particularly troubling for northern blacks who wished to discredit the image of black female impropriety. Observing the give and take between female passengers and male suitors on excursion trains, Downs exclaimed that even the most innocent of women are given over to the "hounds": "The abandoned women glories and exults in her shame. She sits in the laps of men associates, who regard it as fun." Even respectable females, Downs acknowledged, became entangled in the seditious trap of crude language, binge drinking, and sexual

"Black Excursionists in Atlantic City," 1895. Courtesy of the Heston Collection.

gropes. "Females, who respect themselves," he narrated, "hurridly [*sic*] leave one coach to go to another, while the polluted queens of the slums display their degradation and beastly propensities." Husbands who dropped off innocent young women returned later to collect "disgraced wives," their homes thereafter fouled by "enraged husbands." In 1896, the Federated Colored Women's Club thus moved to abolish all excursions to the shore, explaining, as Downs did, that "not a too few ruined women can date the beginning of their downfall to their first ride on one of these short trips."[9]

In his critiques of black excursions, Downs was accompanied by the editorial rebukes of the northern black press, which kept a watchful eye on blacks' recreational outings. A reporter for the *New York Age* recounted to black leaders the "deplorable acts" of black men and women who arrived in excursion cars. "Just picture in your mind a tarin of eight or ten coaches," the *Age* reporter declared, "literally packed with men, women, and children until standing room is at a premium." Add to that the "whiskey in abundance, cigars, tobacco, bad language, whooping and yelling, and you have a fair sample of the average Sunday excursion." The concerns expressed by the *Age* and other periodicals troubled many northern blacks who worried about the negative public image leisure outings inflicted on white observers. Bystanders who witnessed an 1883 brawl in Lakeside Park recounted later that even respectable African American tourists were sometimes taken to violence when "loaded up with bad rum." On one Sunday afternoon in particular, an excursion party descended into a street brawl as "knives, razors, and blackjacks flashed through the air," an event that one black observer acknowledged was the "most boisterous crowd of excursionists that ever visited Lakeside Park."[10]

It was not just violence, however, that attracted the judgment of black elites and religious figures. Seemingly innocent popular cultural traditions like the "cakewalk" became scenes for white ridicule and black moral instruction. Made popular by a local dance troupe, the Cake Walkers, the cakewalk was a choreographed series of dance moves in which the most intricate performance won a prize. The entertaining attraction for black audiences of all social classes appeared to many African American participants to be an innocent amusement activity. Yet, to white audiences, the cakewalk became a voyeuristic stage on which to ridicule black comportment and social expression. The *Philadelphia Record* recorded that white attendees "enjoy the antics of the carefree colored folks." Attuned to these Jim Crow judgments, cautionary black leaders saw within the theatrical displays of the cakewalk a minstrel act for white amusement and a cultural justification for exclusionary public policies. Observing the scene for himself, Pastor Elijah Jenkins of Atlantic City instructed his congregation to avoid the cakewalk competition, an act that in his view was the "most degrading spectacle which Atlantic City offers her visitors." He instructed skeptical black participants to observe the smiling faces and mocking gestures of white onlookers, reiterating, "White people go because they always like to see the colored man make a fool of himself."[11]

In Asbury Park, where racial tension and civil rights protests had been a definable part of the political culture during the 1880s and 1890s, divisions among blacks over civil rights became most pronounced. To some church leaders, civic reformers, and local business owners, Asbury Park was more than an excursion destination. Many long-standing residents operated cottages, inns, and other modest enterprises, and in the off-season managed social welfare agencies for seasonal workers. They formed partnerships with Asbury Park's white officials, including James Bradley, whose collegial relationship with local black community leaders and generous financial contributions led many longtime residents to defend the mayor's policies during the 1880s and early 1890s.

In a public defense of James Bradley in 1890 Reverend Gould of West Asbury Park noted angrily that black citizens were routinely the beneficiaries of the mayor's generosity. Denouncing civil rights protests, he argued that those who objected to the color line were members of the community who had made their presence unwelcome by unruly and "objectionable behavior." Although he acknowledged that recently instituted segregation laws concerned many year-round residents, he also insisted that the "spirit" of Asbury Park was "as liberal as is generally found" in any other northern community. "There may be traces of the color line visible," Gould acquiesced, yet "when the average colored man or woman shall meet the average white with the same gentlemanly and ladylike courtesies and bearings, I do not believe the color line will amount to much." Objecting further to the "uncouth and unbecoming manners" of black working-class citizens and tourists, Gould called on his community to be as vigilant in enforcing fairness and equality as they were in calling on the town's white citizens to uphold. "While we ask our white brother and sister to lay aside their prejudices, we must not forget," he insisted, "to lay aside our own, and if possible treat them with more of a Christ-like spirit than is manifested by them toward us."[12]

Gould was not the only one in Asbury Park calling for a referendum on the behavior of working-class blacks. The Reverend John P. Sampson of the African Methodist Episcopal Church broke rank with his fellow ministers and approved Bradley's actions, refusing to attend the civil rights meetings or to endorse the group's political protests. Along with A. W. Lowrie, pastor of the Baptist Mission, the two defended Bradley to the *Asbury Park Press*, noting that, "in regard to bathing facilities for the colored people, the colored people as a rule were satisfied with the change." To mobilize against the West End's civil rights coalition, they joined outspoken members of the black ministry and neighboring black civic leaders in Philadelphia and New York. These groups insisted that class, not race, should dictate the shore's social and cultural boundaries. Labeling themselves the "better elements," they sought to distance themselves from "the speakers at the indignation meeting." Instead, they singled out the agitation to the "floating colored population" who "abused their privileges," and promised to hold their own meeting "at which they will approve Mr. Bradley's action in the matter."[13]

Echoing the sentiments of Asbury Park's conservative black clergy was Col. William Murrell, a politician and editor of the *New Jersey Trumpet*, who spent most of his summers at Asbury Park meeting with James Bradley and other influential white officials in the shore town. Defending the policies initiated by the mayor to separate white and black vacationers, Morrell offered a scathing rebuke of black workers and their integrationist backers. In particular, Murrell criticized civil rights protestors who refused to recognize or endorse traditional interpretations of market theory and social customs: "In ordering the scum of my race to keep away from the pavilions, Mr. Bradley is right." For Murrell and others who defended the actions of Bradley, the denial of equal access to leisure did not just illuminate accommodationist rhetoric and class-infused moral judgment, but dovetailed with disagreements about political economy. Civil rights advocates argued that the right to consumption was equal to the right to labor and the right to property. Conservative black leaders like Murrell offered a more traditional explanation of public space and market relations. "Decent color people are not obtrusive and do not monopolize seats or make loud and insulting remarks," Murrell pointed out. "Mr. Bradley owns the pavilions and can keep anybody out if he liked to." Reiterating that consumer rights were not absolute, he concluded by stating that "it is nobody's business" but his. "If I owned Asbury Park I would drive these people away."[14]

The argument against civil rights activism by some of Asbury Park's conservative black leaders represented the judgment evoked by many successful conservative nineteenth-century black activists that the route to success in life was not to be found through collective action, political protests, or the rejection of traditional marketplace principles. In an earlier nineteenth-century debate over the proper path to prosperity, the famous political activist Samuel Cornish exclaimed, "Each one for himself, must commence the improvement of his condition." It is "not in mass," he declared, but in "individual effort, and character, that we are to move onward." In *Up from Slavery*, Washington reiterated Cornish's earlier warning, regretting the way that "members of this race or that race" had begun to look to the government to claim special privileges "regardless of their own individual worth or attainments." Like Cornish and Washington, Murrell and other prominent entrepreneurs considered their own humble origins and successful careers a blueprint for entrepreneurial success and social satisfaction. Dreams of integration were not only impractical as business-minded black leaders reasoned, but they also pushed black workers to the vice-ridden activities that stunted their upward mobility, left them impoverished, and hardened the exclusionary resolve of segregationists.[15]

Eager to highlight the political arguments of the region's conservative black leaders, the white press picked up on their announcements and activities to marginalize the West End's civil rights protests, praising Gould, Sampson, Lowrie, and Murrell for their reasoned approach to racial politics. Covering Asbury

Park's racial tension in 1890, the *New York Times* noted that civil rights activists were "a few too conspicuous colored men," and that the "attack was promptly resented by the better class of colored people." Given the continued racial tension and civil rights protests that gripped Asbury Park throughout the decade, the *Times* coverage appears ill informed and premature. Yet its in-depth look at blacks' political disagreements displayed the contentious nature of black politics over the issue of integrated leisure and consumer rights, as conservative black leaders debated with black activists in defining civil rights, public behavior, and political economy.[16]

Despite their reluctance to embrace civil rights protests during the 1880s, Asbury Park's black business class remained sensitive to their economic and political vulnerability, even when they supported local authorities. The *Christian Recorder*, for example, explained that its defense of James Bradley was rooted in the financial backing and generosity of the Asbury Park mayor. "He gave us a lot on which the Church property stands today," the town's ministers declared, "and he gives employment to hundreds of our people . . . It would come in bad taste for us to lead in a crusade against the good name of founder Bradley." Yet, to many local black businessmen, such statements reiterated and reinforced the lack of viable entertainment and consumption options for black consumers.[17]

Since the antebellum period, many leading black intellectuals and activists spoke openly and frequently about solving the dilemma, as Martin Delany aptly put it, where "white men are producers" and "we are consumers." In a sentiment drafted by many black entrepreneurs at the Jersey shore a half century later, Henry Bibb declared defiantly in 1851, "We must consume what we produce." For those who embraced the market revolution during the antebellum era, the goal was often economic interdependence rather than isolation. "An Address to the Colored People" of Cleveland, Ohio, dated September 6, 1848, declared to those in attendance that northern blacks should strive to "make white persons as dependent on us, as we are upon them." Turn-of-the-century black advocates, however, were not so ambitious to reconfigure the market culture or Jim Crow system of the Jersey shore. Instead, in an effort to protect their right to consume, they called on black workers and tourists to boycott Jim Crow leisure spaces.[18]

The urgency with which many black civic leaders and entrepreneurs approached these matters in the 1890s and early 1900s reflected, in part, the rapid development of segregation at the Jersey shore in the preceding decade. In 1883, a correspondent for the *New York Globe* noted that in Atlantic City, "we learn of one of two kept" places that refuse black patrons, "but it is not general and our race does a good deal of business." "Prejudice," the *Globe* exclaimed, "is not felt here." Although Atlantic City would not begin to officially institute segregation until 1904, many black leaders of the resort town's "Northside" felt the pressure of Jim Crow's cultural and economic power rapidly mounting in the 1880s and 1890s. Black domestic workers, for example, who had been a mainstay in northern resort towns since the antebellum period, were slowly being replaced by white female "help" at the turn of the century. White tourists welcomed the change as long overdue by expressing their distain for the "poor service" and incessant political demands exhibited by the city's black domestic servants. A drummer for a white traveling band in 1903 noted that many whites began to abandon hotels that employed only black waiters. "It is not the tip they object to," he explained, "for girls get that, too; but it is the poor service they get unless a colored waiter feels sure beforehand he is going to get something."[19]

In the years immediately following the *Plessy* decision, it was not enough for black leaders and capitalists to push for behavior modification or to consolidate class status. In northern resort towns, and elsewhere, black consumers faced a tightening of entertainment options in white-controlled service economies, and black workers found their employment opportunities increasingly restrained by a diversified labor pool. By the 1890s, religious leaders, civic boosters, and small-business owners began to boycott Jim Crow restrictions—resorting to collective action and individual creativity—to combat the shifting racial politics and financial realities of the region's political economy. In keeping with the moral reform impulse of many black progressives, local blacks also sought to reconfigure the ideas associated with public leisure and consumption, moving to eliminate degrading amusements and scandalous entertainment venues that made black communities the focus of national ridicule, local police raids, and curious "slummers" in other northern cities.

In an effort to promote intraracial consumption, northern black activists scorned the influx of "Black and Tans" and other interracial social clubs that proliferated in many urban centers in the post–Civil War North. Throughout major northern cities, the "Black Bottoms," "Badlands," and "Tenderloins" of Chicago, New York, and Philadelphia became synonymous with social recklessness and sexual deviancy that the white sociologist Walter Reckless described as the defining features of "open Negro community life." In an era in which segregation was best understood through the political vocabulary of privacy and property rights, the idea of an "open community life" symbolized to many white northerners an alternative political economy that ignored the critical benchmarks and boundaries that generated economic growth and contained social disorder.[20]

One such individual who best understood the economic and moral stakes of segregation was George Walls. A longtime resident of Atlantic City, Walls was a familiar face to both white and black tourists in the shore town during the early Jim Crow period. In 1894, he teamed with other local businessmen to fund the Northside's first YMCA after recognizing the lack of recreational venues available to black consumers. Walls's entrepreneurial ventures were not limited to the Northside, and in the years that followed he founded and helped run a popular bathhouse for both white and black sunbathers on Texas Avenue. As with the publicity that accompanied the opening of the Dale Hotel, the northern black press hyped Walls's establishment as a glowing example of financial ingenuity and racial progress. One northern newspaper touted it as the "Great Mecca" of black leisure accommodations, noting with pride that "this place is of the colored people, by the colored people, and for the colored people." Unlike many black venues that were tucked away from Atlantic City's boardwalk marketplace, Walls's bathhouse straddled the city's informal Jim Crow line. On sun-soaked summer days, white bathers carved out convenient spots in the sand directly in front of Walls's establishment. Black bathers, however, were "encouraged" to walk two blocks to the assigned Jim Crow beach on Missouri Avenue. The spatial parameters of northern segregation culture on crowded beaches prompted many black residents and local businessmen and women to reconfigure their approach to leisure and consumption.[21]

Joining Walls in building a separate amusement district for black tourists was B. G. Fitzgerald. Fitzgerald, who had moved to Atlantic City from the South in the 1890s, quickly discovered the lack of leisure accommodations for black consumers. Traveling Atlantic City's famed boardwalk upon his arrival, he observed the seemingly endless array of amusement venues, snack stands, and bathing pavilions operated and attended by white businesses and guests. Yet not only did many of these businesses exclude black patrons, but none of them was owned by African Americans. In response, he opened his own multipurpose venue in the heart of the Northside's excursion district in 1899. Like Walls's bathhouse, Fitzgerald Hall became a popular destination for out-of-town black guests as well as local residents. Admission to the two-story structure invited guests to seek relaxation and companionship in the building's café, saloon, dance hall, or poolroom, each of which became a go-to stop for black consumers on hot summer nights. To members of the black northern press who had championed the construction of black resorts since the 1880s, the Fitzgerald auditorium solved a pressing economic and cultural need. In 1906, the *Colored American* praised Fitzgerald for

"George Walls," 1900. Courtesy of the Heston Collection.

highlighting the solvency of investing in black leisure and consumption. "The few places that may object to our presence," a local correspondent noted, "are teaching us a lesson the meaning of which is to spend your money among your own people."[22]

In a bold move to shield black patrons from public ridicule, as well as to ensure the economic solvency of these early black businesses, George Walls petitioned the city council in 1906 to segregate the beaches by law. In Walls's mind, the move served two purposes. First, he saw the measure as a protection for black business owners and a legal sanction to what had already been established by custom. Second, he and other black business owners and politicians realized the danger inherent in the political bargaining power some members of the community waged against white proprietors. While black protests and mass demonstrations undermined the cultural value that whites assigned to certain leisure spaces and helped secure early civil rights victories, the political tactics were also economically damaging to black workers. When black waiters at the Albion Hotel went on strike in 1899, the hotel's manager dismissed the workers from their posts and replaced them with an all-white wait staff the next day. Several years later,

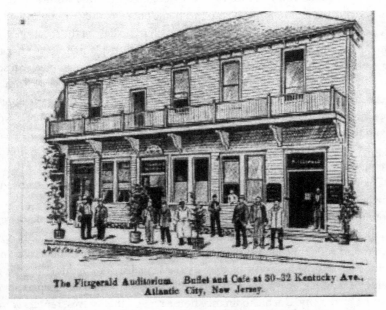

"Negro City by the Sea." Fitzgerald's Hall. *Colored American*, May 26, 1900.

another labor strike threatened to end black domestic work in the city. In 1906, waiters at the Marlborough Blenheim Hotel struck for a five-dollar-per-month increase in wages. The waiters argued that the proposed wage increase would compensate them for the service requirements that management added to their daily duties following an expansion of the hotel's major dining rooms. After refusing to work until the wage increase was instituted, the hotel's management promised to adjust the staff's wages to twenty-five dollars per month, up from the twenty dollars per month they had been receiving. By the end of the 1906 summer season, though, management refused to make good on their promise. When the 1907 summer season opened, the Marlborough Hotel no longer employed black waiters.[23]

By the early 1900s, domestic service workers were not the only ones feeling whites' resolve to enforce Jim Crow. The popular shore town underwent a construction boom during the first two decades of the twentieth century. Bricklayers, hod carriers, and road-crew workers were needed to keep up with the bevy of new projects that contributed to Atlantic City's expansion, and many black workers believed they would be again called on to complete the work. However, many black applicants increasingly found themselves excluded from such projects. A mechanic who took odd jobs for the city throughout this time admitted, "As soon as white mechanics knew of a Negro mechanic on a job, they would immediately refuse to proceed with the construction of a job regardless of the location." Harry Jump, a white contractor employed in Atlantic City, explained to another black job seeker that "if you are alone and in dire need of work, I can give you something to do but not with white mechanics, because they will not work with you." These developing Jim Crow restrictions led many black laborers to seek private work, which excluded them from membership in local unions. As one worker recounted years later, "I went to work on private jobs for myself and needed the support of the union, which I was denied. They refused to furnish me with men, forcing the curtailment of several jobs."[24]

The reevaluation of black labor by white businesses and contractors led to a growing unemployed class that languished in Atlantic City's Northside. Even in boom times, living conditions for many black workers had been bleak. Most seasonal lodgers were jammed together in cramped, dingy, and unsanitary spaces. Year-round residents often suffered the worst. Unemployed, in debt, and in bad health, they faced the brunt of the city's seasonal work rhythms. By the early twentieth century, many sections of the Northside were falling apart or condemned by the city. Unable to finance home repairs themselves, renters were left to suffer from the abuse of unresponsive, negligent, and exploitative landlords.

Just as damaging was the decrepit visual picture that black poverty rendered to whites, who used the imagery of urban decay to degrade black living situations and forestall integrated leisure and free consumption. An illustrated handbook of Atlantic City, edited by the town's major tourist promoter Alfred Heston typified this view. Ignoring the economic origins of black poverty and the social consequences of segregation, Heston instead painted a picture of black duplicity, explaining that the region's "colored people come here for the purpose of doing laundry and waiting, and their children are bottle-fed and neglected."[25]

These factors forced many black reformers to abandon their early ideas about the roots of black poverty. Instead, they argued that the exploitative practices and policies of Jim Crow rendered many hardworking men and women trapped in an increasingly segregated service economy maintained and promoted by white authorities. Black entrepreneurs and local civic leaders like George Walls and B. G. Fitzgerald thus pushed to reconfigure the labor and consumption options of the Northside. With her husband, Alonzo, local activist and entrepreneur Maggie Ridley spearheaded efforts to shield black tourists and workers from both the indignities of the city's Jim Crow hotels as well as the unseemly slums of the Northside. Together they funded and operated affordable, safe, and sanitary boardinghouses for workers in the 1880s and 1890s. In 1900, the Ridleys used the profits from these early ventures, along with a loan secured from the Northside Credit Union, to open a more lavish hotel, the Hotel Ridley. The Hotel Ridley quickly became a popular and sought-after spot for out-of-town black guests, particularly middle-class tourists who were eager to pay higher rates in order to enjoy respectable accommodations worthy of their striving status.[26]

In marketing the development of the Northside's tourist industry, Walls, Fitzgerald, and the Ridleys used advertisements and other promotional campaigns to counter the disparaging images of and narratives about black leisure. A lengthy profile on the opening of the Grand Hotel in Atlantic City typified the selling features of respectable tourist accommodations and the importance of adequate leisure amenities for black consumers. Unlike many of the city's hotels and boarding houses, the *Colored American* noted that the Grand Hotel was an oceanfront venue with clean sight lines of the sea, boardwalk, and the city's main thoroughfare of shops, restaurants, and cheap amusements. Positioned within the confines of Atlantic City's "white" resort area, the owners of the hotel touted it as a respectable and affordable place for black tourists to enjoy environmentally safe accommodations. "We can breathe in comfort without being ostracized," its proprietors declared, with assurances that an "imposing pavilion" will allow bathers to "freely breathe the ozone from the ocean." Additional consumer features included poolrooms with shuffleboard, a barbershop, dinning rooms, dancing parlors, and an ocean café.[27]

In place of the typical portrait that whites painted of ramshackle tenements and illicit behavior, black proprietors touted clean, comfortable, private rooms, with reasonable rates, ocean views, and modern amenities. Additional advertisements in national publications urged tourists to visit the city's Harlow House, "the largest and most comfortable house for colored people in Atlantic City." In close proximity to local railroad depots, the Harlow House, its proprietors argued, served "first class meals every week." Other local tourists were urged to take up residents in the Clinton Cottage, which offered "moderate prices" and an ice cream parlor, the Ormond, which catered to "guests requesting a European or American style plan"; the Cape May House, which offered "airy rooms," "Hot and Cold baths," and a wide selection of "choice wines and liquors"; or the Banneker House, which invited "friends and visitors" to frequent a summer boarding house where "every effort will be made to provide for the comfort of paying guests."[28]

These early ventures would form the foundation of a much larger mission envisioned by Walls and other local business owners to lure additional black investors and capital to the region. In an 1899 prospectus, Walls explained that Atlantic City's white population endorsed the economic proposals and that black investors could be confident that the resort community "employs more Colored men and women than any other city in the country." For those concerned about the region's developing Jim Crow culture, Walls confidently reassured them that the community's black tourists and working classes "enjoy more privileges than in any other city of its kind in the United States." He was not alone in lobbying for the measure. Throughout the resort town, many black, working-class residents were beginning to see calls for integration as dangerous to employment opportunities and free consumption. These black businessmen and working-class citizens came to use segregation as a cultural and economic defense strategy to provide employment security and disentangle them from the racial confrontation and indignities they sometimes faced in designated white areas. To potential investors, black boosters reassured their constituents that the development of the city's northern sector would serve as a model for other black resorts: a blueprint for black cultural autonomy and economic prosperity, aided by "white friends."[29]

Fitzgerald Hall, the Grand Hotel, the Hotel Ridley, and the Dale Hotel thus served to persuade national readers that black-owned leisure establishments were popular, respectable, and profitable. An advertisement for a proposed Atlantic City hotel in 1921 alerted investors of the financial possibilities for savvy

Invest in a Sound and Worth-While Race Proposition!

The Ovington Hotel
To be Erected At
Atlantic City, N. J.

Cor. Pacific Ave., One Square off Board Walk

Stock now selling at $10.00 per share, 6 per cent accumulative preferred in blocks of five, with one share of common with each block of preferred.

For Further information address:

JOHN W. LEWIS, 1938 12th St., N. W.
Washington, D. C.

Get into an Enterprise that the public will support, and get into it before most people awake to its possibilities; here lies the secret of fortune.—*Rothchild.*

"Invest in a Sound and Worth-While Race Proposition!" Advertisement for proposed black-owned hotel in Atlantic City. *Washington Times*, May 31, 1921.

and creative entrepreneurs. Published in black newspapers throughout the East Coast, John W. Lewis called on black entrepreneurs to buy shares in the Ovington Hotel, which was to be built on the corner of Pacific Avenue, one block from the center of Atlantic City's main boardwalk complex. Marketing the financial potential of the project as a "sound and worth-while race proposition," Lewis called on skeptical investors to "get into an enterprise that the public will support, and get into it before most people awake to its possibilities, here lies the secret of fortune." As Lewis's proposal indicates, the attraction of black-owned leisure lay not only in its reaction to segregation, but also in its unique and profitable potential for black capitalists. Indeed, the unique position of the proposed project, which sought to place it near many white-owned establishments, informed northern blacks that the emergence of segregation at the Jersey shore did not mean that African Americans needed to abandon recreational and economic pursuits, nor would they necessarily have to confine themselves to the margins of consumer life.[30]

The development of Atlantic City's Northside in the first two decades of the twentieth century was indicative of black investors' and entrepreneurs' efforts to construct a black resort industry nationwide. Throughout the South and Midwest during the Reconstruction period, black businessmen began to cater to tourists in "black Chautauquas" and other black-owned resort communities. Besides serving as a recreational sanctuary for safe and secure fun, these resorts were self-improvement retreats that offered a place for political organization and racial uplift. By the early twentieth century they became part of a broader postwar leisure tradition—championed by both whites and blacks—of balancing recreation with self-improvement. For many northeastern black boosters, however, these black resorts offered a more practical and profitable solution to the endemic racial confrontations and economic exploitation they faced from white tourists and financial institutions.[31]

In addition to the problem of adequate housing and tourist accommodations, the development of segregation along the Jersey shore also forced many African Americans to reconsider their labor options. In a reversal of the "wages of whiteness," the increased reliance on white domestic labor in Atlantic City significantly depressed wages for all waiters, hotel attendants, and service workers and in particular for African American workers. The effects of these changes threatened not only to end the golden period of available and lucrative work for African Americans, but also to close off sites of consumption to black workers and tourists. As many local residents and reformers understood, the civil rights achievements of the 1880s centered on the availability and desirability of black labor. Unable to secure other labor alternatives, white business owners were often forced to concede to the integrationist demands of black working-class consumer advocates. Yet, as more and more white proprietors secured affordable and socially acceptable labor alternatives after 1900, many African Americans decided that the availability of work and the promise of free consumption could only be attained through a regional boycott of white establishments and a reconfiguration of black labor.[32]

What had begun as a solution to housing deficiencies set off a broader debate over the role of black labor and consumption in leisure settings, particularly communities that housed a sizable year-round population. This was not necessarily a new discussion. In the 1840s and 1850s, many northern black leaders spoke resolutely about the problem of domestic service. They declared that "the occupation of domestics and servants among our people is degrading to us as a class, and we deem it our burden and duty to discountenance such pursuits." For a brief period, preoccupation with the Civil War, emancipation, and Reconstruction politics shifted national priorities to political and legal matters. However, the reemergence of segregation at the Jersey shore after 1900 renewed calls from many black leaders to rethink their economic position in the labor market. For black workers eager to leave behind their posts in domestic service, Maggie Ridley's Atlantic City chapter of the Young Women's Christian Association was a necessary and popular destination. To fund the operation, Maggie secured funds from the successful Hotel Ridley along with additional money procured from private donations. At the YWCA, a gathering place for female professional development, Maggie and her associates taught aspiring white-collar women occupational skills and marketable professional traits. Although the staff also provided a centralized system for locating domestic work in the city, the YWCA's primary function was to coordinate the staffing needs of black businesses and prepare market-ready and talented black women for work in a largely white-dominated professional service industry.[33]

Throughout the early twentieth century, the increasing role of intellectual agencies and employment networks like Maggie Ridley's YWCA were indispensable for northern black job seekers. Besides the influx of white service workers, by 1900, black community organizers were beginning to professionalize retail and service work in the city. Attuned to the changing makeup of their service industry, longtime headwaiters, hotel attendants, and other members of the black service "elite" instituted entrance exams and tightened employment qualifications for black applicants in order to retain their jobs and consolidate their class status. Many of them also joined the growing number of "colored waiters unions" to combat unequal pay and degrading treatment, and to mobilize against resort communities who no longer regarded their labor as indispensable. Not only did these decisions isolate the resorts' most marginalized and vulnerable black laborers, they significantly cut down on the civil rights agitation and racial tension of the city's main marketplaces, forcing many black tourists to seek out alternative consumer choices.[34]

These shifting economic dynamics significantly affected the employment roles and options of black women, prompting female entrepreneurs at the Jersey shore to carve out new consumer industries that black female workers staffed and cater to the unique and in-demand consumer tastes and styles of black women. Like Maggie Ridley, Madame Sara Spencer Washington resented the notion that women were relegated to domestic service. An innovative pioneer in beauty culture and black consumer tastes, Madame Washington moved to Atlantic City in 1913 and quickly established herself as a fashion mogul and formidable entrepreneur among Northside residents. Throughout the first half of the twentieth century, she built a profitable and popular beauty culture empire that included a beauty school, hotel and resort complex, industry newsletter, delivery and distribution service, golf course, and an untold army of beauty school agents who bought, sold, and manufactured her products nationwide.

Trained in chemistry, Madame Sara Washington bought raw materials wholesale from local and regional distributors and mixed her own products, peddling makeup and hair products door-to-door to customers in the Northside. By 1920, she saved up enough money to open the APEX Hair and News Company. Training local young women, she eventually established the APEX Beauty College that marketed products and beauty training to black clientele throughout the Mid-Atlantic region. During an age in which northern employment patterns were spatially coded by racial customs and exclusionary public policies, the APEX business model offered successful female beauty agents the opportunity to transcend the political and cultural boundaries of Jim Crow.[35]

By the 1920s, Madame Washington's APEX enterprises formed part of a broader style war being waged in Jim Crow America. For much of the late nineteenth century, the black beauty industry was viewed as a frivolous activity that sidetracked young women from more professional and refined pursuits. Washington, however, saw a more enterprising, empowering, and uplifting message in the promotion of beauty products among black women consumers. She used her APEX enterprises to uplift struggling and poor black women, marketing the APEX system as a "scientific" profession that led working-class women toward financial independence and race pride. Through relentless ambition and clever marketing, the APEX business model promoted respectability and lucrative work. An advertisement marketed to aspiring agents displayed the image of a professionally dressed and confident black female agent. Above the image was printed the message "Now I am my own boss." The signage was accompanied by a short biography of the agent, noting her humble origins, early struggles to find suitable employment, and financial independence after becoming an APEX agent. "Several years ago," the ad narrated, "she wondered what to do about her future." Yet, after completing the necessary course work to become an APEX agent, the woman was now "her own boss" and "owns her own home." Mirroring the individual effort and relentless ambition of Washington's own rise to wealth and fame, the ad motivated young women to believe that the path to prosperity was achieved through "your own efforts." For black women stuck in the marginalized and anonymous sector of domestic service, the APEX Beauty College offered

Madame Sara Spencer Washington, "World's Finest Beauty Preparations: Beauty Products and Their Use," 1922. Courtesy of the Heston Collection.

profitable trade skills in a modern service industry that championed beauty, individual style, and social recognition for African American women.[36]

To black female consumers in Atlantic City, the APEX product line touted individual cultural expression, race pride, and feminine virtue—traits and skills that were denied to many black women by a northern Jim Crow culture that regularly mocked and ridiculed the public appearances, activities, and consumer tastes of striving black women. In a promotional brochure distributed to aspiring agents and interested consumers, Washington used the sale and consumption of beauty products to teach black women to think as individuals. "The use and selection of cosmetics should be made on an individual basis," she explained, in which black women should consider their "own natural coloring of skin and hair together with their texture." Cautioning female consumers to avoid the ideas of beauty marketed by white beauty agents, Washington reminded black women that "what is attractive on some model or even friend of yours, may possibly be unbecoming to you." More important, Washington insisted that there was a direct link between professional women and those who appealed to their individual inner beauty. "A woman who is smartly dressed is one who wears clothes to her physical background," she explained. In place of the degrading images of blackness popularized in Jim Crow renderings of black women, Washington used black consumer culture to persuade African American women to take pride in their natural features. "We did not determine our own individual features," she reminded black consumers, but "we can do much with cosmetics" to highlight the most desirable of those features. Indeed, as Washington explained, the APEX line of beauty products enabled African American women to take pride in the cosmetic advantages of blackness. Unlike blondes and brunettes, who were limited in their cosmetic choices, Washington explained that "those with brown skins, ranging from Cream to Copper are the most fortunate since they can wear cosmetics and clothes of almost any shades to advantage." In a Jim Crow marketplace that threatened to mock, ridicule, and exploit black consumers, Washington's assurances allowed beauty agents to take pride in their work and for black female consumers to take comfort in the promise of cultural expression and black beauty.[37]

Despite her success as a beauty mogul and cultural trendsetter, Washington was unsatisfied with the available leisure outlets for respectable women at the Jersey shore. Using funds from her other successful enterprises, she would later finance the APEX resort, a sprawling modern vacation destination for black tourists that was outfitted with an assortment of amenities and choice accommodations. The palatial estate was regularly filled with area beauty agents who mingled with out-of-town guests to create a unique social network for striving black women. For those just starting out in the business, the APEX resort was an invaluable meeting place where entrepreneurs acquainted themselves with new customers, future business partners, and potential financial backers. In a city where white businessmen shaped patterns of labor and consumption, the developing social and economic marketplace created by Washington and her APEX consortium competed openly with the exclusive service sector of Atlantic City's "boardwalk men."[38]

The promotional messages of the APEX school were symbolic of a broader realization of the potential of black consumption. Washington, Ridley, and Walls turned the Jersey shore's consumer-driven political economy into a respectable leisure district that competed openly with white businesses, promoting black entertainment and consumption without sacrificing respectability and prosperity. In an age in which northern employment patterns were spatially coded by racial customs and exclusionary public policies, the APEX business model offered successful female beauty agents the opportunity to advance socially and economically despite the political and cultural obstacles of Jim Crow.

Despite these social and economic advancements, the Jersey shore's respectable black men and women faced open competition from the proprietors of the region's low resorts and "cheap amusements" who threatened to undermine their hard-fought status and prestige. Yet, while many black civic reformers argued that such venues only sold sex and sin to vulnerable consumers, the proliferation of these low resorts was integral to the cultural and fraternal cohesion of Atlantic City's Northside nightlife. For many black tourists and seasonal laborers, the ability to enjoy simple pleasures and intimate sociability was often only found in the comfortable and safe confines of social clubs, poolrooms, dancing halls, and saloons. It was in these pleasure-seeking spaces where many working-class black consumers were free to create a personal style and cultural profile all their own. Unlike the voyeuristic venues of Atlantic City's main shopping district, the Northside's juke joints and pleasure dens took care of the rudimentary amusements and social desires of black consumers without the spectacle and legal maneuverings of Jim Crow's vigilant surveillance system. On hot summer nights, an untold number of public venues, including a great many "off-the-books operations," came alive to add to the allure and popularity of the Northside's exciting nightlife.

Like civil rights activists who pushed for a free consumer society, these anonymous bootleggers, pimps, and cardsharps pushed for an unregulated and guilt-free leisure marketplace that catered to the desires and expressive demands of black laborers. Among the most notorious venues were Charles Coleman's and Alexander Cook's gambling dens. Both men built a reputation as reckless and transient dealers whose checkered pasts often found them the targets of vice raids and consternation from local black leaders. To avoid detection from police and Progressive-era moral reformers, many low spaces hid their profile inside respectable neighborhoods. Newspaper accounts from early police raids mention a few of these consciously nondescript operations, but unfortunately little else is known. Because of the need to evade public detection and the Republican Party's inclination to protect them, the activities of these scandalous places were often buried with the men and women who ran them.[39]

If African Americans became somewhat less focused on fighting for integrated leisure by the 1920s, they retained, nonetheless, their relentless pursuit of consumption in the decades that followed. The politics of mass consumption that informed early civil rights victories was not relinquished, but instead transformed by the potential of institution building, black entrepreneurship, and fraternal solidarity. Far from "voluntary segregation," the realities of Jim Crow forced black residents, civic leaders, and entrepreneurs to rethink traditional ideas about class, morality, and economic freedom. In devising economic and political strategies for social survival, black entrepreneurs and local religious leaders shifted their priorities from moral instruction to consumer-based remedies. They turned Atlantic City's Northside and Asbury Park's West End into incubators of productive work, fraternal comfort, and free cultural expression by boycotting the Jersey shore's white marketplaces.

Rather than a symptom of black criminality, sexual deviancy, and urban decay, they promoted inclusive black-owned recreational venues as safe, secure, and healthy retreats that shielded consumers from the intrusive and degrading policies of Jim Crow. Although most black citizens postponed direct civil rights activism in favor of intraracial leisure, few saw themselves as apologists for white supremacy or Jim Crow accomodationists. Instead, they viewed their economic initiatives and political decisions as practical and potentially profitable solutions to political and economic problems that mass demonstrations and other forms of political protest had not fully eradicated. As John Cell has asked, "What was it like to be exposed, continually and relentlessly, to the double jeopardy of race and class discrimination in a segregated society?"[40] To those unfamiliar and uncomfortable with the disapproving stares, quizzical glances, and hushed sneers of the Jersey shore's public leisure spaces, the racial politics of the boardwalk, beaches, and amusement venues seemed to breed self-doubt rather than confident personal expression. For every black leader who admonished black tourists or championed civil rights, there were many others who worked independently to promote and build black businesses and entertainment venues of their own, hoping that while such ventures might not defeat Jim Crow, the availability of affordable consumer choice and fraternal comfort would prevent the cultural weight of segregation from crushing its most vulnerable citizens.

To compartmentalize, then, the political loyalties of those who failed to participate in direct civil rights activities would be to deny African Americans the sophistication of political thought often afforded to white participants. Many northern blacks—both those who operated businesses and those who worked for whites—preferred to operate in the more comfortable political circles of friends and allies. Not only did combative civil rights politics not suit their personalities, many believed that direct political acts of rebellion obscured the urgent economic concerns that faced black communities, leaving many impoverished, financially dependent, propertyless, and excluded from a developing consumer-driven society.

Those who lobbied for integrated leisure space as well as those who preferred to be left alone during their leisure hours confounded the expectations white citizens constructed for African Americans after the Civil War. For black workers who sought an integrated leisure community, segregation represented the denial of their citizenship rights and a reminder that contemporary market-based rules did not protect the consumer rights of black workers and tourists with money to spend. For other black citizens, acts of civil disobedience threatened their economic security and prevented them from enjoying their leisure hours in peace. Yet, both options reflected the black community's faith in a capitalist economy to provide profitable work, peaceful relaxation, and consumer choice.

At the same time, the decision to embrace intraracial consumption hindered long-term campaigns for integrated leisure. In choosing to boycott Jim Crow, black business interests reinforced the growing convictions of white authorities that the future direction of the consumer marketplace hinged on efforts to regulate social behavior and political actions that threatened the free choice of white consumers and the future profits of local merchants. More important, such actions worked to strengthen the wisdom and governing culture of "separate but equal" that white business interests employed to enforce segregation and deflect charges of racism. In a capitalistic society where private property, profits, and respect for the outcomes of the "invisible hand" often served as rhetorical cover for white supremacy, African Americans found little economic and personal alternatives but to pursue capitalistic civil rights strategies and tactics in their fight against Jim Crow. While many of these various endeavors produced quite remarkable levels of comfort, recreation, economic advancement, and protection, they also strengthened the overall project of segregation and institutionalized inequalities in labor and housing that could not be addressed through consumer-based solutions.

In the first two decades of the twentieth century, these evolving campaigns for equalization rather than integration increasingly required the cultivation and maintenance of partnerships with white authorities that strengthened the bonds of Jim Crow and the paternalistic culture ascribed by the logic of the *Plessy* decision. Far from undermining Jim Crow, the pursuit of free consumption and property ownership led to a greater reliance on white partners and allies for protection and legitimacy against law enforcement raiders and civic planners eager to rein in black consumption by redeveloping and repositioning the economic and cultural profile of the region and the political boundaries of the public sphere.

5   Cleaning Up Jim Crow

On September 13, 1909, the *Atlantic City Daily Press* declared, "The lid went down on the tenderloin last night." The first in a series of vice raids on black pool halls, juke joints, and other illegal gambling dens, the raids were greeted ambivalently by Republican Party city officials who worried that police intrusions into Atlantic City's black business district would upset racial harmony in the resort community and threaten the party's segregation pact with black leaders. When the raids turned to riots following an attempt by state detectives to close a gambling operation on Natter's Alley—a notorious street known for illicit amusement venues—efforts to police black communities became a referendum on the town's segregation policy and free consumption. Under the direction of New Jersey state prosecutor Clarence Goldenberg, three of the state's detectives attempted to close down the venue when local black residents and tourists blocked their entry. Shouting and jeering at the men as they made their way down the alley, the group soon gathered bats, clubs, and other weapons to ward off the vice detectives. When a plainclothes white police officer shot into the crowd, black residents fired back, igniting a riot that ended when one of the detectives accidentally shot and wounded an unarmed woman watching the proceedings from her hotel balcony. Following the incident, all three of the white detectives were arrested and found guilty of disorderly conduct.[1]

In the days that followed, local black residents and Republican Party officials condemned Goldenberg and his detectives for "inciting a riot," while a coalition of "hotel men" and local Democrats blamed the city's law enforcement and political brass for coddling black vice owners and perpetuating a corrupt political culture that purportedly allowed illegal black votes to finance local Republican Party operations. As subsequent events in Atlantic City and Asbury Park would prove, the Goldenberg raid and riot became emblematic of efforts to solve the unforeseen political conflicts and economic consequences of segregation and consumerism during the early 1900s. From 1893 to 1900, segregation policy at the Jersey shore rested on the containment of African American claims to integrated leisure and free consumption by excluding black tourists from the beaches, boardwalks, and local amusement venues, and isolating them in marginalized and unsanitary sections of town, where seasonal work patterns, exclusionary social policies, and negligent landlords threatened their financial and political well-being.[2]

Despite these challenging and discriminatory conditions, by the turn of the century many black businessmen and women managed to construct a popular and modestly profitable black leisure district. Yet, as settlement in these areas increased year after year, so did whites' discussions about how to manage and contain black consumer behavior and business activities. By the early 1900s, it became clear to many white locals that segregation had entered a critical phase. Unable to halt the complaints of social reformers to clean up the area's vice districts, incapable of expanding commercially because of Jim Crow boundaries, and facing politically damaging inquiries from local Democrats about voting fraud, the region's merchants and local politicians undertook a sweeping reevaluation of its segregation policy. Yet, unlike earlier Jim Crow debates, which concerned questions of economic rights and consumer access, debates about segregation and consumption after 1900 focused on the moral and physical health of consumers. Free consumer advocates advanced and protected the underground economy of leisure, and advocates of consumer protection advanced a program of economic growth and environmental justice. The outcome of these debates and battles provided mixed results for African Americans. Intent on making issues of consumption central to the segregation debate, black activists in Atlantic City and Asbury Park succeeded in protecting black businesses and securing municipal reforms to clean up their neighborhoods. Yet these victories came at a cost, as whites used the concessions to drown out and neutralize earlier civil rights claims to integrated leisure. By the 1920s, black activists and white business leaders constructed a shared vision of economic freedom, defined exclusively in terms of commercial development and greater prosperity. Together they helped build a consumer society at the Jersey shore that separated the right to consume from the right to integrate.[3]

In northern cities during the early 1900s, the trafficking of liquor and women and the widespread proliferation of gambling joints dominated urban consumer marketplaces. Although just as accessible in many modest cities, sprawling metropolitan areas like New York City, Chicago, Philadelphia, and Boston witnessed the public consumption of these illicit economies on an unprecedented scale. Facing pressure from Progressive-era moral reformers, many city governments and private organizations engaged in a variety of reforms and state-sponsored initiatives throughout the first decade of the twentieth century to regulate and close the most scandalous venues. By the 1910s, temperance advocates were widely successful in eradicating and rerouting the disreputable places from the main (and white) thoroughfares and marketplaces. The result of these reforms, however, did not officially end the availability of low resorts. From Chicago to Boston, juke joint operators, pool hall proprietors, pimps, and cardsharps set up shop in designated "interzones"—unregulated spaces located in many African American neighborhoods, where the popular businesses served an interracial clientele under the unspoken cloak of immunity.[4]

Few of these areas were more notorious than Atlantic City. The spiritual home of "booze, broads, and gambling," the "world's playground" became, by the early 1900s, the go-to summer destination for those seeking simple pleasures and "something for nothing." Atlantic City's unique appeal owed its reputation to the civic planners and resort promoters, who in tandem with local businesses and public officials had long marketed the idea that politics should serve consumption. By the mid-1890s, though, other political interests coalesced to redefine and reshape Atlantic City's scandalous public image. Not immune to the Progressive-era impulse to halt the racial impact of urbanization, Republican Party bosses found themselves increasingly attacked from moral reformers, muckrakers, and local Democrats who called on the city's power brokers to end the vice-ridden political economy that earned the city the unfortunate moniker of the "Sodom and Gomorrah of New Jersey." In a startling exposé on Atlantic City's illicit venues, the *Philadelphia Inquirer* detailed an alarming comfort among city residents with "Atlantic City's Foul Blots." "The elements of low life have been allowed to gain what may be truthfully termed a dangerous ascendancy," the article declared, noting that particular leniency had been granted to brothels and prostitutes. "Notorious women are free to lure their victims to their gilded dens," in a city (the *Inquirer* proclaimed in a follow-up story) where "everything goes, and it is not one better than Coney Island."[5]

Despite sporadic raids to wipe out the resort's disreputable venues, the proliferation of sex and sin seemed to be increasing in Atlantic City, while other northern cities were cracking down on their underground economies. By the middle of the decade, compliant hotel keepers, restaurant owners, and boardwalk operators abandoned the official party line and called on local officials to enforce New Jersey's "Bishop's Law"—forbidding the sale of alcohol on Sunday—and to close the thriving red-light districts in the city's Northside that threatened to undermine Atlantic City's white establishments. Home to the coastal community's black excursion district, the Northside soon became the public face of Atlantic City's vice problem. Republican Party bosses, headed by the notorious

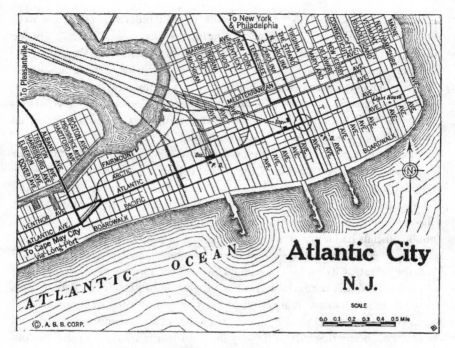

Atlantic City, 1900. Courtesy of the Atlantic City Public Library.

"Commodore" Louis Kuehnle, forged a political coalition with the Northside to protect black businesses in exchange for party loyalty. The pact was central to the racial politics of consumption in the city, whereby blacks' support for party candidates and an understanding to keep away from designated "white beaches" and "cheap amusements" bought political autonomy for the Northside's developing black leisure industry.[6]

In facing public pressure to end vice in the city, Atlantic City's ruling class confronted the prospect of losing their grip on the fragile and unofficial segregation policy that divided the town (but ultimately kept the peace). Unwilling to crack down on noncompliant white establishments that bankrolled the party establishment and funded municipal improvements and commercial projects, the Commodore and his associates ambivalently adopted a hidden-hand approach to the problem of vice by singling out, through show raids and other staged law enforcement operations, the most notorious gamblers, bootleggers, and brothels of Atlantic City's Northside. As a show of support to their white supporters, the

Commodore tipped off the city's white establishments, leaving the owners and proprietors of black-owned venues to face the brunt of police raids and indicting Jim Crow headlines alone. After Chief Eldridge raided and closed down Joshua Foreman's gambling joint on Arctic Avenue, the local press angrily noted the shameful theatrics of the raid. "Even the police laughed at the farcical attempt," the paper explained, "at a general raid, and within an hour after the colored men were arrested, they had been bailed out by white politicians and all the dens opened up again." Black establishments raided during the summer of 1907 followed a similar pattern as police alerted white vice operators before condemning Joseph Ford and Bud Griffin's gambling houses.[7]

Although the raids were generally not injurious financially to those arrested and the Northside's respectable establishments were left alone, they contributed to the public image of black leisure and consumption as dangerous, corrupt, and illegitimate. Whites who might only read the headlines or glance at the pictures showing a huge bar across the door of a black establishment registered a set of images that confirmed the racialized depictions of poverty, vice, and criminality in turn-of-the-century popular culture narratives of black leisure communities. Even the most well-intentioned sociological surveys of the city's black community affected and implicated the racial politics of the city. A 1912 representation of the Northside's slum districts by sociologist Margaret Brett stirred up the complaints of Democrats, who pushed for a firmer boundary line separating the two communities and a more aggressive law enforcement policy. In attempting to explain the challenging seasonal employment patterns for service workers, Brett's findings instead confirmed the environmental fears that many hard-line segregationists expressed about the need to condemn black leisure establishments in the Northside. One black employee of an Atlantic City hotel revealed to Brett that he often "accumulated boardwalk feet, nervous prostration and a plentiful lack of clean linen" that he took home with him every day. Lacking "proper facilities" for tuberculosis and other debilitating diseases themselves, city residents, Brett explained, became a blighted spot on the resort city's public image, threatened the hygiene of respectable whites, and endangered the consumer health of white marketplaces.[8]

To Democrats, though, the most troublesome effects of these arrangements were that they left many of the city's black residents beholden to Republican Party officials who used the "slack seasons" to recruit needy residents onto its welfare rolls. In a city defined by consumption, the winter months meant that only the "steady" were kept on, while the city, Brett explained, was left to deal with "unpaid landlords and overtaxed city funds." The result, Democrats explained, was a corrupt political culture defined by the "cheerful philosophy" of black residents and Republican Party officials that it was the party's "duty to care for them." By highlighting the prevalence of black poverty and unsanitary living conditions in the Northside, Progressive reformers gave fodder to Democrats who complained about black voting fraud, and provoked fears in the minds of tourists and business owners who worried whether the immoral behavior and corruption that seemed to underwrite politics in the Northside would inflict economic and social damage to the city's main beach economies.[9]

To Kuehnle and his Republican cronies, however, the purpose of the raids were not to support law and order, but to reclaim the promotional edge over a Progressive-era moral constituency dedicated to reframing Atlantic City's politics and social profile. Mirroring Reconstruction-era promotional efforts that once claimed Atlantic City as the nation's preeminent middle-class resort, Kuehnle and his supporters used battles with temperance agents and segregationists to remarket the resort town as a glowing modern symbol of free consumption. "Atlantic City is one of the most remarkable manifestations of American life," officials declared to a *Philadelphia Bulletin* reporter. Defining the boardwalk and other consumer marketplaces as the "greatest illustration of 'Triumphant Democracy' in this country," the *Bulletin* agreed, touting the popular marketplace as the only one of its kind where "the rich and the poor, the millionaire and the bootblack, the owner of the luxurious cottage, and the denizens of the excursion homes all meet on common ground."[10]

For Republicans, battles over vice venues and disagreements over the city's segregation policy revealed a fundamental difference over political economy. Kuehnle and his black supporters helped to popularize a new consumer-based governing philosophy that identified individual and economic liberty with the freedom to consume. Democrats and moral reformers, on the other hand, scorned Atlantic City's free consumer society because it provided normally responsible citizens unregulated license to abandon the social protocol of industrial order by imbibing in the sinful desires and forbidden pleasures of illicit marketplaces. Holdovers from an older—but no less politically potent—free labor ideology, they found themselves in competition with a modern political culture increasingly beholden to consumer interests and interracial constituents.

Yet, when Goldenberg and his detectives arrived in Atlantic City in the summer of 1909, the Republican Party's delicate Jim Crow pact was left exposed. Since the segregation pact was meant to keep the peace, the Goldenberg riot unveiled to many opponents the extent to which extralegal maneuverings held the fragile peace together. Democrats used the fallout from the riot to investigate the city's police department, and to inquire about the electoral activities of the Republican Party's African American supporters. Charles White, president of the Hotel Men's Association, criticized Republicans and the city police department for openly undermining attempts to control black leisure activities. "The business element of this city, not those so-called reformers," White declared, "have been for some time trying to close the gambling houses in the negro section in the back part of town." Yet "we found," White explained, "that they were reopening one by one, and that all appeals to the police were in vain." The city's police chief, Malcomb Woodruff, rebuffed charges of impropriety and cautioned Democrats to avoid inflaming additional racial tension by "making sensational issues at critical times." Yet, to White and his supporters, the government's response revealed the great lengths to which Republican Party officials would go to appease their relaxed Jim Crow policy and protect their black constituents.[11]

Democrats had alleged black voter fraud in Atlantic City since 1892, when Democratic challenger William Riddle lost his bid for the New Jersey State Senate to Republican Party incumbent Samuel Hoffman. In the aftermath of the senatorial campaign, Riddle complained that Republicans had won only by "colonizing the colored Republicans in the city." At a senate investigation the following January, Riddle testified to multiple cases of election fraud in which fictitious black residents cast votes for Republican Party candidates. In addition, he claimed that other unidentified black voters were registered to vote in Philadelphia, Washington, D.C., and "more distant points," and shipped in on Election Day to support Republican candidates. Following the 1909 riot, Democrats again attempted to link Republican Party political success to a systemic black voting scandal. Speaking to the *Philadelphia North American*, local Democrats explained that the "protection" Republicans provided to the Northside's black leisure district was "granted to the dives, not for money, but for votes." Noting the susceptibility of the local black population "to the blandishments of the gambling house and the resort of evil," officials linked this evil with even greater political offenses: "The balance of power rests with the Negro and the vicious white element in the Third Ward. This is Kuehnle's stronghold. It is the tenderloin of Atlantic City as McNichols' Tenth Ward is the tenderloin of Philadelphia. From this source, Kuehnle and his partners get the political strength to control the government of Atlantic City. From this lair marched the arrogant mobs of thugs and crooks, which the other night defied the law, broke into the regions of respectability, from which they hitherto been excluded, and ended a riot with potential murder."[12]

However, as Democrats scoured the Republican Party and degraded black leisure enterprises, they were also busy courting the Northside's votes in the fall

of 1909. Having defected from Kuehnle's grip, prominent hotel owners did the
party's bidding, reminding black workers that it was they, and not the Commodore, who provided them work and steady pay. Charles White explained to the
Atlantic Review that "every colored voter must realize that his welfare depends
upon the welfare of the hotel men." As White and others explained, the black
worker was no longer the cheap commodity he had once been, and hotels could
easily secure "white waiters and waitresses just as cheaply as they could colored
men." To Democrats, the threats were designed to mark a clear distinction between the employment they provided and the welfare assistance Republicans
doled out. As Lawrence McCoy explained, "This is the one time in local politics
when it is a black man's fight as well," before hinting that black voters should
support the men who profited from their labor over public officials who bought
their dependency.[13]

African Americans in Atlantic City responded to these scandals and the larger
political contest to win their vote along similar lines. Tired of being pawns for
the Republican Party, and unwilling to support local Democrats who routinely
appealed to conventional racist tactics to win support from segregationists, local black leaders in the Northside's Third Ward attempted to stake out a middle
ground. Yet, after they were reprimanded by Republican officials for attempting
to form an alternative wing of the party in 1906 and 1907, Northside leaders were
left to support the new coalition of hotelmen whose loyalties were suspect, or
faithfully serve the Republican Party platform.[14]

Throughout the fall campaign, a small contingent of black workers attempted
to challenge the new Hotel Men's Association by threatening to strike for higher
wages. Yet, when many seasonal workers abandoned the campaign, the remaining few activists lost political momentum. At a mass meeting in Fitzgerald Hall,
five hundred black workers voted to approve measures to support Charles White
and the hotel men, declaring that "self preservation demands a duty to the merchants who give us employment." Rebuffed by Kuehnle and the Republicans and
facing a newly formed and hostile hotel coalition, those who refused to attend
the meeting were left to offer little but scathing rhetorical rebuttals. A. L. Murray,
who had attempted—alongside Gus Parker—to organize a "Colored Republican
Club" in 1906 and later the racially neutral "Atlantic City Progressive Club" in the
fall of 1909, challenged White and the hotel men's assertions that the black vote
went to the highest bidder. "It has been said that the organization gives protection to the gamblers and saloonkeepers, and by this forces them to vote as they
dictate," Murray declared, reiterating the now familiar charge of White and the
Democrats. At the same time, he countered these insinuations by asking the ho-

tel men whether "men and women who are employed are gamblers, thieves, and cutthroats because they support the organization that supports them."[15]

While Murray's claims struck at the hypocrisy of the city's Jim Crow political culture, they did little to influence public opinion or shape racial policy. Indeed, neither the outcome of the 1909 election nor the ouster and indictment of Louis Kuehnle by 1913 effectively challenged or reshaped the Republican Party's segregation pact with the Northside. Despite continued allegations from Democrats and other detractors, Kuehnle's successor and political heir, Enoch "Nucky" Thompson, continued the party's self-serving support of the segregation pact. However, the continuation of the policy does not effectively explain the long-term effects of the agreement. Although even Democrats eventually abandoned confiscation of black property in the name of political reform in the years to come, the political parameters of the Jim Crow system had effectively ended attempts to reform the social boundaries of the city's segregation policy. In a city where politics served consumption, and where the unique system of boss rule limited alternative political possibilities, black residents and workers were socially resigned to bathe in the restricted area of sand and surf known as "Chicken Bone Beach" and forced politically to support Republican Party officials who offered the lesser of two evils. In Atlantic City, like Asbury Park, black business interests and local residents faced the choice of free consumption or integration, and for much of the ensuing decades the need to preserve their right to consume overrode earlier campaigns for integration.

Although he failed to see it at the time, the 1902 summer season would be James Bradley's last as leader of Asbury Park. As the twentieth century commenced, Bradley's once thriving resort had become unable to keep up with municipal improvements and was increasingly resistant to relaxing its temperance policies or to update its social standards. In the early months of 1903, prominent merchants pressured Bradley to relinquish his authority and cede power to the newly formed Board of Trade Annexation Committee instituted to remarket and reenergize the shore town. By July 1903, they succeeded. Marking the occasion, New Jersey governor Frank Murphy applauded the new regime for its plans to "outdo Atlantic City" and for "leaving off the old to put on the new."[16]

The ouster of Bradley from power also meant that changes were coming to Asbury Park's segregation policy. Since 1893, Bradley's strict segregation ordinances had blocked efforts to develop and modernize the West End. To longtime businessmen and future developers, the Jim Crow plan, which made sense to many whites in the 1880s and early 1890s, was now working against the financial and political interests of the resort park. By the early 1900s, developers discovered that they were unable to locate or secure available real estate under the town's present boundaries, and that tax revenue failed to finance the seemingly unending municipal improvements and sanitation concerns that mounted in the years that followed. To make matters worse, in order to preserve his control over Asbury Park's social character and maintain his paternalistic hold over the West End, Bradley routinely declined offers to commercialize Asbury Park and its surrounding districts. To modernize its infrastructure and racial policies, the resort town's new governing body set in motion plans to annex the territory known as "West Park" or the "West End"—Asbury Park's outlying areas "across the tracks" that were home to the town's 2,500 African Americans and Italian, Polish, Jewish, and Chinese residents and merchants.

In promoting its plans for consolidation in February 1906, the Board of Trade Annexation Committee indicted the economic and racial policies of the past. "Realizing that these effects retard the growth of realty, valuations, and desirability of that particular district as a residential section," the committee explained that "we have adopted the proposition of annexation with an enthusiasm, which if met with the proper spirit by the residents of Asbury Park" could alleviate the pressing political and environmental conditions of its "sister city." Calling on both white and black residents to free Asbury Park from its "swaddling clothes," committee members, in a subtle attack on Bradley's segregation policy, insisted that any plans to annex the West End should be pursued and "conducted on broad and liberal lines." In its proposal to city residents, the Board of Trade struck a particularly unique racial stance. As it attempted to drum up support for its expansive reorganization of government and industry, the decision to annex or not to annex Asbury Park's West End became tied to discussions about the fate of segregation and consumption in the resort city. Unlike Atlantic City's cleanup efforts, which conformed to conventional patterns of racial control, Asbury Park's annexation proposals announced a subtle desire to confound and transcend Jim Crow practices in order to make "better representative government" work for consumption and protect environmental equality.[17]

To the West End's prominent black residents and community leaders, the proposed annexation project was greeted with applause. Bradley's refusal to modernize Asbury Park's public utilities and infrastructure was compounded by the outright neglect of its outlying communities, which he considered incubators of illicit consumption protected by an ungovernable constituency. Mirroring some of Atlantic City's own slum districts, black residents and leaders worried that unless it was consolidated with Asbury Park, the West End would become just another underfunded and publicly ridiculed segregated black ghetto in the Jim Crow North. The support that annexation garnered among black residents of various classes explains the extent to which Asbury Park's segregation policy had matured since the 1880s. Forced to enjoy their "beach days" in a section of secluded sand known as the "mudhole"—the dumping ground for Asbury Park's insufficient sewer system—black leaders and area residents made environmental reform, public health, and residential safety a cornerstone of their annexation support. "The annexation of West Park will solve the intricate sewage problem," Earl Stone, a resident and businessman in West Park, explained to reporters. Placing the West End's sanitation epidemic in humanitarian terms, a laundress residing in the West End explained to the *Atlantic City Evening Press*, "We are suffering in many ways for sewers to carry our dirty water as we now are compelled to throw on the ground and in the backyards, then inhale it, until the sun and the wind may take the smell away." And even then, she explained, "when there is not a heavy rain for a long time the ground becomes poisonous and our families must suffer."[18]

The West End's protests for municipal modernization and environmental advocacy drew on a critical and developing component of the turn-of-the-century consumer movement that remade the politics of consumption through appeals to product safety and public health. Organizations like the National Consumer League argued that consumers as well as governing bodies too often marketed and consumed items based on superficial qualifications such as personal style and cultural trends that ignored the broader public dangers and hazards of these seemingly innocent private choices. Calling on annexationists to make sanitation and prosperity one and the same, L. C. Hubbert acknowledged, "I am in favor of annexation, but not in a cowardly way . . . let us have sewers and better heath protection, which is the best wealth we can have." Like Hubbert, neighbors William Labaw and Walter T. Hubbard touted incorporation as the "only solution of our defects and lack of modern conveniences"; they explained that unless public health became a priority for local businesses, "better government, improved streets, and additional fire fighting abilities" would be incapable of keeping Asbury Park protected from an outbreak of influenza and small pox that routinely went untreated throughout West Park. Thus, like Progressive-era suffragists, black annexation supporters called on public officials to make the public's welfare an important criterion for crafting and implementing consumer policy.[19]

Agreeing with the West End's black community, Asbury Park's Board of Trade marketed public health as a cornerstone of its agenda to reform the resort town's economic and segregation policy. "There can be no more forcible argument,"

annexation proponents asserted, "than the need of sanitation." To the more progressive members of the annexation committee, incorporation of the West End
meant more than a gateway to commercial expansion. To several outspoken and
influential members, it also meant a thorough cleansing and modernization of
West Park. As one committee member succinctly explained, annexation would
bring "purification" and the "expelling of all possible causes of diseases and epi-
demics." The result would be a healthier and more productive beach community
that could reclaim its "reputation as a health resort," a "safe place for women and
children to live happily by the seashore, away from the heat of the cities and the
atmosphere of contagion." Echoing those sentiments in an editorial to the local
press, one white resident of Asbury Park chided skeptical voters to put aside their
prejudices and elevate the mutual health of all involved. "Their cry is give us sewers and remove these unsanitary conditions," the citizen explained, before asking
uncommitted whites whether "it is right that we should place the health of their
children in danger."[20]

Despite agreement on public health reform, the committee's annexation plan
was temporarily stalled when plans were implemented to include the West End's
Springwood Avenue section. Although less prominent than Atlantic City's red-
light districts, the section of gambling dens, pool halls, and juke joints that
lined Springwood Avenue were no less notorious to city residents—both black
and white—who worried about the moral and physical effects of ungovernable
shadow consumer economies. Board of Trade Annexation Committee members
made the case, as did African Americans, that annexation of all territory was
necessary for government oversight and sanitation control. Exhibiting the racial
condescension that accompanied most discussions of the Springwood Avenue
district, longtime white resident Dr. J. Turner Rose explained that any annexation agreement must include the divisive thoroughfare. Rose acknowledged that
while the incorporated section would be difficult to control in its present condition, any proposed creation of a "Greater Asbury Park" would not be supported
by many whites who no longer desired to "live with that thoroughfare continuing
in its present condition under our nose."[21]

Making segregation reform inseparable from issues of public health and consumer protection allowed annexationists to build a broader coalition of support
among white residents. Like black proponents, white annexationists appealed
to the new consumer maxim of "long-distance solidarity," which stressed an
interconnected system of production and consumption. As many turn-of-the-
century municipal reformers explained, citizens who entered venues dedicated
to purchasable entertainment—especially places known for providing indecent

amusements—were no longer engaging in private decisions, but were instead making choices with public consequences. As one editorial to the local press noted, if "Springwood wasn't incorporated," it would be Asbury Park businesses and seasonal tourists who would "suffer the evils that breed there without having the power to apply corrective or punitary punishment."[22]

In a decision that shows the serviceable language of consumer politics, Asbury Park's Board of Trade Annexation Committee used this point to persuade white skeptics—including ardent segregationists—to consolidate Springwood Avenue. Adopting the language of Progressive-era liberals who believed in the "managerial state," as well as appealing to Reconstruction-era racial politics that stigmatized black consumer behavior as dangerous and corrupt, committee members asserted that "West Park needs a stern hand in its local government." They explained to doubters that "Asbury Park suffers because of the disorders of West Park." Yet they also reassured Asbury Park voters that the "plague spots could be wiped out within a year" if they supported present measures to annex and clean up the divisive neighborhoods and shopping districts. "The disorderly houses, the speakeasies, the houses which are made the nightly resort of the lowest classes of blacks," members explained, could be "wiped out of existence." As the committee's reasoning and rhetoric reveals, the flexible language of public health—as the various uses of the word "plague" indicate—could be adopted in the name of humanitarian cleanup efforts, as well as to promote the eradication of immoral consumer behavior.[23]

To broaden additional support for annexation among both white and black voters, the Board of Trade Annexation Committee cited the commercial advantages of a unified government dedicated to free consumption. Citing the unavailability of land in the present boundaries of Asbury Park, as well as the moral benefits annexation would bring to black residents with the accompanying expansion, annexationist claims ran the gamut of turn-of-the-century imperialist ideology. Mirroring the rhetoric of Frederick Jackson Turner and other "open-door" contemporaries, annexation committee officials linked the future prosperity of the resort to its "capacity to build." As one official noted, "Being already built to capacity," Asbury Park "must by nature of its superior accommodations be always and only, with normally expanding territorial lines, the great business and residential section of the township." Citing statistical models that marked West Park's valuation at $1,042,250, conservative committee estimates predicted an annual increase of 29 percent for the first two years, a total gain of $208,450. Others, like committee member George W. Pittinger, were more optimistic. In a public forum hosted by the Board of Trade on February 16, 1906, Pittinger exclaimed that "the Annexation of West Park to Asbury Park will increase the property values of the former municipality 50 percent within a short time." Reflecting the developing speculative fever of the evening, Harry A. Borden went even further, predicting that if West Park followed the example of Spring Lake (a neighboring borough annexed to Neptune, New Jersey), black prospectors could foresee "the price of lots advanced 100 percent."[24]

In anticipating the claims of some critics that annexation was nothing more than a self-serving mission that aimed to dominate the real estate and consumer markets of the region, prominent members of the committee, like chairman J. L. Kinmonth, offered the trickle-down benefits of "one-government" rule. First, he explained that "it helps the business district to first concentrate and then expand by slow degrees . . . its wealth in the sections already improved and allow room for expansion to territory equally well situated." This would in turn, he pointed out, "expand property prices in the already improved areas and naturally expand property prices in the section to be improved." Thus each section would share in the financial benefits of consolidation through increased consumption and rising property values. Asbury Park would be "proportionately benefited" by "concentrating and enlarging its wealth," and, by comparison, so would the incorporated black communities by "sharing in the benefits of the compulsory expansion."[25]

In an editorial published in the local papers, one white resident, exclaiming the need to fulfill "our moral duty," applied the period's "white man's burden" logic to the case of Asbury Park. "Left to its own devices, drifting aimlessly like a ship without a rudder," the individual asked, "What would become of this little rejected settlement? How could finances be managed, how protected from its vicious class and how able to perpetuate even the semblance of government?" Drawing a line between the poverty and unfitness for self-government that many identified with West Park to the nation's occupation of the Philippines, the editorial echoed the Progressive reasoning of the period by asserting, "We can conceive of no argument based upon supreme selfishness and cruel indifference to the fate of these poor people strong enough to release this city from an obligation quite as imperative and absolutely parallel in the conditions to the taking of the Philippines by the American government. It was the cry of moral duty that justified the transfer of the Philippines that justifies their (West Park) retention."[26]

Although few annexationists made such bold comparisons, the point was an instructive one. Progressive-era committee members, although united in their support of public health, commercial expansion, and a reconfiguration (and perhaps eradication) of the city's segregation policy, were of many minds when it approached the political character and racial destiny of black communities.

While they rejected the explicitly racist maxims of some segregationist contemporaries—since such logic defied their claims that government and politics
should serve consumption—they nonetheless revealed a virulent strand of ra-
cialist thinking that continued to view black political and economic autonomy as
financially threatening, politically corrosive, and environmentally hazardous.

Among black residents in West Park, the financial possibilities of annexation
were met with equal division. While they were united in their calls for public
health reform, black residents and developers proceeded with cautious optimism
when it came to commercial expansion and official political incorporation. To
prominent businessmen and property owners, annexation offered the same benefits that white merchants foresaw. S. H. Labaw exclaimed to the local press that
"as a property owner of West Park it is my opinion that annexation is the best
thing that could happen for us. It will increase our property values and give us
better government." William A. Berry agreed. Explaining the financial dispari-
ties between residents in Asbury Park and the West End, Berry pointed out that
"property in Asbury Park has increased during the past few years, while in the
township of Neptune, our values have remained practically the same for the past
20 years. If Asbury Park doesn't want us we will incorporate as a borough."[27]

The West End's skeptical residents, however, saw a more insidious plan at
work. One cautious observer noted that while annexation might provide mod-
ernized facilities and public utilities to West Park, he feared that the expenses
would be passed onto the West End's already feeble and insolvent economy. Instead of rising property values, he instead foresaw a scenario where "Asbury Park
will arbitrarily require the above improvements, but they will assess the property of the annexed district accordingly, and will charge the assessment again the
same." In an editorial published on March 31, 1906, businessman and property
owner John H. Richardson echoed the skeptics by explaining, "I am against the
project . . . because I see coming to that same people destitution, deprivation,
and evacuation." Highlighting the tendency of well-intentioned whites to turn on
black communities and businesses who could not meet the financial burdens of
municipal reform elsewhere, Richardson noted that financial destitution would
increase in West Park "because of the inability of my people to meet the financial
demands it will bring with it."[28]

As many black property owners and communities knew all too well, municipal reforms and commercial expansion projects were routinely accompanied
with unforeseen financial obligations and hidden costs that often reappropri-
ated burdensome taxes and regulations onto black constituents. Indeed, white
opponents of annexation had openly promoted such requirements in citing their

refusal to finance the welfare of the West End. They informed the Board of Trade Annexation Committee that any plan for consolidation would need to realign the tax system in order to pass along the financial responsibility to those citizens who needed the reforms most. In a meeting with the committee on February 19, 1906, councilman Jesse Minot voiced his reservations for a revenue-sharing plan under the proposed annexation proposal. Explaining that it would be a "financial burden" to the city, he noted that it should be "considered significant that sanitary and police protection—chief reasons for the union—were more required in the section left out than in the section sought to be taken in." To counter the optimistic property value estimates of the Board of Trade, James Bradley's secretary, William Wells, explained to the committee that any annexation proposal should consider the alternative boundary of Mattison Avenue, which was valued at $750,000 compared to the proposed Springwood Avenue boundary, which carried a paltry $330,000 valuation. Annexing the Springwood Avenue district, Wells argued, would thus "leave the burden of government upon Asbury Park" to finance a district with unending municipal deficiencies and heavy accompanying political and social risks.[29]

In a debate that foreshadowed the desegregation battles of the 1950s and 1960s, the political contest over the financial responsibilities of annexation revealed competing visions of welfare, taxes, and the role of government. While Progressive-minded annexationists believed that government should intervene to protect consumption by adopting a revenue-sharing plan, white anti-annexationists believed the city's black residents should fund municipal improvements themselves. Black activists meanwhile threatened to withdraw support for annexation unless municipal resources were allocated according to public need. Fearing that squeamish annexation supporters would adopt burdensome tax proposals to appease skeptical whites, John Richardson threatened to "defend the rights of my race first" if vulnerable black residents were "sold out" by the city's change of heart. He cautioned black property owners not to idly dismiss the proposals of anti-annexationists, reiterating that "this affects each and every property owner where these improvements are to be made," including "the poor widow, the lone woman, and the old woman" whose livelihoods, he argued, should be considered just as important as those of the wealthy developers.[30]

While the Board of Trade, black activists, and skeptical councilmen like Jesse Minot debated the merits of resource allocation in mostly race-neutral tones, other, more ardently racialized arguments were put forth by James Bradley to retain the present Jim Crow boundaries and municipal structure. With his segregation policy under attack from both white Progressives and black annexationists, Bradley took to the press to defend his scrutinized policies and to reject the proposed plans for incorporating the West End. In scathing attacks on the West End's political and social character, Bradley argued that not even annexation could contain or control the criminal element of Springwood Avenue, which if incorporated would corrupt and corrode the moral foundations and public appeal of the resort town. Ignoring the market-based arguments of earlier debates, Bradley denounced the innate criminality of northern black consumer culture. Reminding voters of the "shanties that have been erected in the Springwood Avenue district," Bradley exclaimed that "much disorder prevails in that locality." Although he acknowledged that many "respectable colored people reside there," the "percentage of disreputable people is much greater," he pointed out, "than in other colored communities in our state." Pass the resolution, he explained, and whites "could say goodbye to the present boom in Asbury Park real estate."[31]

To traditional segregationists like Bradley, the scandalous vices of the West End were proof enough of the incompatibility of the two towns and the foolish utopian vision of annexation. While annexationists painted consolidation as a move to clean up the region's public health and strengthen the resort's consumer economy, Bradley argued that integration would devalue the profile of the resort town and also pave the way for a black political coalition that would work against the interests of consumption within the leisure economy. "To make the Wesley Lake brook (Springwood Avenue) the boundary line at the present time," he asserted, "is for Asbury Park to commit hari kari."[32]

Yet, for Bradley, who cared less than others did about consumer interests, the fear of black political power worried him most. In their rush to raise revenue and court the black vote, Bradley believed that annexationists were inviting the same level of corruption that drew scandalous headlines in Atlantic City. "To annex the objectionable district," he explained, "is to give over the destiny of Asbury Park to the scheming politicians who will secure this colored vote to serve his own ends regardless of how Asbury Park suffers." Worse still, the city would assume responsibility for the "largest number of colored voters pro rata of any city in the state of New Jersey," a fact compounded in Bradley's estimation since "the majority of the colored vote in Monmouth County is a purchasable article." Asbury Park mayor Charles Atkins, who was Bradley's ally in the fight against annexation, agreed. Worried that consolidation would allow black residents to "elect a candidate for Mayor or councilman, thus taking the governing power away from Asbury Park," Mayor Atkins called on West Park to "prove that they can assimilate" socially before considering the Board of Trade's annexation plans. "Let them become a part of us in every sense of the word," he exclaimed, "and we can begin to seriously consider the advisability of consolidating the Springwood Avenue district."[33]

Black activists and community residents responded to the racial rebukes of Bradley and Mayor Atkins by denouncing the narrative of criminality and political corruption popularized by the region's segregationist supporters. Longtime resident L. C. Hubbert pointed out that "for the last few years we have had three murders, six men shot, and three badly cut." Yet "none of the above crimes," he explained, "were committed by colored people." Citing the assertion of Bradley and others that the "colored voter was a purchasable lot," the Reverend S. G. Kelly explained that the "day of foggyism is past. The negro thinks for himself and votes as he pleases regardless . . . of 'long green' offered by our kind 'White Friends' in politics." More important, though, Hubbert and Reverend Kelly reminded whites that black voters were taxpayers, too, according to Hubbert's estimates, in the range of "at least $100,000" per year, which justified financing the construction of sewers and other sanitary improvements that were lacking in the West End.[34]

Fearing the potential political fallout from their attempts to court segregationists, the Board of Trade Committee renewed their commitment to the progressive promises of sanitation reform and desegregation in the days and weeks leading up to the vote. To many members, the escalating racial tension of the debate revealed fundamental differences over the scope of government in a service economy. Indeed, the effort to provide better care for the well-being and health of a community's laboring classes was in keeping with the service culture reform movement developing among prominent merchants at the turn of the century. Foreshadowing more expansive institutions of welfare capitalism in the late 1920s, leading retail moguls like John Wannamaker instituted a Progressive system of welfare assistance to its workers that included health care benefits, educational assistance, and "legal wages." The racial implications of this "service ideal" were most felt in Asbury Park, where several prominent business leaders dropped the marketplace conservatism of earlier segregation debates in favor of integration.[35]

To mark this rhetorical departure, committee members stressed the interrelated political, economic, and environmental interests of the two communities. Denouncing the "claims of pleaders" who pushed to maintain "existing lines of demarcation," Klinmonth called on other whites to reject even the "selfish view of annexation" that is asserted from "certain alarmists who care nothing for the conditions of their neighbor's moral and physical welfare, provided everything looks smooth and rosy in their own locale." An editorial from an Asbury Park resident and voter agreed, noting that all residents, black and white, are "friends and neighbors and if perchance there are more spots to lift up to a higher and more acceptable purchase," then it was the duty of government to "let us be heal- ers." Reiterating the rhetorical return of the common law culture of old, annex- ationists reworked the "greatest good for all" ideal to fit the developing therapeu- tic state maxims of a "uniform government for one people and one community," whose future prosperity and consumer interests, Klinmonth declared, are all "tied up in one thing, the resort business." Yet, in pursuing the ideal of a con- sumer democracy, Klinmonth and others rejected the notion that it should be accompanied through segregation, a system he denounced, since it pitted "one man's plot of ground against any other man's plot." As recent experience had shown, "every case of dividing a territory," another resident declared, "has been unsatisfactory and an expensive experiment for the people."[36]

In rejecting the economic judgments that once justified segregation, annex- ationists also attacked the political fears of Bradley and others who cautioned whites to fear "the purchasable" tendencies of the West End voter. To Klinmonth and other Progressive advocates of political integration, the notion that black voters would elect corrupt politicians who would then work against the interests of the popular resort were unfounded. "There is reason to believe," Klinmonth argued, "that West Park, realizing the destiny of the new city, would be proud to aid in the building of it," especially since, he reminded whites, "its own well-being is wrapped up and controlled in the success of Asbury Park." Reiterating the Pro- gressive ideals of democratic consumption, Klinmonth acknowledged that the new system would work to ensure "that one man's vote is as good as another," explaining to critics that the town was not "reaching for fame as an exploitative resort." Remarketing Asbury Park as a "cosmopolitan city with no ruling class to the exclusion of the other," Klinmonth and the committee proposed a new era for the beach resort, one in which "more wealth and social standing is no more the badge of respectability and honesty of purpose in the community than the toil hardened and begrimed hands."[37]

On May 16, 1906, the annexationists were finally victorious. In a landslide de- cision favoring consolidation, the West End was annexed to Asbury Park. While the *New York Times* applauded the efforts of the committee to put an end to the scandalous section of black-owned businesses on Springwood Avenue, the local papers expressed cautious optimism about future cooperation. A cartoon printed on the front page of the *Asbury Park Journal* featured a newly married couple with the words, "Now you're married, you must obey," printed below the picture. Indeed, while the annexation ruling brought the possibility of sanitation and public health improvements to the West End, consolidation failed to eliminate the color line or the environmental conditions of black residential areas. In the 1920s, a hostile coalition of segregationists, backed by the Ku Klux Klan, emerged in the beach town to temper and control black excursions to beaches and boardwalks, reminding many black locals that even the most dedicated of consumer economies could not completely repel the long-standing desire to segregate.

In both Atlantic City and Asbury Park, the new consumer politics of environmental reform and commercial growth enabled local African American communities to protect their businesses, improve their neighborhoods, and, in Asbury Park, reform residential segregation. Yet, by tying economic rights to business development and municipal reform, black activists lost the struggle over integrated leisure and a consumer rights discourse framed around issues of unregulated access that served as a critical component of earlier civil rights victories. For much of the next few decades, the segregation debate at the Jersey shore would be about the allocation of resources and consumer protection, rather than the rights to space. In the end, the eradication of residential segregation and the institutionalization of free consumption helped naturalize, not end, segregated leisure.

Conclusion

In the mid-1960s, consumer changes to America's built environment and gradual economic decline rerouted northern tourists away from the Jersey coast. As local merchants and city officials looked for ways to rebrand and rebuild, they applauded their ability to avoid the urban unrest and racial tensions that plagued nearby cities like Newark, Camden, and Philadelphia during the turbulent decade. Speaking to reporters in 1966, Atlantic City mayor Joseph Altman went so far as to exclaim that "America's Favorite Playground" was still the "most integrated city in the country." The mayor's inability to tell the difference between de facto segregation and integration underscored the impact of consumer forces in hardening Jim Crow and limiting civil rights activism during the twentieth century. Beginning in the 1880s, white and black northerners initiated a sweeping conversation about the rights and health of consumers that permanently framed debates about segregation at the Jersey shore. By the 1920s, the result was the consumer conquest of civil rights. In the years that followed, changes in America's consumer culture, in tandem with the rising popularity and profitability of black entertainment in Atlantic City's "Northside" and Asbury Park's "West End," institutionalized the prevailing wisdom of "separate but equal" and halted more expansive civil rights campaigns that persisted elsewhere in the Jim Crow North. Guided by the popular consumer maxim "we give the people what they want," white and black business interests helped fortify the consumer walls—both spatial and cultural—that sustained segregated leisure at the Jersey shore.[1]

Between 1920 and the mid-1960s, segregated leisure endured, in part, due to the continued economic development of the Jersey's shore's black commercial districts and the interracial appeal they amassed after World War II. Outside of Harlem, Atlantic City's Northside became the most popular place to catch emerging black talent in the Jim Crow North. Popular performers like Sam Cooke, James Brown, Billie Holiday, and Sammy Davis, Jr., dazzled black audiences in nightclubs like Club Harlem, Timbuktu, the Wonder Gardens, and the Paradise Club. In Asbury Park, middle-class black tourists and local New Jersey residents sought out jazz clubs like the Orchid Lounge on Springwood Avenue. The focus of white ridicule during the annexation debates of the early 1900s, Springwood

Avenue, like Kentucky Avenue in Atlantic City, became Asbury Park's premier music showcase for white and black audiences interested in taking in performances by top acts like Jack McDuff, Lonnie Liston Smith, and Jimmy Smith. Even white performers like Frank Sinatra and Jerry Lewis made sure to book shows in the region's black clubs.[2]

As a result of shrewd marketing by men like Larry Steele, local booking agents and nightclub owners made Atlantic City's Northside and Asbury Park's West End into two of the premiere stops on the thriving "chitlin' circuit." Denied access to many white clubs in the Jim Crow South, black booking agents created the "chitlin' circuit" to give inexperienced black singers, dancers, and comedians an opportunity to hone their acts in front of welcoming and often interracial crowds. White authorities, too, found ways to promote black entertainment and make Jim Crow work for consumption. Atlantic City's Chamber of Commerce enticed middle-class whites to the resort town throughout the post–World War II era by highlighting the region's black nightlife. In addition, they recruited black tourists in nearby northern cities by advertising in regional black newspapers and sending flyers to parishioners in local black churches. By the mid-1950s, the result, according to local musician Sid Trusty, was a place where "people were united in their desire to have fun." On the Northside, the fun included an array of musical and performative styles as soloists, house bands, chorus girls, and burlesque troupes fused jazz, soul, and rhythm and blues into the early morning hours. Both on stage and in the audience, the Northside's nightclubs helped popularize the prevailing wisdom of "separate but equal" by becoming a safe recreational space where whites and blacks learned to "jump Jim Crow" together. Like the industrious men and women who helped construct the Jersey shore's black commercial base at the turn of the century, promoters and local entrepreneurs like Larry Steele turned black entertainment and consumer culture into the region's marquee recreational spectacle. On hot summer nights, this new form of reverse integration emerged to contain racial tensions and stymie the possibility of civil rights disorders on the white boardwalks and beaches.[3]

The growing popularity of the Northside and West End paralleled the declining appeal of the white boardwalk economy in the postwar years. To the disappointment of many white tourists, boardwalk merchants and boosters failed to offer rival entertainment districts. Instead, local white authorities remained committed to an outdated carnival marketplace dedicated to conspicuous consumption and cheap amusements. Throughout the 1950s, white crowds still flocked to New Jersey's beaches, but they often spent their money elsewhere. White single men and women crossed the color line and paid cover charges to dance to modern music in black nightclubs. Middle-class white families, on the other hand, sought out privatized accommodations closer to home. Spurred by the highway construction boom of the postwar period, the opening of the Garden State Parkway in 1947 allowed suburban developers to offer modern, safe, and private shopping experiences in air-conditioned malls, amusement parks, and members-only swimming clubs.[4]

To keep their declining enterprises afloat, local white business owners in Atlantic City and Asbury Park gradually reduced staff or skimped on repairs. Ornate movie houses, once the decadent showpieces for striving northerners who came to flaunt "making it in America," struggled to fill seats. By the early 1960s, empty theaters and unkempt accommodations undercut the privileged appeal that once made them part of the Jersey shore's premiere consumer spectacle. As door receipts declined and cost-cutting measures turned away customers, many longtime owners sold their properties to discount chains, liquor stores, and pawn shops, effectively ending the turbulent fiscal reign of what local historian Nelson Johnson has affectionately termed the "boardwalk empire." Indeed, while historians often point to the modern civil rights movement as inciting white flight, the construction of a segmented consumer marketplace proved just as vital to the nation's retreat from public leisure and mass consumption. Between 1945 and the mid-1960s, the creation of niche consumer markets in New Jersey's developing suburban landscape bankrupted the boardwalk economies of the Jersey shore and aided the gradual—and in many ways invisible—destruction of segregation.[5]

Segregation endured during the 1950s even as white crowds began to splinter because the black merchant class exploited the gradual decline of white entertainment spaces and the rising appeal of black consumer culture to lure in white customers and to downplay direct civil rights action. Like earlier black capitalists, the black merchant class calculated the economic costs of accommodation against the negative political costs of civil rights agitation. When some black community members protested the absence of integrated swimming pools in 1935, black business owners and members of the Negro Chamber of Commerce overrode their plans and instead lobbied Atlantic City's mayor to build a segregated facility. Driven by the promise of profits, peace, and fraternity, rather than ideological agreement, black officials unwittingly aided the maintenance of segregation and the accompanying economic inequalities that indicted the region after segregation fell.[6]

Not all local black residents and activists, however, shared the producer-driven vision of mass consumption espoused by the region's entrepreneurial class. In the 1920s, the northern black press complained that too many "average negroes" simply "steered their wife or sweethearts" to black leisure venues when confronted with the response "We don't serve colored people." With "Jim Crow poking its head into Atlantic City, Asbury Park, and other northern summer resorts," the *Baltimore Afro-American* called on the northern "Afro-American who is dressed all up with no place to go" to demand integrated admission to moving picture houses, cabarets, restaurants, soda fountains, and boardwalk shops. During the summer of 1929, the local NAACP chapter in Asbury Park guided black tourists and workers to demonstrate in favor of integrated leisure after lifeguards blocked access to designated white beaches. After weeks of demonstrations and letters to the city's Board of Commissioners, local officials conceded to the demands of black protestors and instructed area lifeguards to readmit black bathers.[7]

In their campaigns for integrated leisure, black protesters and the NAACP directed their harshest critiques at members of the black business class. Marking their victory over segregated bathing in 1929, one black journalist regrettably noted that the delayed action against segregated leisure by black community activists prompted the hardening of Jim Crow laws and customs throughout the Jersey coast. "It is the feeling," one unnamed member of the NAACP complained, "that had the Negroes maintained a united front against discrimination or segregation, the present issue would never have arisen." In similar attacks against local black business interests who lobbied local whites to build a segregated beach for black bathers, the Asbury Park NAACP exclaimed, "We are citizens and not cattle and we will not be silent under the practices or conditions that seek to deprive us of our inalienable rights." Refusal to demand integration, the letter continued, led to "many instances where colored people have been ordered away from certain parts of the beach."[8]

After World War II, members of the Asbury Park Black Progressive Party, headed by Louis Kaplan, spearheaded additional campaigns against segregated hotel swimming pools and beach attendants who refused to sell beach tags to black tourists. Lobbying the New Jersey State Commission against Discrimination in 1952, Kaplan informed the state delegation that repeated attempts by black activists to seek admittance to the Monte Carlo Pool Club were routinely denied, even though "no other white person was asked whether they belonged to the club." Two years later, local authorities proclaimed the issue resolved after a "satisfactory and amicable agreement was reached." However, as many black protestors exclaimed to local reporters, prospective black patrons were routinely denied entry in the years that followed. In effectively confronting Jim Crow, black tourists and workers were able to reclaim the earlier consumer rights initiative that was abandoned in favor of intraracial leisure and consumption at the turn of the century. Yet, despite the pressure that occasional civil rights campaigns exerted, they were often piecemeal victories that failed to incite a more formal and sustained movement against segregated leisure. The ability of white business owners to delay enforcement of mandated state non-discrimination statutes, alongside face-saving denunciations of "prejudiced views" from local authorities, ultimately derailed more sustained civil rights campaigns after 1920.[9]

At the same time, the gradual decline of local mass protests did not completely shield the region from the effects of civil rights campaigns nationwide. Integration in nearby northern marketplaces during the late 1950s and early 1960s gradually admitted black workers and tourists to local public and commercial leisure venues. When outside precedent was not enough, local activists exerted direct pressure to finish the job. In the early 1960s, longtime Northside activists like Horace Bryant pushed reluctant boardwalk merchants to fully integrate white theaters and hotels. Faced with fewer white tourists, local business owners hesitantly agreed. Such actions, however, decimated the commercial enterprises in Asbury Park's West End and Atlantic City's Northside. Declining attendance and decreased profits in black commercial establishments led to bankruptcies, layoffs, and unfunded social services for black workers left behind. As black businesses closed, poverty, crime, and anger intensified. In response, displaced black workers lobbied local officials to provide work beyond service jobs, and they joined local NAACP activists in demonstrations on the Atlantic City boardwalk in 1966, proclaiming "Don't buy where you can't work" and "Better jobs for the negro." These protests, however, were less successful than those aimed at campaigns for free consumption. Unable to secure sustainable employment, black teenagers in Asbury Park rioted in 1970, burning the West End in protest against property owners and local officials who failed to provide affordable housing, well-paying jobs, and adequate social services.[10]

The race riots and economic decline that accompanied the end of segregation at the Jersey shore exposed the fragility of consumer economies to deliver systemic economic change. While national civil rights organizations used sites of leisure and consumption to defeat de jure segregation during the 1950s and 1960s, the decision to separate the right to consume from the right to integrate at the Jersey shore prolonged the underlying economic injustices that de facto segregation masked. However eagerly Jersey Shore retailers and local officials worked to promote the inclusiveness of northern beach resorts, they ultimately proved incapable of finding a solution other than segregation to manage racial conflict and sustain consumer growth. Together, black and white merchants constructed a segregation system and culture that entrapped black workers and consumers in a debate that became more about consumption than about integration.[11]

The story of segregation at the Jersey shore is not, then, the familiar and triumphant march to freedom that is routinely evoked in civil rights literature. Instead, it is the more typical narrative of retreat and retrenchment, a history of piecemeal victories and more long-standing defeats. By severing the right to consume from the right to integrate, white and black business interests articulated an alternative vision of civil rights defined by equal enjoyment, rather than equal access. As a result, the politics of mass consumption aided the desire of the region's producer classes to maintain a system in which good service eclipsed equal service. In treating beach resorts as private enterprises, rather than actual cities, local officials were able to ignore social problems, environmental concerns, or racial boundaries that did not directly threaten future profits. When such problems did become a threat to the public image and finances of resort owners in the late 1950s and early 1960s, local urban redevelopers responded by tearing the resorts down. Replicating the model enacted by urban renewal programs nationwide, local authorities in Atlantic City bulldozed the "undesirables" on the Northside's Absecon Boulevard, tearing down housing projects, schools, and private homes to make way for more consumer-minded and financially rewarding enterprises that would, in minds of one local official, "better decorate the boulevard." Over the long haul, these decisions greatly diminished the opportunity to stave off the festering inequalities in housing and labor that plagued the black working class and exacerbated the destructive effects of the region's economic decline and blighted profile by the late 1960s. When integration arrived by default, it exposed the underlying injustices that segregation held at bay, and officially ended the long and gradual retreat from the more radical civil rights promises first offered and promoted by black consumer activists and white Progressives during the Reconstruction era.[12]

The decision to divide cities never arises naturally, and it is rarely retained without varying degrees of control, accommodation, and compromise. In the late nineteenth century, African Americans recognized changes in the nation's political economy and class divisions within the white community as opportunities to formally contest the emergence of segregated leisure and to push for free consumption. In successfully claiming their rights as free consumers, black workers disputed claims by whites that calls for integration were part of a larger plot to promote social equality. In doing so, they also challenged long-standing assumptions about the morality of markets. While white progressives touted the market economy as the gateway to economic success and social change, black consumer activists disputed the notion that markets were morally inflatable. In demonstrations against the "visible hand of race," black activists insisted that the degrading racist images and denunciations about black culture and entertainment employed by white opponents of integration directly influenced the marketplace outcomes that sustained white supremacy and produced segregation. Moreover, by making consumer rights and public health central to the struggle against segregation, African Americans did more than just challenge the cultural authority of white supremacy. They moved as consumer activists, and later as entrepreneurs and environmental advocates, to contest and sometimes defeat the imposition of Jim Crow in the post–Civil War North, making leisure a critical battleground in a national campaign for civil rights, market equality, and environmental justice.

Even after many African Americans retreated from making formal claims to integration in favor of consumer protection and public health, whites and blacks debated the merits of segregation through conflicting attitudes about market change. In the end, the rise of segregation at the Jersey shore did not witness the conservative triumph of free labor ideology, as many scholars have intimated, but instead heralded the burgeoning ambiguities—and later power—of a new consumer society that helped contain civil rights. Initial uncertainties about the rights of consumers and producers intersected with competing attitudes about race and public health to unsettle traditional segregationist practices and civil rights tactics. By the turn of the century, disputes over consumer rights descended into squabbles over the allocation of resources and space rather than sustained demonstrations in favor of integration.[13]

Beginning in the early 1900s, the promise of consumption and the accompanying culture of growth spurred the region's long retreat from civil rights. In binding the fate of segregation to market forces, moderate businessmen supplanted talk of race with a capitalist vocabulary of free choice, commercial development, and greater prosperity that sought to promote segregation as reform. This strategy not only aided local officials in their attempts to retain segregation, but it also allowed for the required flexibility in reforming the color line when it worked against the consumer interests of property owners. Despite the various organs of power that segregationists held at their disposal, the political work of dividing a resort community often forced whites to accommodate and cede power to black business interests and local residents. At the turn of the century, local white authorities discovered that the decision to divide Asbury Park blocked attempts to expand commercially or to shelter the town's white recreational spaces and commercial establishments from the environmental inequalities that inflicted neighboring black residents and businesses. In joining with black activists to approve annexation in May 1906 and by promoting black entertainment in the 1940s and 1950s, white business interests conceded to demands to erase the formal boundary of Jim Crow. Yet, by effectively separating the right to consume from the right to integrate, the propertied classes on both sides of the Jersey shore color line drove civil rights activists away from strategies of protest and confrontation to those that favored compromise and economic self-defense.[14]

The conscious adoption of this strategy by the business community belies the traditional image of northern-style Jim Crow as orderly, informal, and uniform, ideas which have become synonymous with de facto segregation. Indeed, one of the main premises about segregation is that it arises through legislation, court order, and violent repression, or in more subtle ways, is put into place through informal measures and maintained by the rhetorical cover of tradition. Neither of these distinctions accurately explains the making of segregation at the New Jersey shore. The decision by officials in Atlantic City and Asbury Park to endorse segregation led to a policy and culture that, like the fluctuations of the market system itself, proved disorderly and rarely settled. The various policy changes and "cultural turns" that business owners undertook to sell segregation as a product of market outcomes, as well as the various accommodations they made to promote consumption, underscores the complicated and unpredictable history of de facto segregation in the consumer-driven economies of the Jim Crow North.

By the 1890s, business owners understood that traditional ideas and beliefs alone were not enough to "make" segregation. Although early efforts to market and manage segregation drew on traditional social rules and etiquette manuals— much of which were drawn from Victorian culture and assisted the rhetoric of free labor ideology—such appeals to cultural persuasion had to be manufactured within the proper local and political context in which they arose. For example, ideas about propriety on their own were not enough to sell segregation or compel political action. Instead, business leaders and local officials had to imbed such Victorian pronouncements within the language of the emerging consumer marketplace and in accordance with the specialized business profile of the region. To the local business class, segregation became more than a policy to pacify the racist claims of white tourists. Throughout the Jim Crow era, area merchants and local authorities often embraced segregation to manage the necessary profile required to ensure profits and preserve the boardwalk economy against a rising tide of consumer activism and municipal deficiencies. In a service economy in which political compromise served the consumer interests of the white and black propertied classes, maintaining segregation compelled the maintenance of a nat-

ural and informal color line against consumer forces that were constantly fighting to destabilize it. What is more, the instability of consumer opinion required
that business owners consistently repackage the desired profile to meet shifting
economic realities brought about by disruptive social agendas and environmental threats. Thus, while the absence of official laws and rampant violence seemed
to present a Jim Crow culture that was often informal, such informality was a
product of careful business planning and creative packaging by marketing agents
and local boosters whose disguised impartiality was critical to maintaining the
appearance of a neutral market system unbound by the regulatory hand of race.

This system depended on considerable "buy in" from black business interests.
In quite extraordinary ways, black capitalists proved that prosperity and property ownership were possible under Jim Crow. Investments in coastal property
created a profitable and popular black leisure district in Asbury Park and Atlantic City that discredited prevailing ideas about black recreation. The profits that
black property owners generated from a reliable black consumer base helped
finance the storefronts, churches, schools, relief organizations, and recreational
facilities that worked to make separate more equal. By turning exploitation into
segregation, black merchants used proceeds from door receipts and bar tabs to
fund the Northside Federal Credit Union and black booster organizations like
the Atlantic City Board of Trade. Over time, these investments extracted gradual
freedom from Jim Crow and helped soften the effects of poverty and recreational
displacement that might have otherwise facilitated more debilitating social and
economic costs for the region's laboring classes. In addition, these operations
helped carve out a cultural space for middle-class black northerners looking to
escape the social indignities of America's segregation culture. From "Chicken
Bone Beach" to local nightclubs like Club Harlem, black northerners created an
economically competitive and socially progressive consumer marketplace that
rivaled more established black entertainment districts in the Jim Crow North.[15]

In seeking out economic alternatives to direct political action, these trailblaz-
ing black activists and their supporters reflected and advanced the prevailing
doctrines and approaches espoused and outlined by a range of leading black
thinkers during the twentieth century. Although they moved beyond the free
labor advocacy of Booker T. Washington and other late-nineteenth-century contemporaries, local black merchants and entrepreneurs like George Walls and
Madame Sara Spencer Washington still promoted black capitalism as a gateway
to personal advancement that was in keeping with the core philosophies of even
more militant leaders like T. Thomas Fortune, W. E. B. Du Bois, and later Marcus
Garvey. Yet, at the same time, they predated these leading thinkers in promoting

mass consumption as a guide to spur and protect economic growth and advance race pride for African American producers and consumers, a producer-driven vision of mass consumption that aligned with the individualistic and market-oriented orthodoxy of the Jim Crow age.

The associated costs that flowed from these consumer-minded compromises were far-reaching and extended beyond the denial of integrated leisure options. As present-day inequalities have proven, consumer economies are adept at acquiescing to civil rights claims that appear to confirm one or more critical elements of the capitalistic system. The collapse of the boardwalk economy in the late 1960s coincided with the failure of American policy makers to affectively confront inequalities in housing and labor nationwide. Writing for the *New Republic* in 1920, Robert Bliven asked white tourists to explain why they often stiffed black waiters out of hard-earned tips. In a moment of honest reflection, one patron admitted, "We only spend where it shows." In many ways, this acknowledgment reflected the producer-driven vision of mass consumption that local authorities used to stifle economic and political reform. In separating the right to consume from the right to integrate, white and black business interests spent only where it showed. Despite repeated promises to provide equal municipal services and higher wages, those who controlled the economies of Asbury Park and Atlantic City foreclosed on these guarantees because they grew assured that segregationist compromises could contain the accompanying blowback.[16]

None of this is particularly surprising. As many urban and economic historians have shown, undisclosed inequalities are endemic to consumer economies that celebrate affluence and temporary pleasure at the expense of long-ranging economic and public service investments. With a year-round population inhabited by a largely dependent and politically unconnected black laboring class, the men who governed the Jersey shore's boardwalk economy found little motivation to address systemic inequalities that offered little promise of aiding the cultural profile or financial value of its pleasure-driven enterprises. Segregation proved profitable to the economically and politically connected on each side of the color line because it stabilized a consumer economy uniquely prone to volatile market shifts and shifting personal tastes. The financial collapse and declining cultural appeal of the Jersey shore by the late 1960s coincided with the failure of local authorities to foresee or prepare for the undocumented costs of segregation's political economy. Yet, unlike in other postwar cities, the origins of the "urban crisis" in Asbury Park and Atlantic City were not confined to the effects of deindustrialization, nor were they a product of postwar black radicalism. As early as the Reconstruction era, disputes over the public sphere and the rights of free individuals set the stage for a prolonged battle over the legality of segregation and the accessibility of the marketplace in northern leisure venues. White and black northerners created and contested public and social life during summers at the seashore as they synthesized the broader meanings of capitalism and the rights and health of consumers, political concepts that were left unresolved in the wake of Reconstruction's—and later segregation's—collapse.[17]

Acknowledgments

The men and women who fought for freedom on the beaches of the Jersey shore reminded me that we owe most of our personal triumphs to those who walk beside us. Over the past nine years, this project has benefited from an untold number of professors, advisers, editors, archivists, students, classmates, roommates, friends, family members, conference panelists, and anonymous reviewers who helped shape and influence this book. Time and again, I was struck by their devotion, knowledge, and patience as I shared early drafts and occasional frustrations.

This project started with the helpful suggestion of Judy Giesberg, who challenged me to uncover the understudied post–Civil War northern civil rights movement. Because she was the original champion of this topic, I owe immense gratitude to her for her thoughtful reading of early drafts and continued support throughout the years. Peter Carmichael next directed the project through its intermediate stages. Pete's "tenacious" and satirical editing helped fine-tune its arguments and clarify its prose. He continues to shape and guide my career in immeasurable ways, and I thank him for his continued support, friendship, and impressive network of connections within the profession. I especially wish to thank Aaron Sheehan-Dean, whose seamless guidance of this project's later stages is a reflection of his immense editorial talent. I am particularly indebted to Brian Luskey, who consistently went above and beyond in commenting, editing, and offering constructive feedback on many earlier drafts. Ken Fones-Wolf, John Ernest, and Walter Greason each brought a diverse set of skills and individual expertise to the project, and I hope they will find that the this book is a reflection of their consistent interest and many conversations about how to make it better.

I especially wish to thank Andrew Slap, William Cerbone, and Fredric Nachbaur at Fordham University Press. Andy enthusiastically embraced this project and has continued to offer critical insight that has made this a much better book than it would have otherwise been. Through many productive conversations, he went above and beyond his role as editor, sharing not only suggestions related to the book, but also invaluable guidance and professional connections that have helped me navigate my early career. All first-time authors should be as lucky to have Andy, Will, and Fred directing their work.

Between writing and researching, I had an opportunity to teach hundreds of students at Villanova University, West Virginia University, and the University of Pittsburgh at Johnstown. These talented and inspiring men and women provided welcome reprieves from the anonymity of the scholar's life. It was my pleasure to be their professor, and I wish them all the best in their own professional careers. Nate Hall and Timmy Poydenis, you're still the best! These research and writing breaks were also spent in the company of many friends and family members, especially those from my days at Elizabethtown College. To Matt Woehnker, Eric Wetzel, Mike Grecco, Brian Bonner, Steve Luongo, Rachel Jones Williams, Jackie Woehnker, Craig Woehnker, and the countless other Blue Jays, thank you for the glory days.

Since then, I've had the privilege of meeting many important colleagues and graduate school friends. While I was an undergraduate student Dr. David Brown taught me how to be a scholar, and his career continues to be a model for aspiring historians. At WVU, I was lucky to serve as a teaching assistant for Tyler Boulware, who has proven repeatedly to be an important teaching mentor and professional sounding board. A very special thank-you to my graduate school roommates and forever friends Brandon Williams, Joe Rizzo, and Cara Snider. I also wish to recognize Josh Esposito, Karina Esposito, Lauren Thompson, Joel Christenson, Jake Ivey, David Williams, Stuart Collins, and Jonathan Nicholson. Each of you greatly aided in the personal and scholarly enjoyment of my time at Villanova and WVU. Thank you for your guidance, patience, and, most important, the much-needed comic relief.

More recently, I've benefited from the professional encouragement and friendly advice of my colleagues at the University of Pittsburgh at Johnstown, including Kay Reist, Paul Newman, Veronica Wilson, Bob Matson, Dan Santoro, Jeremiah Coldsmith, and Ray Wrabley. They have each gone out of their way to welcome me into their department, their homes, and their community. They are impeccable scholars and teachers, and even greater people.

Of course, I especially wish to thank my parents. My mom was my first editor and continues to nourish my personal and professional life with her boundless love, unyielding support, and daily conversation. From the ball fields to the classroom, my father has consistently proven to be an impeccable model of what it means to be a man, father, and professional. I hope this book resembles the values they both continue to exude. Thank you as well to my sisters, Gabrielle and Lena; my grandparents Barney and Elaine Goldberg; my godfather, Gregg Christenson; and my "ever-loving grandmother" Josie Christenson.

Last, I wish to thank two people who provided the "spiritual" introduction to this project. In 2003, Matt Woehnker introduced me to the music and songbook of Bruce Springsteen. Since then, the Boss's lyrics and anthems have not only bonded our friendship, but also served as a constant source of rejuvenation and inspiration during this project's lengthy tenure. In them I discovered the magic of the Jerseys shore's mystical and enigmatic hold over American culture and was inspired to narrate the stories and activism of those who also "had a notion" to fight for a free and socially responsible society. Thanks Bruce and Matt!

Notes

Introduction

1. *Philadelphia Inquirer*, July 23, 1893, 10.

2. For a short list of studies that detail the political uses of vacation destinations and tourist sites during the Gilded Age and Progressive era, see esp. Cindy Aron, *Working at Play: A History of Vacations in the United States* (New York: Oxford University Press, 1999); Jon Sterngrass, *First Resorts: Pursuing Pleasure at Saratoga Springs, Newport, and Coney Island* (Baltimore: Johns Hopkins University Press, 2001); John F. Kasson, *Amusing the Millions: Coney Island at the Turn of the Century* (New York: Hill & Wang, 1978); David Nasaw, *Going Out: The Rise and Fall of Public Amusements* (Cambridge, Mass.: Harvard University Press, 1999); Catherine Cocks, *Doing the Town: The Rise of Urban Tourism in the Unites States, 1815–1915* (Berkeley: University of California Press, 2001); John F. Sears, *Sacred Places: American Tourist Attractions in the Nineteenth Century* (New York: Oxford University Press, 1989); Marguerite S. Shaffer, *See America First: Tourism and National Identity, 1880–1940* (Washington, D.C.: Smithsonian Institution Press, 2001); Dona Brown, *Inventing New England: Regional Tourism in the Nineteenth Century* (Washington, D.C.: Smithsonian Institution Press, 1997); Olive Logan, "Long Branch, 1876," *Harper's New Monthly Magazine* 53, no. 316 (September 1876); Stephen Crane, "Asbury Park as seen by Stephen Crane," *Kansas City (Mo.) Star*, August 22, 1896. See also Stephen Crane, "Joys of Seaside Life," *New York Tribune*, July 17, 1892.

3. Although there have been other studies done on African American communities and activists at the Jersey shore, this will be the first to fully document and conceptualize the totality of civil rights campaigns and segregation efforts from the end of the Civil War to 1920. Studies that document the early history of African American communities in Atlantic City include Henry James Foster, "The Urban Experience of Blacks in Atlantic City, New Jersey: 1850–1915" (Ph.D. diss., Rutgers University, 1981); Richlyn F. Goddard, "'Three Months to Hurry, Nine Months to Worry': Resort Life for African Americans in Atlantic City, 1854–1940" (Ph.D. diss., Howard University, 2001); and Nelson Johnson, *The Northside: African Americans and the Creation of Atlantic City* (New York: Plexus, 2010). For works that mention the persistence of race relations at the Jersey shore, as well as neighboring resorts in Philadelphia, see esp. Charles E. Funnell, *By the Beautiful Sea: The Rise and High Times of That Great American Resort, Atlantic City* (New Brunswick, N.J.: Rutgers University Press, 1975); Martin Paulsson, *The Social Anxieties of Progressive Reform: Atlantic City, 1854–1920* (New York: New York University Press, 1994); Bryant T. Simon, *Boardwalk of Dreams: Atlantic City and the Fate of Urban America* (New York: Oxford University Press, 2004); Daniel Wolff, *4th of July, Asbury Park: A History of the Promised Land* (New York: Bloomsbury, 2005); and Brian E. Allnut, "The Negro Excursions: Recreational Outings among Philadelphia African

Americans, 1876–1926," *Pennsylvania Magazine of History and Biography* 129 (January 2005): 73–104. For a small sample on the history of race in the United States, see Winthrop Jordan, *White over Black: American Attitudes toward the Negro, 1550–1812* (Chapel Hill: University of North Carolina Press, 1968); Thomas F. Gossett, *Race: The History of an Idea in America* (1963; repr., New York: Oxford University Press, 1997); George Fredrickson, *The Black Image in the White Mind: The Debate on Afro-American Character and Destiny, 1817–1914* (New York: Harper & Row, 1971); Lee D. Baker, *From Savage to Negro: Anthropology and the Construction of Race, 1896–1954* (Berkeley: University of California Press, 1998); James Brewer Stewart, "The Emergence of Racial Modernity and the Rise of the White North, 1790–1840," *Journal of the Early Republic* 18 (Spring 1998): 181–217; and William L. Van Deburg, *Hoodlums: Black Villains and Social Bandits in American Life* (Chicago: University of Chicago Press, 2004); C. Vann Woodward, *The Strange Career of Jim Crow* (New York: Oxford University Press, 1955). Following Woodward's example, Leon Litwack surveyed the pervasiveness of racial discrimination in framing segregation in the antebellum North, concluding that "virtually every phase of existence" was closed off to black Americans. See Litwack, *North Slavery: The Negro in he Free States: 1790–1860* (Chicago: University of Chicago Press, 1961). Recent work by Blair Kelley, Judy Ann Giesberg, and Kate Masur has begun to qualify these conclusions by documenting the persistent African American resistance efforts to desegregate public accommodations during the Civil War era. See Kelley, *Right to Ride: Streetcar Boycotts and African American Citizenship in the Era of Plessy v. Ferguson* (Chapel Hill: University of North Carolina Press, 2010); Giesberg, *Army at Home: Women and the Civil War on the Northern Home Front* (Chapel Hill: University of North Carolina Press, 2009); and Masur, *An Example for All the Land: Emancipation and the Struggle over Equality in Washington, D.C.* (Chapel Hill: University of North Carolina Press, 2010). Thomas Sugrue's sweeping survey of civil rights in the North gets us closer to understanding how segregation functioned in various spheres of everyday life, but he does not begin his look at the "long civil rights movement" until 1920. See Sugrue, *Sweet Land of Liberty: The Forgotten Struggle for Civil Rights in the North* (New York: Random House, 2008); George Fredrickson, *Black Image in the White Mind*; Masur, *Example for All the Land*; William Gillette, *Retreat from Reconstruction, 1869–1879* (Baton Rouge: Louisiana State University Press, 1979); Saidiya V. Hartman, *Scenes of Subjection: Terror, Slavery, and Self-Making in Nineteenth-Century America* (New York: Oxford University Press, 1997); Kirt H. Wilson, *The Reconstruction Desegregation Debate: The Politics of Equality and the Rhetoric of Place, 1870–1875* (East Lansing: Michigan State University Press, 2002); Douglas Blackmon, *Slavery by Another Name: The Re-enslavement of Black People from the Civil War to World War II* (New York: Doubleday, 2008); David Roediger, *The Wages of Whiteness: Race and the Making of the American Working Class* (New York: Verso, 1991). Although not all the authors mentioned in the following list of works would classify themselves as "whiteness scholars," they have each focused on the inner workings and public affirmations of white supremacy in the nineteenth-century North. See Joanne Pope Melish, *Disowning Slavery: Gradual Emancipation and "Race" in New England, 1780–1860* (Ithaca, N.Y.: Cornell University Press, 1998); Benjamin Reiss, *The Showman and the Slave: Race, Death, and Memory in Barnam's America* (Cambridge,

Mass.: Harvard University Press, 2010); Alexander Saxton, *The Rise and Fall of the White Republic: Class Politics and Mass Culture in Nineteenth Century America* (New York: Verso, 1990); Roediger, *Wages of Whiteness*; Matthew Frye Jacobson, *Whiteness of a Different Color: European Immigrants and the Alchemy of Race* (Cambridge, Mass.: Harvard University Press, 1999); Noel Ignatiev, *How the Irish Became White* (New York: Routledge, 1995); Thomas C. Holt, "Racism and the Working Class," *International Labor and Working-Class History* 45 (Spring 1994): 86–95; Andrew Neather, "'Whiteness' and the Politics of Working-Class History," *Radical History Review* 61 (Winter 1995): 190–96; and Jerome Bjelopera, *City of Clerks: Office and Sales Workers in Philadelphia, 1870–1920* (Urbana: University of Illinois Press, 2005). Historians have often treated African Americans as the objects of public ridicule and consumer exploitation, while also suggesting that Jim Crow policies permanently segregated blacks from northern leisure venues. See Myra B. Young Armstead, *"Lord Please Don't Take Me in August": African Americans in Newport and Saratoga Springs, 1870–1930* (Urbana: University of Illinois Press, 1999); Bjelopera, *City of Clerks*; Nasaw, *Going Out*; and Cocks, *Doing the Town*.

4. On nineteenth-century free labor ideology, see Eric Foner, *Free Soil, Free Labor, Free Men: The Ideology of the Republican Party before the Civil War* (New York: Oxford University Press, 1970); Heather Cox Richardson, *The Greatest Nation of the Earth: Republican Economic Policies during the Civil War* (Cambridge, Mass.: Harvard University Press, 1997); William E. Gienepp, *The Origins of the Republican Party, 1852–1856* (New York: Oxford University Press, 1987); John Ashworth, *Slavery, Capitalism, and Politics in the Antebellum Republic, Vol. 1: Commerce and Compromise* (New York: Cambridge University Press, 1995); Alex Gourevitch, *From Slavery to the Cooperative Commonwealth: Labor and Republican Liberty in the Nineteenth Century* (New York: Cambridge University Press, 2014); and Mark A. Lause, *Free Labor: The Civil War and the Making of an American Working Class* (Urbana: University of Illinois Press, 2015).

5. The history of why northerners withdrew support for Reconstruction remains a contentious one. Some classic interpretations include David Montgomery, *Beyond Free Labor: Labor and the Radical Republicans, 1862–1872* (New York: Vintage, 1967); John G. Sproat, *"The Best Men": Liberal Reformers in the Gilded Age* (New York: Oxford University Press, 1968); Gillette, *Retreat from Reconstruction*; Robert Wiebe, *The Search for Order, 1877–1920* (New York: Hill & Wang, 1966); David Tucker, *Mugwumps: Public Moralists of the Gilded Age* (Columbia: University of Missouri Press, 1995); Amy Dru Stanley, *From Bondage to Contract: Wage Labor, Marriage, and the Market in the Age of Slavery Emancipation* (New York: Cambridge University Press, 1998); Wilson, *Reconstruction Desegregation Debate*; Heather Cox Richardson, *The Death of Reconstruction: Race, Labor, and Politics in the Post–Civil War North, 1865–1901* (Cambridge, Mass.: Harvard University Press, 2001); Nancy Cohen, *The Reconstruction of American Liberalism, 1865–1914* (Chapel Hill: University of North Carolina Press, 2002); and Andrew L. Slap, *The Doom of Reconstruction: The Liberal Republicans in the Civil War Era* (New York: Fordham University Press, 2006); Eric Foner, *Reconstruction: America's Unfinished Revolution, 1863–1877* (New York: Harper & Row, 1988); David Quigley, *Second Founding: New York City, Reconstruction, and the Making of American Democracy* (New York: Hill & Wang, 2004).

6. My guiding question here—Is the right to consume equal to the right to work?—
is adopted from Joanna Cohen's statement about consumption in the antebellum era,
"The right to purchase is as free as the right to sell." See Cohen, "The Right to Purchase
Is as Free as the Right to Sell: Defining Consumers as Citizens in the Auction-House
Conflicts of the Early Republic," *Journal of the Early Republic* 30, no. 1 (2010): 25–62. For
works that detail the rise of consumption in the eighteenth and nineteenth century, see
esp. T. H. Breen, *The Marketplace of Revolution: How Consumer Politics Shaped Ameri-
can Independence* (New York: Oxford University Press, 2004); Drew McCoy, *The Elusive
Republic: Political Economy in Jeffersonian America* (Chapel Hill: University of North
Carolina Press, 1980); Richards L. Bushman, *The Refinement of America: Persons, Houses,
Cities* (New York: Vintage, 1992); Richard Butsch, *For Fun and Profit: The Transformation of Leisure into Consumption* (Philadelphia: Temple University Press, 1990); Richard
Wightman Fox and T. J. Jackson Lears, eds., *The Culture of Consumption: Critical Essays
in American History, 1880–1980* (New York: Pantheon, 1983); Roy Rosenzweig, *Eight
Hours for What We Will: Workers and Leisure in an Industrial City, 1870–1920* (Cambridge, Mass.: Harvard University Press, 1983); William Leach, *Land of Desire: Merchants, Power, and the Rise of a New American Culture* (New York: Pantheon, 1994). In
contrast, Jackson Lears and Daniel Horowitz have stressed the social anxieties that a free
consumer society created for Progressive-era cultural elites. See Lears, *No Place of Grace:
Antimodernism and the Transformation of American Culture, 1880–1920* (New York:
Pantheon, 1981); Horowitz, *The Morality of Spending: Attitudes towards the Consumer in
America, 1875–1940* (Chicago: University of Chicago Press, 1992); Lawrence Glickman,
Buying Power: A History of Consumer Activism in America (Chicago: University of Chi-
cago Press, 2009); Kelley, *Right to Ride*; Margaret Finnegan, *Selling Suffrage: Consumer
Culture and Votes for Women* (New York: Columbia University Press, 1999); Nan Enstad,
*Ladies of Love, Girls of Adventure: Working Women, Popular Culture, and Labor Politics
at the Turn of the Century* (New York: Columbia University Press, 1999); Grace Elizabeth
Hale, *Making Whiteness: The Culture of Segregation in the South, 1890–1940* (New York:
Vintage, 1998); Lizabeth Cohen, *A Consumers' Republic: The Politics of Mass Consump-
tion in Postwar America* (New York: Vintage, 2003), 188; Eric Foner, *The Story of American Freedom* (New York: Norton, 1998).

7. The prevalence of Reconstruction-era debates in discussions about civil rights and
consumption after 1877 requires that historians rethink how we characterize and name
the post–Civil War era. While it is common to refer to the years after 1877 as the "Gilded
Age," this characterization often assumes that issues directly related to the Civil War and
Reconstruction—particularly those pertaining to race—faded as northern Americans
took up new discussions about class, robber barons, and the consequences of industrial
capitalism. Any lingering Reconstruction-era disputes are usually reserved for treat-
ments of southern communities and do not account for how the continued saliency
of Reconstruction-era issues—many of them unresolved—shaped the segregationist
debates and practices in northern communities. Prior to the Compromise of 1877, the
politics of public amusements in conjunction with discussions about the 1875 Civil
Rights Act made clear that debates about Reconstruction were already transitioning
from concerns about the rights to labor to a wider political conversation about con-

sumption and the rights of citizens to access commercial spaces. In defending the rights of business against consumers, the Supreme Court's ruling in the 1883 *Civil Rights Cases* intimated the new ways in which white northerners were moving beyond free labor as an organizing principle of economic growth and as a defense of segregation. While many summer tourists preferred to escape these disputes during their leisure time, many white northerners who visited the beach resorts of the Jersey shore continued to ground their beliefs about the place of African Americans in the public sphere and their ideas about the rights of consumers in relation to their recreational experiences and conflicting interpretations and memories of Reconstruction. Although this is not a book about the memory of Reconstruction, it is clear that white and black northerners constructed vastly different interpretations of Reconstruction that, at certain critical junctures, framed their discussions about segregation as they struggled to understand the social boundaries of new public and commercial spaces without clear precedents. For the best book on the memory of Reconstruction, see Bruce Baker, *What Reconstruction Meant: Historical Memory in the American South* (Charlottesville: University of Virginia Press, 2007). Unlike most works that focus on the contested meanings of the Civil War, Baker's zeroes in on how understandings of the Reconstruction era shaped the future politics and segregationist policies of the New South. Unfortunately, there is no comparable study of the North.

8. Sterngrass, *First Resorts*, 3. The fears about consumer activism expressed by moderate business owners at the Jersey shore in the 1880s and 1890s were similar to those articulated by Radical Republicans in response to the northern labor movement after the Civil War. See Montgomery, *Beyond Free Labor*; Cohen, *Reconstruction of American Liberalism*; Slap, *Doom of Reconstruction*.

9. My reliance on northern periodicals, advice literature, and other visual sources is not meant to conclude that these sources speak any more accurately or authentically than do other records. White authorities and black activists each exhibited clear biases and conveyed misrepresentations about events as they fought to shape the vocabulary and practices of segregation. Yet, due to the incomplete and often scarce availability of letters, diaries, and other "official" policy-related papers, it is necessary that these sources be consulted in an attempt to uncover the "voice of the public" in an age before public opinion polls. More than that, these sources reveal the idealized visions that northern participants constructed of public and commercial leisure space as they sought to influence social behavior and economic activity in the absence of official policies and laws. I consult them disproportionately because those in charge of shaping and contesting segregationist boundaries viewed them as important political weapons in a fight that each side understood to be highly unsettled.

10. *The Sun* (New York), June 29, 1887; "Denouncing Mr. Bradley: The Colored People of Asbury Park Resent the Slurs of Its Founder," *The Sun* (New York), June 28, 1887. William Novak reminds us that for much of the nineteenth century, the promotion of a "well-regulated" society trumped the primacy of property rights, which were "social, relative, and historical, not individual, absolute, and natural." See Novak, *The People's Welfare: Law and Regulation in Nineteenth-Century America* (Chapel Hill: University of North Carolina Press, 1996). For a look at how race and the law were influenced

by common law ideas, see Barbara Welke, "When All Women Were White, and All the Blacks Were Men: Gender, Class, Race, and the Road to *Plessy*, 1855–1914," *Law and History Review* 13, no. 2 (1995): 261–316; A. K. Sandoval-Strauss, "Travelers, Strangers, and Jim Crow: Law, Public Accommodations, and Civil Rights in America," *Law and History Review* 23, no. 1 (2005): 53–94; Kelley, *Right to Ride*; Giesberg, *Army at Home*; Masur, *Example for All the Land.*

11. My conceptual understanding of infrapolitics and "hidden transcripts" is drawn from the work of Michel de Certeau, Robin D. G. Kelley, Stephen Hahn, and James C. Scott. See Certeau, *The Practice of Everyday Life* (Berkeley: University of California Press, 1984); Kelley, *Race Rebels: Culture, Politics, and the Black Working Class* (New York: Free Press, 1994); Hahn, *A Nation under Our Feet: Black Political Struggles in the Rural South from Slavery to the Great Migration* (Cambridge, Mass.: Harvard University Press 2003); Scott, *Domination and the Arts of Resistance: Hidden Transcripts* (New Haven, Conn.: Yale University Press, 1992). Elizabeth Abel's study of Jim Crow signs in the postwar South is particularly useful in gauging what constituted legitimate and illegitimate forms of segregation notices. As Abel points out, signs that were handwritten, lacked proper grammar, or appealed to folkish traditions were often seen as invalid and fraudulent since they betrayed the official, state-sanctioned authority and conformity necessary to compel obedience. See Abel, *Signs of the Times: The Visual Politics of Jim Crow* (Berkeley: University of California Press, 2010).

12. "The Color Line at Asbury Park," *The Sun* (New York), June 29, 1893; "Africa and Asbury Park," *New York Times*, July 7, 1893.

13. For a sampling of post–World War II desegregation efforts, see esp. Thomas Sugrue, *The Origins of the Urban Crisis: Race and Inequality in Postwar Detroit* (Princeton: Princeton University Press, 1996); Martha Biondi, *To Fight and Stand: The Struggle for Civil Rights in Postwar New York City* (New York: Cambridge University Press, 2003); Gary Gerstle, "Race and the Myth of the Liberal Consensus," *Journal of American History* 82, no. 2 (1995): 579–86; Cohen, *Consumer's Republic.*

14. N. D. B. Connolly, *A World More Concrete: Real Estate and the Remaking of Jim Crow South Florida* (Chicago: University of Chicago Press, 2014), 241; Andrew Kahrl, *The Land Was Ours: African American Beaches from Jim Crow to the Sunbelt South* (Cambridge, Mass.: Harvard University Press, 2012); J. Douglas Smith, *Managing White Supremacy: Race, Politics, and Citizenship in Jim Crow Virginia* (Chapel Hill: University of North Carolina Press, 2002); Adam Green, *Selling the Race: Culture, Community, and Black Chicago, 1940–1955* (Chicago: University of Chicago Press, 2007); Earl Lewis, *In Their Own Interests: Race, Class, and Power in Twentieth-Century Norfolk, Virginia* (Berkeley: University of California Press, 1993); Andrew Weise, *Places of Their Own: African American Suburbanization in the Twentieth Century* (Chicago: University of Chicago Press, 2004); Michele Mitchell, *Righteous Propagation: African Americans and the Politics of Racial Destiny after Reconstruction* (Chapel Hill: University of North Carolina Press, 2004); and Touré Reed, *Not Alms but Opportunity: The Urban League and the Politics of Racial Uplift, 1910–1950* (Chapel Hill: University of California Press, 2008).

15. "Bradley Is Only Opponent," *Asbury Park Evening Press*, March 20, 1906; "Annexation Demanded," *Asbury Park Evening Press*, February 17, 1906. While other northern metropolitan areas were undertaking measures to seize black property throughout the

early twentieth century, Asbury Park's annexation victory served notice to local black activists that even within such highly charged racial times, a shared commitment to environmental justice, consumer safety, and municipal efficiency could reform certain forms of segregation (even if it meant having to surrender their earlier claim to integrated leisure). Khalid Muhammad, Kevin Mumford, Marcy Sacks, and Andrew Kahrl remind us of the serious efforts whites pursued to police and control black leisure spaces in the early 1900s. See Muhammad, *The Condemnation of Blackness: Ideas about Race and Crime in the Making of Modern Urban America* (Cambridge, Mass.: Harvard University Press, 2010); Mumford, *Interzones: Black/White Sex Districts in Chicago and New York in the Early Twentieth Century* (New York: Columbia University Press, 1997); Sacks, "'To Show Who Was in Charge': Police Repression of New York City's Black Population at the Turn of the Twentieth Century," *Journal of Urban History* 31 (September 2005): 799–819; Kahrl, *The Land Was Ours.* For studies that link environmental inequality to public policy, as well as African American attempts to combat public health deficiencies in black communities, see esp. Robert D. Bullard, *Dumping in Dixie: Race, Class, and Environmental Quality* (Boulder, Colo.: Westview, 1990); Diane D. Grave and Mark Stoll, *"To Love the Wind and the Rain": African Americans and Environmental History* (Pittsburgh: University of Pittsburgh Press, 2006); Andrew Hurley, *Environmental Inequalities: Class, Race, and Industrial Pollution in Gary, Indiana, 1945–1980* (Chapel Hill: University of North Carolina Press, 1995); and Julie Sze, *Noxious New York: The Racial Politics of Urban Health and Environmental Justice* (Cambridge, Mass.: MIT Press, 2007).

1. Reconstructing Jim Crow

1. "Negro by the Sea," *Philadelphia Times*, July 25, 1890.

2. For many years, historians have emphasized the continuation of racist feelings in shaping segregation in the post–Civil War North. This chapter maintains that historians have often taken racism for granted. For example, scholars who have documented the history of Jim Crow in the North have assumed that very little changed between the antebellum era and the hardening of Jim Crow during Reconstruction. See George Fredrickson, *The Black Image in the White Mind: The Debate on Afro-American Character and Destiny, 1817–1914* (New York: Harper & Row, 1971); William Gillette, *Retreat from Reconstruction, 1869–1879* (Baton Rouge: Louisiana State University Press, 1979); Saidiya Hartman, *Scenes of Subjection: Terror, Slavery, and Self-Making in Nineteenth-Century America* (New York: Oxford University Press, 1997); Kirt H. Wilson, *The Reconstruction Desegregation Debate: The Politics of Equality and the Rhetoric of Place, 1870–1875* (East Lansing: Michigan State University Press, 2002); Alessandra Lorini, *Rituals of Race: American Public Culture and the Search for Racial Democracy* (Charlottesville: University of Virginia Press, 1999); Douglas Blackmon, *Slavery by Another Name: The Re-enslavement of Black People from the Civil War to World War II* (New York: Doubleday, 2008); and David Roediger, *The Wages of Whiteness: Race and the Making of the American Working Class* (New York: Verso, 1991).

3. "Cape May, 1848: Rebecca Sharp and Henrietta Roberts," in Margaret Thomas Buchholz, ed., *Shore Chronicles: Diaries and Travelers' Tales from the Jersey Shore, 1764–1955* (Harvey Cedars, N.J.: Down the Shore Publishing, 1999).

4. "Cape May, 1850: Frederika Bremer," in Buchholz, *Shore Chronicles*, 65; Olive Logan, "Long Branch, 1876," *Harper's New Monthly Magazine* 53, no. 316 (September 1876).

5. *Frank Leslie's Illustrated Newspaper*, August 22, 1857.

6. "The Close of the Watering Season," *New York Herald*, September 22, 1861; "The Watering Places," *New York Herald*, June 10, 1861; "Our Fashionable Summer Resorts—North and South," *New York Herald*, June 2, 1861.

7. *New York Herald*, September 22, 1861; "The Watering Places—Close of the Season," *New York Herald*, August 29, 1861; "The Watering Places—Recreation and Retrenchment," *New York Herald*, June 17, 1862; *New York Herald*, September 22, 1861.

8. For examinations of antebellum-era free labor ideology, see Eric Foner, *Free Soil, Free Labor, Free Men: The Ideology of the Republican Party before the Civil War* (New York: Oxford University Press, 1970); John Ashworth, *Slavery, Capitalism, and Politics in the Antebellum Republic, Vol. 1: Commerce and Compromise* (New York: Cambridge University Press, 1995); Sean Wilentz, *Chants Democratic: New York City and the Rise of the American Working Class, 1788–1850* (New York: Oxford University Press, 1984); Bruce Laurie, *Artisans into Workers: Labor in Nineteenth-Century America* (New York: Hill & Wang, 1989); Charles Sellers, *The Market Revolution: Jacksonian America, 1815–1846* (New York: Oxford University Press, 1994); David Walker Howe, *What Hath God Wrought: The Transformation of America, 1815–1848* (New York: Oxford University Press, 2007); Heather Cox Richardson, *The Greatest Nation of the Earth: Republican Economic Policies during the Civil War* (Cambridge, Mass.: Harvard University Press, 1997); Nancy Cohen, *The Reconstruction of American Liberalism, 1865–1914* (Chapel Hill: University of North Carolina Press, 2002); Roediger, *Wages of Whiteness*; Alex Gourevitch, *From Slavery to the Cooperative Commonwealth: Labor and Republican Liberty in the Nineteenth Century* (New York: Cambridge University Press, 2014); Mark A. Lause, *Free Labor: The Civil War and the Making of an American Working Class* (Urbana: University of Illinois Press, 2015).

9. T. Robinson Warren, *Shooting, Boating, and Fishing for Young Sportsmen* (New York, 1871); "The Watering Places," *New York Herald*, April 7, 1862; "The Watering Place Season—New Developments," *New York Herald*, August 23, 1862.

10. "The Next Season at the Watering Places," *New York Herald*, April 21, 1863; Melinda Lawson, "Imagining Slavery: Representations of the Peculiar Institution on the Northern Stage: 1776–1860," *Journal of the Civil War Era* 1, no. 1 (2011): 25–55. The prevalence of racism in antebellum era popular culture is well documented. For a small sample of prominent works, see Roediger, *Wages of Whiteness*; Dale Cockrell, *Demons of Disorder: Early Blackface Minstrels and Their World* (New York: Cambridge University Press, 1997); Robert C. Toll, *Blacking Up: The Minstrel Show in Nineteenth-Century America* (New York: Oxford University Press, 1974); Hazel Waters, *Racism on the Victorian Stage: Representations of Slavery and the Black Character* (New York: Cambridge University Press, 2007); Heather S. Nathans, *Slavery and Sentiment on the American Stage, 1787–1861* (New York: Cambridge University Press, 2009); Errol G. Hill and James V. Hatch, *A History of African American Theatre* (New York: Cambridge University Press, 2003); Eric Lott, *Love and Theft: Blackface Minstrelsy and the American Working Class* (New York: Oxford University Press, 1995); W. T. Lhamon, Jr., *Raising Cain: Blackface*

Performance from Jim Crow to Hip Hop (New York: Cambridge University Press, 1998); Alexander Saxton, *The Rise and Fall of the White Republic: Class Politics and Mass Culture in Nineteenth-Century America* (New York: Verso, 1990); and Benjamin Reiss, *The Showman and the Slave: Race, Death, and Memory in Barnum's America* (Cambridge, Mass.: Harvard University Press, 2001).

11. *Freedom's Journal*, March 14, 1828; *Hazard's Register of Pennsylvania*, 14, 1834, 126–28, 200–3, 265–66; John Runcie, "'Hunting the Nigs' in Philadelphia: The Race Riot of August 1834," *Pennsylvania History* 29 (April 1972): 187–218; Gary Nash, *Forging Freedom: The Formation of Philadelphia's Black Community, 1720–1840* (Cambridge, Mass.: Harvard University Press, 1988); *Pennsylvania Gazette and Democratic Press*, February 29, 1828; *Pennsylvania Monthly Magazine* 2 (1828): 53–57.

12. Chandra Manning, *What This Cruel War Was Over: Soldiers, Slavery, and the Civil War* (New York: Vintage, 2007); Kate Masur, "'A Rare Phenomenon of Philological Vegetation': The Word 'Contraband' and the Meanings of Emancipation in the United States," *Journal of American History* 93, no. 4 2007): 1050–1084; Alice Fahs, *The Imagined Civil War: Popular Literature of the North and South, 1861–1865* (Chapel Hill: University of North Carolina Press, 2001).

13. "The Watering Places during the Dog Days," *New York Herald*, August 7, 1863; "The Excitements of the Day: The War and the Watering Places," *New York Herald*, May 17, 1863; "The Reign of Terror and the Watering Places," *New York Herald*, June 6, 1863.

14. Marguerite S. Shaffer, *See America First: Tourism and National Identity, 1880–1940* (Washington, D.C.: Smithsonian Institution Press, 2001); John Walton, *Histories of Tourism: Representation, Identity, and Conflict* (New York: Multilingual Matters, 2005).

15. "Mr. Bradley of Asbury Park," *New York Times*, October 22, 1893; James A. Bradley, "A History of Asbury Park," *Asbury Park Journal*, 1882.

16. Thomas Chambers, *Drinking the Waters: Creating an American Leisure Class at Nineteenth-Century Mineral Springs* (Washington, D.C.: Smithsonian Institution Press, 2002); Richard Butsch, *For Fun and Profit: The Transformation of Leisure into Consumption* (Philadelphia: Temple University Press, 1990); Catherine Cocks, *Doing the Town: The Rise of Urban Tourism in the United States, 1850–1915* (Berkeley: University of California Press, 2001); John Sterngrass, *First Resorts: Pursuing Pleasure at Saratoga Springs, Newport, and Coney Island* (Baltimore: Johns Hopkins University Press, 2001); Cindy Aron, *Working at Play: A History of Vacations in the United States* (New York: Oxford University Press, 1999); John F. Kasson, *Amusing the Millions: Coney Island at the Turn of the Century* (New York: Hill & Wang, 1978); Roy Rosenzweig and Elizabeth Blackmar, *The Park and Its People: A History of Central Park* (Ithaca, N.Y.: Cornell University Press, 1992).

17. *Harper's New Monthly Magazine* 56, no. 333 (February 1878); James Hannay, "Atlantic City: 1914," in Buchholz, *Shore Chronicles*.

18. Stephen Crane, "Joys of Seaside Life," *New York Tribune*, July 17, 1892.

19. For works that stress the impact of commercialization and consumption in postwar recreation and amusement, see Alan Trachtenberg, *The Incorporation of America: Culture and Society in the Gilded Age* (New York: Hill & Wang, 1982); T. J. Jackson Lears, *Fables of Abundance: A Cultural History of Advertising in America* (New York: Basic,

1994); Richard Ohmann, *Selling Culture: Magazines, Markets, and Class at the Turn of the Century* (London: Verso, 1999); Lawrence Levine, *High Brow/Low Brow: The Emergence of Cultural Hierarchy in America* (Cambridge, Mass.: Harvard University Press, 1988).

20. Joanne Pope Melish, *Disowning Slavery: Gradual Emancipation and "Race" in New England, 1780–1860* (Ithaca, N.Y.: Cornell University Press 1998); Dona Brown, *Inventing New England: Regional Tourism in the Nineteenth Century* (Washington, D.C.: Smithsonian Institution Press, 1997).

21. Camden and Atlantic Railroad, *Annual Report*, 1873, 10; and *A Complete Guide to Atlantic City* (Philadelphia: Burk & McFetridge, 1885), 19, both in Atlantic City Public Library, Atlantic City, N.J. For local histories of Atlantic City, see Charles E. Funnell, *By the Beautiful Sea: The Rise and High Times of That Great American Resort, Atlantic City* (New Brunswick, N.J.: Rutgers University Press, 1975); Martin Paulsson, *The Social Anxieties of Progressive Reform: Atlantic City, 1854–1920* (New York: New York University Press, 1994); Bryant Simon, *Boardwalk of Dreams: Atlantic City and the Fate of Urban America* (New York: Oxford University Press, 2004).

22. *New York Recorder*, July 26, 1891; quoted in Sterngrass, *First Resorts*, 100; quoted in William Novak, *The People's Welfare: Law and Regulation in Nineteenth-Century America* (Chapel Hill: University of North Carolina Press, 1996), 33, 41; Francis Couvares, *The Remaking Pittsburgh: Class and Culture in an Industrializing City, 1877–1919* (Albany: State University of New York Press, 1984); Steven Reiss, *Touching Base: Professional Baseball and American Culture in the Progressive Era* (1983; repr., Urbana: University of Illinois Press, 1999); Roy Rosenzweig, *Eight Hours for What We Will: Workers and Leisure In An Industrial City, 1870–1920* (Cambridge, Mass.: Harvard University Press, 1983); Kathy Peiss, *Cheap Amusements: Working Women and Leisure in Turn-of-the-Century New York* (Philadelphia: Temple University Press, 1986); Nan Enstad, *Ladies of Labor, Girls of Adventure: Working Women, Popular Culture, and Labor Politics at the Turn of the Century* (New York: Columbia University Press, 1999).

23. *New York Times*, August 10, 1890.

24. *Colored American*, August 25, 1900; "In the Merry Throng down by the Sea," *Philadelphia Inquirer*, August 18, 1897; Richlyn F. Goddard, "'Three Months to Hurry, Nine Months to Worry': Resort Life for African Americans in Atlantic City, 1854–1940" (Ph.D. diss., Howard University, 2001); Nelson Johnson, *The Northside: African Americans and the Creation of Atlantic City* (New York: Plexus, 2010).

25. "West Side Story: Profile of a Black Community," *Asbury Park Press*, May 21, 1882. See also *Atlantic City Daily Union*, September 1, 1892; *Atlantic City Press*, September 8, 1900; Milton Palmer, "Earning a Living in Atlantic City," New Jersey Writers' Project, New Jersey Ethnological Survey Records, Box WK-2, 1940, New Jersey State Archives, Trenton, N.J., 2; Henry James Foster, "The Urban Experience of Blacks in Atlantic City, New Jersey: 1850–1915" (Ph.D. diss., Rutgers University, 1981); Daniel Wolff, *4th of July, Asbury Park: A History of the Promised Land* (New York: Bloomsbury, 2005); Mark S. Foster, "'In the Face of Jim Crow': Prosperous Blacks and Vacations, Travel, and Outdoor Leisure, 1890–1945," *Journal of Negro History* 84 (Spring 1999): 130–49.

26. *Philadelphia Inquirer*, September 3, 1891; "Colored People Invade Atlantic," *Philadelphia Inquirer*, September 2, 1897, 2.

27. James Bradley, *Three Ways of Telling The History of Asbury Park* (Asbury Park, N.J.: M., W., and C. Pennypacker, 1887); "Summer at the Seaside: The Growing Attractiveness of the New Jersey Coast," *New York Times*, April 14, 1882.

28. *Atlantic City Daily Union*, August 1, 1893, 4.

29. "Many New Yorkers at Saratoga Springs," *New York Times*, August 1, 1902.

30. Casting black workers as a dependent subaltern class was a key component of the postwar racial contract and an integral part in racially marking occupations and access to consumer culture. See Charles Mills, *The Racial Contract* (Ithaca, N.Y.: Cornell University Press, 1997); Matthew Frye Jacobson, *Barbarian Virtues: The United States Encounters Foreign Peoples at Home and Abroad, 1876–1917* (New York: Hill & Wang, 2001).

31. *Philadelphia Inquirer*, August 7, 1885; "Impudents," *Daily Journal*, July 7, 1885; "Two Distinct Factions," *Shore Press*, October 22, 1885.

32. "Too Many Colored People," *Daily Journal*, July 17, 1885; "Their Jubilee Day," *New York Times*, July 21, 1887; Masur, "Rare Phenomenon of Philological Vegetation"; Fahs, *Imagined Civil War*.

33. *Philadelphia Public Ledger*, July 12, 1876; *West Jersey Press*, July 2, 1879; *Philadelphia Public Ledger*, August 8, 1876; See also Brian E. Allnut, "The Negro Excursions: Recreational Outings among Philadelphia African Americans, 1876–1926," *Pennsylvania Magazine of History and Biography* 129 (January 2005): 73–104; *Philadelphia Inquirer*, June 26, 1885.

34. "The Offenders," *Daily Journal*, June 29, 1887.

35. Nina Silber, *The Romance of Reunion: Northerners and the South, 1865–1900* (Chapel Hill: University of North Carolina Press, 1997); Shaffer, *See America First*. For a sample of the large body of scholarship on race and memory during the Reconstruction period, see David Blight, *Race and Reunion: The Civil War in American Memory* (Cambridge, Mass.: Harvard University Press, 2001); W. Fitzhugh Brundage, *The Southern Past: A Clash of Race and Memory* (Cambridge, Mass.: Harvard University Press, 2005); Andrew Kahrl, "The Political Work of Leisure: Class, Recreation, and African American Commemoration at Harpers Ferry, West Virginia, 1881–1931," *Journal of Social History* 42, no. 1 (2008): 57–77; Kirk Savage, *Standing Soldiers, Kneeling Slaves: Race, War, and Monument in Nineteenth-Century America* (Princeton, N.J.: Princeton University Press, 1997); Leslie Schwalm, *Emancipation's Diaspora: Race and Reconstruction in the Upper Midwest* (Chapel Hill: University of North Carolina Press, 2009); Gary Gallagher, *Causes Won, Lost, and Forgotten: How Hollywood and Popular Art Shape What We Know about the Civil War* (Chapel Hill: University of North Carolina Press, 2008); Caroline E. Janney, *Remembering the Civil War: Reunion and the Limits of Reconciliation* (Chapel Hill: University of North Carolina Press, 2013); Barbara Gannon, *The Won Cause: White and Black Comradeship in the Grand Army of the Republic* (Chapel Hill: University of North Carolina Press, 2014).

36. *Daily Journal*, June 29, 1887.

37. "The Negro by the Sea," *Philadelphia Times*, July 25, 1890; *Philadelphia Times*, July 20, 1890; *New York Times*, August 23, 1885, 3.

38. *Atlantic City Review*, August 21, 1884, 1; "The Colored Controversy," *New York Times*, July 21, 1885; "Colored Invasion," *Daily Journal*, August 5, 1886.

39. *New York Times*, October 22, 1893; "Asbury Park: Why People Are Living in Hotels Rather Than Cottages," *New York Times*, July 13, 1890. The *Times* noted that "for years the question, 'What to do about the colored people,' has been a vexed one. Their presence on the beach in large numbers was last year for a time offensive . . . This trouble was overcome by appointing certain hours, late in the evening, for their pleasure along the beach walks. This year, the same difficulty will be met in the same way." *Camden (N.J.) Courier*, June 5, 1880; *Camden (N.J.) Courier*, July 28, 1883; *West Jersey Press*, August 20, 1884; *Philadelphia Times*, August 16, 1890.

40. *Camden (N.J.) Courier*, June 25, 1887.

41. "The Color Line at Asbury Park: Visitors Annoyed at Colored Servants on the Beach," *New York Times*, June 30, 1889; "Colored People Indignant: Likely to Place Obstacles in Founder Bradley's Way," *New York Times*, July 20, 1893.

42. *New York Times*, June 30, 1889.

43. "The Tables Are Turned," *Asbury Park Press*, July 19, 1890; "Bradley Statement," *Shore Press*, July 8, 1887.

2. Occupying Jim Crow

1. "Defining the Color Line," *Asbury Park Press*, June 27, 1889; "Palace Guard Incident," *Shore Press*, June 28, 1889.

2. "Riots Feared at Asbury Park: Colored Waiters Will Resist Their Supplanting by Whites," *Evening World*, August 4, 1893.

3. Blair Kelley's *Right to Ride* is one of few works that addresses the Gilded Age civil rights campaigns of northern black activists and consumers. See *Right to Ride: Streetcar Boycotts and African American Citizenship in the Era of Plessy v. Ferguson* (Chapel Hill: University of North Carolina Press, 2010). In contrast, southern scholars have done a much better job exploring the civil rights achievements between the end of Reconstruction and the formal declaration of Jim Crow in 1896. See Jane Dailey, *Before Jim Crow: The Politics of Race in Postemancipation Virginia* (Chapel Hill: University of North Carolina Press, 2000); Glenda Gilmore, *Gender and Jim Crow: Women and the Politics of White Supremacy in North Carolina, 1896–1920* (Chapel Hill: University of North Carolina Press, 1996); and Leslie Schwalm, *Emancipation's Diaspora: Race and Reconstruction in the Upper Midwest* (Chapel Hill: University of North Carolina Press, 2009). For an excellent treatment on the ways in which African Americans negotiated leisure space and historical memory in the postwar border South, see Andrew W. Kahrl, "The Political Work of Leisure: Class, Recreation, and African American Commemoration at Harpers Ferry, West Virginia, 1881–1931," *Journal of Social History* 42, no. 1 (2008): 57–77.

4. A. K. Sandoval-Strauss, "Travelers, Strangers, and Jim Crow: Law, Public Accommodations, and Civil Rights in America," *Law and History Review* 23, no. 1 (2005): 53–94; Kelley, *Right to Ride*; Judith Giesberg, *Army at Home: Women and the Civil War on the Northern Home Front* (Chapel Hill: University of North Carolina Press, 2009); John Mercer Langston, "Equality Before the Law," in Philip S. Foner, ed., *The Voice of Black America: Major Speeches by Negroes in the United States, 1797–1971* (New York: Simon & Schuster, 1972); John P. Green, "These Evils Call Loudly for Redress," in Foner, *Voice of Black America*.

5. "Defending Their Race," *New York Times*, July 20, 1885; "Color Line at Asbury Park: Negroes Indignant at Threatened Exclusion from the Beach," *New York Times*, June 25, 1887; "250 People," *Shore Press*, July 1, 1887; "Answering Mr. Bradley: Colored People at Asbury Park Speak Out in Meeting," *New York Times*, June 28, 1887; "Drawing the Color Line at Asbury Park: Negroes Who Offend the Residents of Asbury Park," *New York Times*, July 19, 1885; "Asbury Park Colored Question," *Christian Recorder*, August 3, 1893.

6. "From a Colored Man's View," *Daily Journal*, July 21, 1885; "The Color Line at Asbury Park," *The Sun* (New York), June 29, 1887. In promoting black lawlessness and stigmatizing the "degraded" and "criminal" nature of black leisure, white segregationists pointed to "impartial" empirical evidence to justify racial policies. See Khalil G. Muhammad, *The Condemnation of Blackness: Race, Crime, and the Making of Modern Urban America* (Cambridge, Mass.: Harvard University Press, 2010); William H. Tucker, *The Science and Politics of Racial Research* (Urbana: University of Illinois Press, 1994); Kali N. Gross, *Colored Amazons: Crime, Violence, and the Black Women in the City of Brotherly Love, 1880–1910* (Durham, N.C.: Duke University Press, 2006). Northern efforts to minimize white racism date back to the late nineteenth century when a new generation of race experts argued in favor of a color-blind approach to explaining the "plight of the negro." See Frederick L. Hoffman, *Race Traits and Tendencies of the American Negro* (New York: Macmillan, 1896); Nathan S. Shaler, "The Negro Problem," *Atlantic Monthly* 54 (November 1884): 696–709; "Science and the African Problem," *Atlantic Monthly* 66 (July 1890); The Nature of the Negro," *The Arena*, December 1890, 23–35; Francis A. Walker, "The Colored Race in the United States," *Forum* 11 (September 1891): 501–9; Katherine B. Davis, "The Condition of the Negro in Philadelphia," *Journal of Political Economy* 8, no. 2 (1900): 248–60; *The Sun* (New York), June 29, 1887; *New York Times*, July 19, 1885.

7. *The Sun* (New York), June 29, 1887; *New York Times*, July 19, 1885.

8. "Colored People Indignant: Likely to Place Obstacles in Founder Bradley's Way," *New York Times*, July 20, 1893.

9. "Colored People Aroused: Suits Begun All over the Country against Men Who Have Refused to Recognize Their Rights," *New York Times*, July 26, 1895; "The Cost of Drawing the Color Line," *Boston Transcript*, December 21, 1893.

10. "The Black and White Problem," *Minnesotan-Herald*, March 12, 1870.

11. *New York Times*, July 20, 1893; Green, "These Evils Call Loudly for Redress," 502.

12. "Civil Rights at Indianapolis," *Cincinnati (Ohio) Daily Gazette*, September 1, 1877.

13. "The Trouble at the Grant Hotel," *Indianapolis Sentinel*, September 1, 1877; "That Civil Rights Case," *Cincinnati (Ohio) Daily Gazette*, September 3, 1877.

14. *Camden (N.J.) Courier*, August 25, 1888.

15. Patrick Rael, *Black Identity and Black Protest in the Antebellum North* (Chapel Hill: University of North Carolina Press, 2002); "Proceedings of the National Colored People, 1847," in Patrick Rael, ed., *Pamphlets of Protest: An Anthology of Early African American Protest Literature, 1790–1869* (New York: Routledge, 2001), 167; Charles L. Remond, "Address to a Legislative Committee in the Massachusetts House of Representatives, 1842," *The Liberator*, February 25, 1842.

16. "For Our Colored Friends," *Daily Journal*, July 8, 1885.

17. "Answering Mr. Bradley," *New York Times*, June 28, 1887.

18. *New York Times*, July 20, 1893; *Cincinnati (Ohio) Daily Gazette*, September 1, 1877.

19. "Jubilee Singers' Trials," *New York Times*, December 25, 1885.

20. "Asbury Park's Warfare: Colored People in Mass Meeting Denouncing Mr. Bradley's Actions," *New York Times*, July 6, 1887.

21. "Their Jubilee Day," *New York Times*, July 21, 1887.

22. "Jim Crow Theater Seats," *New York Times*, October 10, 1904.

23. "The Prosperous Season Seems to Have at Last Arrived," *New York Times*, August 10, 1891.

24. "*Washington Post* Complained," *Atlantic City Daily Union*, July 23, 1900; "What Are We Going to Do?" *Atlantic City Daily Union*, July 23, 1893.

25. "Asbury Park's Warfare," *New York Times*, July 6, 1887.

26. Roy Rosenzweig, *Eight Hours for What We Will: Workers and Leisure in an Industrial City, 1870–1920* (Cambridge, Mass.: Harvard University Press, 1983); Kathy Peiss, *Cheap Amusements: Working Women and Leisure in Turn-of-the-Century New York* (Philadelphia: Temple University Press, 1986); Nan Enstad, *Ladies of Labor, Girls of Adventure: Working Women, Popular Culture, and Labor Politics at the Turn of the Century* (New York: Columbia University Press, 1999); "A Colored Man's View," *Daily Journal*, August 12, 1886; "A Travesty upon Justice and Truth," *Christian Recorder*, August 6, 1885.

27. Saidiya Hartman argues that the "social" in nineteenth-century political thought encompassed an "asylum of inequality." See *Scenes of Subjection: Terror, Slavery, and Self-Making in Nineteenth-Century America* (New York: Oxford University Press, 1997), 201. The impact of commercialization on the Gilded Age public sphere is well documented. Few of these works, however, address the influence of northern race relations in reconfiguring the ideological and political parameters of public and private space. See William Leach, *Land of Desire: Merchants, Power, and the Rise of a New American Culture* (New York: Pantheon, 1994); Mary P. Ryan, *Civic Wars: Democracy and Public Life in the American City during the Nineteenth Century* (Berkeley: University of California Press, 1997); David Scobey, *Empire City: The Making and Meaning of the New York City Landscape* (Philadelphia: Temple University Press, 2002); Alan Trachtenberg, *The Incorporation of America: Culture and Society in the Gilded Age* (New York: Hill & Wang, 1982).

28. "Asbury Park Colored Question," *Christian Recorder*, August 3, 1893.

29. *The Sun* (New York), June 29, 1887.

30. *Atlantic City Daily Union*, June 14, 1893, 1; *Atlantic City Daily Union*, August 11, 1899; William M. Ashby, *Tales without Hate* (Newark, N.J.: Newark Preservation and Landmarks Committee, 1980), 36–37.

31. David R. Roediger, *The Wages of Whiteness: Race and the Making of the American Working Class* (New York: Verso, 1991); Heather Cox Richardson, *The Death of Reconstruction: Race, Labor, and Politics in the Post–Civil War North, 1865–1901* (Cambridge, Mass.: Harvard University Press, 2001); "It Must Be Stopped," *Daily Journal*, July 30, 1886, *Evening World*, August 4, 1893.

32. "Founder Bradley's Case," *The Sun* (New York), October 3, 1893; *The Sun* (New York), November 2, 1893.

33. In the 1970s, scholars began to chart the ways that citizens shifted their identity from workers to consumers through a series of strikes, boycotts, and national campaigns for product regulation. Although this study also details boycotts and other forms of labor activism undertaken by black workers, it situates the black consumer movement at the Jersey shore at a critical juncture in the nation's transition from a free labor to a free consumer society. For works that document the link between consumer advocacy and labor rights, see esp. Erna Agnevine, *Roots of the Consumer Movement: A Chronicle of Consumer History in the Twentieth Century* (Washington, D.C.: National Consumers League, 1979); Lawrence Glickman, *A Living Wage: American Workers and the Making of Consumer Society* (Ithaca, N.Y.: Cornell University Press, 1997); Rosenzweig, *Eight Hours for What We Will*; David Montgomery, *Beyond Equality: Labor and the Radical Republicans, 1862–1872* (New York: Vintage, 1967); Michael Gordon, "The Labor Boycott in New York City, 1880–1886," *Labor History* 16 (Spring 1975): 184–229; and Daniel R. Ernst, "Free Labor, the Consumer Interest, and the Law of Industrial Disputes, 1885–1900," *American Journal of Legal History* 36 (January 1992): 19–37.

3. Marketing and Managing Jim Crow

1. "Founder Bradley Explains," *New York Times*, October 24, 1893.

2. Ariela Gross, *What Blood Won't Tell: A History of Race on Trial in America* (Cambridge, Mass.: Harvard University Press, 2008); Leon Higginbotham, Jr., *Shades of Freedom: Racial Politics and Presumptions of the American Legal Process* (New York: Oxford University Press, 1996).

3. The importance of advice literature in directing social boundaries during the late nineteenth century is explored in a few popular works. See John F. Kasson, *Rudeness and Civility: Manners in Nineteenth- Century Urban America* (New York: Hill & Wang, 1990); Saidiya Hartman, *Scenes of Subjection: Terror, Slavery, and Self-Making in Nineteenth Century America* (New York: Oxford University Press, 1997); Timothy Edward Howard, *Excelsior; or, Essays on Politeness, Education, and the Means of Attaining Success in Life, Part I* (Baltimore: Kelly & Piet, 1868); and *Our Manners at Home and Abroad: A Complete Manual on the Manners, Customs, and Social Forms of the Best American Society* (Harrisburg: Pennsylvania Publishing Company, 1883), both in New York Public Library Archives and Manuscripts; quoted in Kasson, *Rudeness and Civility*, 60.

4. "Drawing the Color Line at Asbury Park: Negroes Who Offend the Residents of Asbury Park," *New York Times*, July 19, 1885.

5. Ibid.

6. "Asbury Park: Colored Question Settled," *New York Times*, July 20, 1890.

7. "City by the Sea: Excursion to Atlantic City," *Philadelphia Inquirer*, September 6, 1896; *Philadelphia Record*, September 4, 1898; *Philadelphia Evening Bulletin*, September 8, 1905.

8. *Philadelphia Inquirer*, September 6, 1896. For accounts of working-class women's leisure activities, see Kathy Peiss, *Cheap Amusements: Working Women and Leisure in Turn-of-the-Century New York* (Philadelphia: Temple University Press, 1986); Nan Enstad, *Ladies of Love, Girls of Adventure: Working Women, Popular Culture, and Labor*

Politics at the Turn of the Twentieth Century (New York: Columbia University Press, 1999); Cindy S. Aron, *Working at Play: A History of Vacations in the United States* (New York: Oxford University Press, 1999).

9. Timothy Gilfoyle, *City of Eros: New York City, Prostitution, and the Commercialization of Sex, 1790–1920* (New York: Norton, 1994). For works that address the intersection of race, gender, and sex during the Gilded Age, see Kali N. Gross, *Colored Amazons: Crime, Violence, and the Black Women in the City of Brotherly Love, 1880–1910* (Durham, N.C.: Duke University Press, 2006); Kevin Mumford, *Interzones: Black/White Sex Districts in Chicago and New York in the Early Twentieth Century* (New York: Columbia University Press, 1997); Mason Stokes, *The Color of Sex: Whiteness, Heterosexuality, and the Fictions of White Supremacy* (Durham, N.C.: Duke University Press, 2001); Gail Bederman, *Manliness and Civilization: A Cultural History of Gender and Race in the United States, 1880–1917* (Chicago: University of Chicago Press, 1995); *New York Times*, July 19, 1885.

10. "That Vexatious Bathing Question," *Asbury Park Press*, July 14, 1890; *New York Times*, July 20, 1890.

11. "Africa and Asbury Park," *New York Times*, July 7, 1885.

12. "What Can Be Done?" *Daily Journal*, July 21, 1885; *Philadelphia Inquirer*, July 23, 1893; Daniel Horowitz, *The Morality of Spending: Attitudes towards the Consumer in America, 1875–1940* (Chicago: University of Chicago Press, 1992); John Joseph Goux, *Symbolic Economies: After Marx and Freud* (Ithaca, N.Y.: Cornell University Press, 1990); Stephen Mihm *A Nation of Counterfeiters: Capitalists, Con Men, and the Making of the United States* (Cambridge, Mass.: Harvard University Press, 2007); Jocelyn Wills, "Respectable Mediocrity: The Everyday Life of an Ordinary American Striver, 1876–1890," *Journal of Social History* 37, no. 2 (2003): 323–49.

13. "Intruders," *Daily Journal*, July 29, 1886; Stephen Crane, "Crowding into Asbury Park," *New York Tribune*, July 3, 1892.

14. Kate Masur, "'A Rare Phenomenon of Philological Vegetation': The Word 'Contraband' and the Meanings of Emancipation in the United States," *Journal of American History* 93, no. 4 (2007): 1050–84; Alice Fahs, *The Imagined Civil War: Popular Literature for the North and South, 1861–1865* (Chapel Hill: University of North Carolina Press, 2001); Aron, *Working at Play*, 136.

15. Alfred M. Heston, *Absegami: Annals of Eyren Haven and Atlantic City, 1609 to 1904*, 2 vols. (Camden, N.J.: Sinnickson Chew & Co., 1904), 327, in Heston Collection: African American History in Atlantic City, Atlantic City Free Public Library, Atlantic City, N.J.

16. Tunis Campbell, *Hotel Keepers, Head Waiters, and Housekeepers' Guide* (Boston, 1848); S. A. Frost, *The Laws and By-Laws of American Society* (New York, 1869); R. Vashon Rogers, *The Law of Hotel Life of the Rights and Wrongs of Host and Guest* (San Francisco, 1879); Samuel H. Wandell, *The Law of Inns, Hotels, and Boarding Houses: A Treatise upon the Relation of Host and Guest* (Rochester, N.Y., 1888); John Tellman, *The Practical Hotel Steward* (Chicago, 1900); A. K. Sandoval-Strauss, "Travelers, Strangers, and Jim Crow: Law, Public Accommodations, and Civil Rights in America," *Law and History Review* 23, no. 1 (2005): 62–65; Gregory J. Service, *Hotel-Motel Law: A Primer*

on Innkeeper Liability (Springfield, Ill.: C. C. Thomas, 1983). For examinations on the common law's influence on public accommodations and popular amusement venues, see William Novak: *The People's Welfare: Law and Regulation in Nineteenth-Century America* (Chapel Hill: University of North Carolina Press, 1996); Barbara Welke, *Law and Borders of Belonging in the Long Nineteenth Century United States* (New York: Cambridge University Press, 2010), 261–316; Rebecca Scott, "Public Rights, Social Equality, and the Conceptual Roots of the *Plessy* Challenge," *Michigan Law Review* 106, no. 777 (2008): 777–804; Blair L. M. Kelley, *Right to Ride: Streetcar Boycotts and African American Citizenship in the Era of Plessy v. Ferguson* (Chapel Hill: University of North Carolina Press, 2010); Judith Giesberg, *Army at Home: Women and the Civil War on the Northern Home Front* (Chapel Hill: University of North Carolina, 2009).

17. *New York Times*, July 19, 1885.

18. "The Civil Rights Act," *San Francisco Bulletin*, March 8, 1875.

19. *San Francisco Bulletin*, March 9, 1875; quoted in Michael McGerr, *A Fierce Discontent: The Rise and Fall of the Progressive Movement in America* (New York: Oxford University Press, 2003), 209. See also Cecil B. Hartley, *The Gentleman's Book of Etiquette and Manual of Politeness* (Boston, 1860); George Winfred Hervey, *The Principles of Courtesy: With Hints and Observations on Manners and Habits* (New York, 1852).

20. "Butler on Civil Rights," *Inter Ocean*, March 23, 1875.

21. "Enforcement Guaranteed," *Sunday Times* (Chicago), March 21, 1875.

22. *State v. Whitby*, 5 Har. (Del.) 494 (1854).

23. Horace G. Wood, *A Practical Treatise on the Law of Nuisances*, 2nd ed. (Albany, N.Y., 1883), 21.

24. In several critical ways, northern leisure venues approached the law and individualism in similar ways as southerners did. Ideas about the law, justice, and freedom in the nineteenth-century South were radically particular, often conforming and responding to the interests and values of a specific community and locale. As Laura Edwards writes, southerners applied the law "as their modality of rule, a system that responded to their problems and could express their own conceptions of justice." See *The People and Their Peace: Legal Culture and the Transformation of Inequality in the Post-Revolutionary South* (Chapel Hill: University of North Carolina Press, 2009), 79.

25. "Letter from Wiesbaden," *Daily Journal*, August 17, 1886; "Too Many Colored People," *Daily Journal*, August 17, 1886.

26. *Atlantic City Gazette*, June 29, 1906, 4; *Atlantic City Review*, June 26, 1906, 1.

27. Michael O'Malley, "Rags, Blacking, and Paper Soldiers, Money and Race in the Civil War," in James W. Cook, Lawrence B. Glickman, and Michael O'Malley, eds., *The Cultural Turn in U.S. History: Past, Present, and Future* (Chicago: University of Chicago Press, 2009); Brian P. Luskey, *On the Make: Clerks and the Quest for Capital in Nineteenth-Century America* (New York: New York University Press, 2010); "Drawing the Color Line: Negroes Who Offend the Residents of Asbury Park," *New York Times*, July 19, 1885.

28. "Africa and Asbury Park," *New York Times*, July 7, 1887; *New York Times*, July 19, 1885.

29. "Race Prejudice," *The Sun* (New York), July 17, 1887.

30. "The Colored People at Asbury Park," *The Sun* (New York), August 3, 1893.

31. *The Sun* (New York), August 4, 1893.

32. Ibid.

4. Boycotting Jim Crow

1. "Hotel Dale" (advertisement), *The Crisis*, July 1911.

2. "Atlantic City," *Colored American*, October 1906. For studies that detail the history of Jim Crow boycotts during the early 1900s, see esp. David E. Alsobrook, "The Mobile Boycott of 1902: African American Protest or Capitulation," *Alabama Review* 56, no. 2 (2003): 83–103; David S. Bogen, "Precursors to Rosa Parks: Maryland Transportation Cases between the Civil War and the Beginning of WWI," *Maryland Law Review* 63, no. 4 (2004): 721–51; Cheryl Greenberg, "Don't Buy Where You Can't Work," in Lawrence B. Glickman, ed., *Consumer Society in American History: A Reader* (Ithaca, N.Y.: Cornell University Press, 1999), 241–76; Blair M. Kelly, *Right to Ride: Streetcar Boycotts and African American Citizenship in the Era of Plessy v. Ferguson* (Chapel Hill: University of North Carolina Press, 2010); August Meier and Elliot Rudwick, "The Boycott against Jim Crow Streetcars in the South, 1900–1906," in *Along the Color Line: Explorations in the Black Experience* (Urbana: University of Illinois Press, 1976), 267–89; Andor Skotnes, "'Buy Where You Can Work': Boycotting for Jobs in African American Baltimore, 1933–1944," *Journal of Social History* 27, no. 4 (1994): 735–62; Andrew Wiese, *Places of Their Own: African American Suburbanization in the Twentieth Century* (Chicago: University of Chicago Press, 2004).

3. Many prominent works have long noted the importance of class dimensions in framing political debates in turn-of-the-century black communities. See Willard B. Gatewood, *Aristocrats of Color: The Black Elite, 1880–1920* (Fayetteville: University of Arkansas Press, 2000); Kevin Gaines, *Uplifting the Race: Black Leadership, Politics, and Culture in the Twentieth Century* (Chapel Hill: University of North Carolina Press, 1996); Glenda Gilmore, *Gender and Jim Crow: Women and the Politics of White Supremacy in North Carolina, 1896–1920* (Chapel Hill: University of North Carolina Press, 1996); Joe R. Fergin, *Living with Racism: The Black Middle-Class Experience* (Boston: Beacon Press, 1994); Mark S. Foster, "'In the Face of Jim Crow': Prosperous Blacks and Vacations, Travel, and Outdoor Leisure, 1890–1945," *Journal of Negro History* 84 (Spring 1999): 130–49; Lawrence Otis Graham: *Our Kind of People: Inside America's Black Upper Class* (New York: HarperCollins, 1999); Andrew W. Kahrl, "'The Slightest Semblance of Unruliness': Steamboat Excursions, Pleasure Resorts, and the Emergence of Segregation Culture on the Potomac River," *Journal of American History* 94, no. 4 (2008): 1108–36; Meier and Rudwick, "Boycott Movement against Jim Crow Streetcars in the South"; and Michelle Mitchell, *Righteous Propagation: African Americans and the Politics of Racial Destiny after Reconstruction* (Chapel Hill: University of North Carolina Press, 2004).

4. A number of important works have explored the growth of black business at the turn of the century. See John H. Burrows, *The Necessity of a Myth: A History of the National Negro Business League, 1900–1945* (Auburn, Ala.: Hickory Hall Press, 1988); Horace Cayton and St. Clair Drake, *Black Metropolis: A Study of Negro Life in a Northern City*,

2 vols. (New York: Harcourt Brace, 1945); Walter D. Greason, *The Path to Freedom: Black Families in New Jersey* (Charleston, S.C.: History Press, 2010), 105–24; Kenneth Marvin Hamilton, *Black Towns and Profit: Promotion and Development in the Trans-Appalachian West, 1877–1915* (Urbana: University of Illinois Press, 1991); Sharon Ann Holt, *Making Freedom Pay: North Carolina Freedpeople Working for Themselves, 1865–1900* (Athens: University of Georgia Press, 2000); Juliet E. K. Walker, *The History of Black Business in America: Capitalism, Race, Entrepreneurship* (New York: Twayne, 1988); and Robert Weems, Jr., *Desegregating the Dollar: African American Consumerism in the Twentieth Century* (New York: New York University Press, 1998).

5. W. E. B Du Bois, "The Problem of Amusement," *Southern Workman* 26 (September 1897). Du Bois would later speak more extensively about the problems of public amusements and the exclusionary practices enacted against black pleasure seekers. See Du Bois, "The Color Problem of Summer," *The Crisis*, July 1929; and "About Vacations," *Pittsburgh Courier*, September 18, 1937; "Leisure Hours," *Colored American*, March 18, 1837; "The Cruelty of Idleness," *Colored American*, February 7, 1838.

6. Booker T. Washington, *Up from Slavery* (1901; repr., New York: Dover, 1995), 49–50.

7. Gatewood, *Aristocrats of Color*; Lawrence Glickman, *Buying Power: A History of Consumer Activism in America* (Chicago: University of Chicago Press, 2009); Greenberg, "Don't Buy Where You Can't Work"; Weems, *Desegregating the Dollar*; *Washington Bee*, August 10, 1901; *New York Age*, December 3, 1908; E. M. Woods, *The Negro in Etiquette: A Novelty* (St. Louis, Mo.: Buxton & Skinner, 1899); Richard R. Wright, Jr., "The Economic Condition of Negroes in the North," *Southern Workman* 40 (May 1911): 306; Ida Joyce Jackson, "Do Negroes Constitute a Race of Criminals?" *Colored American* 12 (April 1907): 252–63; R. Henri Herbert, "Our Problems and Our Burdens," *Colored American* 12 (May 1907): 346.

8. Rev. R. R. Downs, *Christian Recorder*, June 29, 1893.

9. "Club Work among Colored Women," *Colored American*, August 1896.

10. *New York Age*, June 2, 1888; *Philadelphia Tribune*, February 24, 1883.

11. *Philadelphia Record*, September 4, 1898; *Philadelphia Evening Bulletin*, September 8, 1905.

12. *Christian Recorder*, August 11, 1890.

13. "The Colored People Satisfied," *Asbury Park Press*, July 15, 1890; "That Vexatious Bathing Question," *Asbury Park Press*, July 14, 1890; "The Better Element's Views," *New York Times*, July 2, 1887.

14. "Commends Mr. Bradley," *The Sun* (New York), July 21, 1893.

15. Quoted in Patrick Rael, "The Market Revolution and Market Values in Antebellum Black Protest Thought," in Scott C. Martin, ed., *Cultural Change and the Market Revolution in America, 1789–1860* (Lanham, Md.: Rowman & Littlefield, 2005), 31.

16. "Asbury Park: The Colored Question Settled," *New York Times*, July 20, 1890.

17. *Christian Recorder*, July 27, 1893.

18. Henry Bibb, "Voice of the Fugitive," March 26, 1851. Patrick Rael writes that "black leaders strove not so much for independence from whites as for a greater degree of mutual dependence between whites and blacks. They strove not so much for the early republic's concern with economic and hence political independence as they did the

Jacksonian era's gradual concession to the developing fact of economic and social inter-dependency among all." "Market Revolution and Market Values in Antebellum Black Protest Thought," 34. See also "An Address to the Colored People of the United States," in *Report of the Proceedings of the Colored National Convention* (Rochester, N.Y., 1848).

19. *New York Globe*, July 28, 1883; "Prefer Girls as Waiters," *New York Times*, July 2, 1903.

20. Quoted in Kevin Mumford, *Interzones: Black/White Sex Districts in Chicago and New York in the Early Twentieth Century* (New York: Columbia University Press, 1997), 41.

21. Lola L. Allen, "Social Agencies"; and Milton Palmer, "The Negro in Business," both in New Jersey Writers' Project, New Jersey Ethnological Survey Records, Box WK-2, 1940, New Jersey State Archives, Trenton, N.J. (hereafter cited as New Jersey Writers' Project); Walls Family Photo Collection, Heston Collection: African American History in Atlantic City, Atlantic City Free Public Library, Atlantic City, N.J. (hereafter cited as Heston Collection).

22. "Atlantic City Industrial Improvement Company" and "Recreation," both in New Jersey Writers' Project; *Colored American*, October 1906.

23. *Atlantic City Daily Union*, August 11, 1899; Milton Palmer, "Labor," in New Jersey Writers' Project.

24. Ibid.

25. Margaret L. Brett, "Atlantic City: A Study in Black and White," *Survey Magazine* 28 (1928); Milton Palmer, "Economic Shifts and Migratory Influences," in New Jersey Writers' Project; Alfred M. Heston, *Illustrated Handbook of Atlantic City* (Atlantic City, N.J.: A. M. Heston & Company, 1889), 124, in Heston Collection.

26. Milton Palmer, "Earning a Living in Atlantic City," in New Jersey Writers' Project.

27. "The Grand Pacific Hotel: The Afro-American Gets a Place on the Boardwalk at Atlantic City," *Colored American*, April 15, 1899.

28. *People's Advocate*, July 21, 1883; *Colored American*, May 6, 1899; *People's Advocate*, July 21, 1883.

29. *Atlantic City Sunday Gazette*, June 29, 1906, 4.

30. "Invest in a Sound and Worth-While Race Proposition!" *Washington (D.C) Times*, May 31, 1921.

31. Cindy S. Aron, *Working at Play: A History of Vacations in the United States* (New York: Oxford University Press, 1999) 213; Adelaide M. Cromwell, "The History of Oaks Bluffs as a Popular Resort for Blacks," *Dukes County Intelligencer* 26, no. 1 (1984); Carroll Greene, Jr., "Summertime: In the Highland Beach Tradition," *American Visions* 1 (May–June 1986); Andrew W. Kahrl, *The Land Was Ours: African American Beaches from Jim Crow to the Sunbelt South* (Cambridge, Mass.: Harvard University Press, 2012); Marsha Dean Phielps, *An American Beach for African Americans* (Gainesville: University Press of Florida, 1997); Lewis Walker and Benjamin C. Wilson, *Black Eden: The Idlewild Community* (East Lansing: Michigan State University Press, 2002).

32. Palmer, "Economic Shifts and Migratory Influences."

33. "Report on the Proceedings of the Colored National Convention Held in Cleveland, 1848," in Patrick Rael, ed., *Pamphlets of Protest: An Anthology of Early African American Protest Literature, 1790–1860* (New York: Routledge, 2001), 186; Palmer, "Eco-

nomic Shifts and Migratory Influences"; see also Nelson Johnson, *The Northside: African Americans and the Creation of Atlantic City* (New York: Plexus, 2010), 130.

34. "Negro Waiters to Organize," *New York Times*, September 17, 1899.

35. Palmer, "Negro in Business"; "APEX Hair Co. Head Lies Critically Ill," *Washington (D.C.) Afro-American*, March 24, 1953.

36. Madame Sara Spencer Washington, "World's Finest Beauty Preparations: Beauty Products and Their Use" (1922), 19; Julia Kirk Blackwelder, *Styling Jim Crow: African American Beauty Training during Segregation* (College Station: Texas A&M University Press, 2003); A'Lelia Perry Bundles, *On Her Own Ground: The Life and Times of Madam C. J. Walker* (New York: Scribner, 2001); Margaret Finnegan, *Selling Suffrage: Consumer Culture and Votes for Women* (New York: Columbia University Press, 1999); Noliwe Rooks, *Hair Raising: Beauty Culture and African American Women* (New Brunswick, N.J.: Rutgers University Press, 1996); Stephanie J. Shaw, *What a Woman Ought to Be and to Do: Black Professional Women during the Jim Crow Era* (Chicago: University of Chicago Press, 1995); and Victoria Wolcott, *Remaking Respectability: African American Women in Interwar Detroit* (Chapel Hill: University of North Carolina Press, 2001).

37. Washington, "World's Finest Beauty Preparations," 2–3. In the 1930s, APEX opened a school and distribution center in Johannesburg, South Africa, which sponsored an annual World Beauty Competition. "The Bantu World Beauty Competition," *Bantu World*, November 12, 1932.

38. "Atlantic City Board of Trade Convention Bureau" (1936), in Heston Collection; *Atlantic City Tide* 3, no. 1 (1936).

39. *Atlantic City Daily Union*, July 25, 1907; *Atlantic City Daily Union*, July 29, 1907; *Atlantic City Daily Union*, August 25, 1907.

40. John Cell, *The Highest Stage of White Supremacy: The Origins of Segregation in South Africa and the American South* (New York: Cambridge University Press, 1982), 234–35.

5. Cleaning Up Jim Crow

1. "Tenderloin Lid Goes Down," *Atlantic City Daily Press*, September 13, 1909; "Sleuths Released on Bail: Serious Charges Sequel to Riot," *Atlantic City Daily Press*, September 16, 1909; "Detectives Adjudged Guilty, but Sentence Was Suspended," *Atlantic City Daily Press*, September 18, 1909.

2. "Goldenberg Says Officer Carroll Fired First Shot," *Atlantic City Daily Press*, September 16, 1909.

3. The efforts of business owners, local politicians, and black activists to both consolidate and phase out the color line at the Jersey shore both qualify and contest historians' ideas about segregation during the Progressive era. For many years, historians have noted the ways in which a new "managerial state" redirected civic and consumer life at the turn of the century. We now have a clearer picture, for example, of how government-sponsored efforts to relocate vice venues and other "shadow economies" into African American neighborhoods became critical to criminalizing and compartmentalizing black consumer behavior in the early years of the "New Negro." See Regina Austin, "'Not Just for the Fun of It!': Government Restraints on Black Leisure, Social Inequality,

158

NOTES TO PAGES 102–6

and the Privatization of Public Space," *Southern California Law Review* 71 (May 1998): 667–714; Marcy S. Sacks, "'To Show Who Was in Charge': Police Repression of New York City's Black Population at the Turn of the Twentieth Century," *Journal of Urban History* 31 (September 2005): 799–819; Khalil G. Muhammad, *The Condemnation of Blackness: Ideas about Race and Crime in the Making of Modern Urban America* (Cambridge, Mass.: Harvard University Press, 2010); Kevin Mumford: *Interzones: Black/White Sex Districts in Chicago and New York in the Early Twentieth Century* (New York: Columbia University Press, 1997); William H. Tucker, *The Science and Politics of Racial Research* (Urbana: University of Illinois Press, 1994); Kali N. Gross, *Colored Amazons: Crime, Violence, and the Black Women in the City of Brotherly Love, 1880–1910* (Durham, N.C.: Duke University Press, 2006). At the same time, while we know much about efforts to create black ghettos during the early twentieth century, we know even less about white consumer-driven movements to reposition and erase Jim Crow boundaries. See Kenneth Kusmer, *A Ghetto Takes Shape: Black Cleveland, 1870–1930* (Urbana: University of Illinois Press, 1976); Alan Spear, *Black Chicago: The Making of a Negro Ghetto, 1880–1920* (Chicago: University of Chicago Press, 1967); Kimberly Phillips, *Alabama North: African-American Migrants, Community, and Working-Class Activism in Cleveland* (Urbana: University of Illinois Press, 1999); Francis M. Fortie, *San Francisco's Black Community, 1870–1890: Dilemmas in the Struggle for Equality* (San Francisco: R & E Associates, 1973); and Thomas Lee Philpot, *The Slum and the Ghetto: Neighborhood Deterioration and Middle-Class Reform* (New York: Oxford University Press, 1986).

4. See Mumford, *Interzones*.

5. *Atlantic City Daily Press*, April 10, 1902. In *Something for Nothing: Luck in America* (New York: Viking, 2003), Jackson Lears describes how gambling and other "games of chance" influenced turn-of-the-century discussions of political economy. See also *Atlantic City Gazette*, July 26, 1906; "Atlantic City's Foul Blots," *Philadelphia Inquirer*, August 4, 1895; *Philadelphia Inquirer*, August 5, 1895.

6. *Atlantic City Daily Union*, July 26, 1906; *Atlantic Review*, July 25, 1907; *Atlantic Review*, August 1, 1907. For surveys on the political career of Commodore Louis Kuehnle and the history of boss rule in Atlantic City, see esp. Charles E. Funnell, *By the Beautiful Sea: The Rise and High Times of That Great American Resort, Atlantic City* (New Brunswick, N.J.: Rutgers University Press, 1975); Martin Paulsson, *The Social Anxieties of Progressive Reform: Atlantic City, 1854–1920* (New York: New York University Press, 1994); and Nelson Johnson, *The Northside: African Americans and the Creation of Atlantic City* (New York: Plexus, 2010).

7. *Atlantic City Sunday Gazette*, June 22, 1900; *Atlantic City Daily Union*, July 25, 1907; *Atlantic City Daily Union*, July 29, 1907; *Atlantic City Daily Union*, August 25, 1907.

8. *Atlantic City Daily Union*, August 25, 1907; Margaret L. Brett, "Atlantic City: A Study in Black and White," *Survey* 28 (September 1912): 723–26.

9. Published findings by New Jersey state officials in the 1930s uncovered that very little had changed in the Northside in the years following Brett's indicting survey. See Interracial Committee: Department of Institutions and Agencies, "Survey of Negro Life in New Jersey: Atlantic City," Community Report No. 14 (July 1932); and "The Negro in New Jersey," Report of a Survey by Interracial Committee of the New Jersey Conference

of Social Work in Cooperation with the State Department of Institutions and Agencies (1932), all in Heston Collection: African American History in Atlantic City, Atlantic City Free Public Library, Atlantic City, N.J.

10. *Philadelphia Bulletin*, August 5, 1895.

11. *Atlantic Review*, September 16, 1909; *Atlantic City Evening Union*, September 15, 1909.

12. "Protest," in New Jersey State Senate, *Testimony Taken before the Committee on Elections, and Reports of the Committee in the Matter of the Contest for State Senator of Atlantic County, New Jersey between William Riddle, Contestant and Samuel D. Hoffman, Incumbent* (Trenton, N.J, 1893), 2; *Philadelphia North American*, September 21, 1909. For additional allegations of election fraud, and in particular the buying of votes in Atlantic City's Northside, see, *Atlantic City Daily Press*, December 14, 1903; "The Rise and Fall of Kuehnle," *Literary Digest*, December 27, 1913.

13. *Atlantic Review*, September 1, 1909; *Atlantic Review*, September 21, 1909.

14. *Atlantic City Sunday Gazette*, September 19, 1909.

15. *Atlantic City Daily Press*, September 13, 1909; *Atlantic City Sunday Gazette*, September 19, 1900.

16. In protesting annexation, Bradley explained that he "opposed the construction of our streets" because the "cost of doing the work has become needlessly excessive." See "Founder Bradley at Odds with Council," *Asbury Park Evening Press*, February 17, 1906; *Asbury Park Evening Press*, July 6, 1903.

17. "Annexation Project Is Renewed with Vigor," *Asbury Park Evening Press*, February 15, 1906.

18. "Annexation Needed," *Asbury Park Evening Press*, April 4, 1906.

19. "Meeting Tonight to Fix Boundary," *Asbury Park Evening Press*, February 17, 1906; *Asbury Park Evening Press*, February 15, 1906, 4; Margaret Finnegan, *Selling Suffrage: Consumer Culture and Votes for Women* (New York: Columbia University Press, 1999).

20. "Township Powerless," *Asbury Park Evening Press*, March 30, 1906.

21. The Board of Trade Annexation Committee proposed two boundaries for consolidation. The first proposal sought to fix the southernmost boundary at Wesley Lake (thus including the Springwood Avenue district). A second option was soon proposed (and supported by James Bradley) that left out the Springwood Avenue district, and instead proposed annexing the northernmost boundary at Mattison Avenue. See, "Sentiment in City Favors Annexation," *Asbury Park Evening Press*, February 16, 1906; *Asbury Park Evening Press*, February 17, 1906, 1.

22. The idea of "long-distance solidarity" is taken from Lawrence Glickman's *Buying Power: A History of Consumer Activism in America* (Chicago: University of Chicago Press, 2009). In a sweeping and wide-ranging survey of consumer activism in the United Stated, Glickman asserts that consumer protestors and organizations popularized the notion that "actions taken at the cash register have a host of effects, most of them bound up in a dense and extensive web and chain." As this chapter argues, the racial consequences of these political ideals were most apparent in northern debates over segregation. See also *Asbury Park Journal*, March 20, 1906.

23. "Should Annex West Park," *Asbury Park Evening Press*, February 22, 1906.

24. "False Comparisons," *Asbury Park Evening Press*, February 21, 1906; *Asbury Park Evening Press*, February 16, 1906; "Asbury Park Council Favors Annexation," *Asbury Park Evening Press*, February 20, 1906.

25. *Asbury Park Evening Press*, February 15, 1906, 3.

26. "Our Moral Duty," *Asbury Park Evening Press*, March 25, 1906.

27. *Asbury Park Evening Press*, February 21, 1906, 4.

28. John H. Richardson, "Against Improvement," *Asbury Park Evening Press*, March 31, 1906.

29. "Annexation," *Asbury Park Evening Press*, February 20, 1906.

30. Kenneth Durr, *Behind the Backlash: White Working-Class Politics in Baltimore, 1940–1980* (Chapel Hill: University of North Carolina Press, 2003). Durr argues that competing visions of political economy, and not just racism, shaped the politics of desegregation during the civil rights era. For a succinct survey on the racial politics of welfare during the first half of the twentieth century, see Linda Gordon, "Black and White Visions of Welfare: Women's Welfare Activism, 1890–1945," *Journal of American History* 78, no. 2 (1991): 559–90. See also Richardson, "Against Improvement."

31. James Bradley, "Annexation," *Asbury Park Evening Press*, March 13, 1906. Bradley's letter to the editor denouncing the annexation proposal ran for two consecutive weeks in March and reappeared in May before the official vote.

32. "Bradley Opposes," *Asbury Park Evening Press*, March 5, 1906.

33. "Atkins Opposed," *Asbury Park Evening Press*, March 8, 1906.

34. L. C. Hubbert, "A Righteous Appeal," *Asbury Park Evening Press*, March 19, 1906, 4; Rev. S. G. Kelly, "Will Vote Intelligently," *Asbury Park Evening Press*, March 28, 1906.

35. William Leach describes the "elaborate employee welfare programs developed throughout the country" that were enacted by Macy's and Wanamaker's to maintain the "service ideal." See *Land of Desire: Merchants, Power, and the Rise of the New American Culture* (New York: Pantheon, 1994), 118–19, 121–22. The widespread intersection of consumption and welfare capitalism in the 1920s is addressed most notably by Lizabeth Cohen in *Making a New Deal: Industrial Workers in Chicago, 1919–1930* (New York: Cambridge University Press, 1990).

36. J. L. Klinmonth, "United in Interest," *Asbury Park Evening Press*, March 27, 1906; "Greatest Good to All," *Asbury Park Evening Press*, March 20, 1906; *Asbury Park Evening Press*, March 29, 1906, 4.

37. Klinmonth, "United in Interest," 4.

Conclusion

1. "Altman Says Season Is Resort's Greatest," *Philadelphia Bulletin*, July 29, 1966; Victoria Wolcott, *Race, Riots, and Rollercoasters: The Struggle over Segregated Recreation in America* (Philadelphia: University of Pennsylvania Press, 2012); Bruce Bliven, "The American Utopia: Atlantic City," *New Republic*, December 29, 1920.

2. Sonny Schwartz, "Spotlight on Larry Steele," *Press of Atlantic City*, August 24, 1975; "Beauties Are His Business: Larry Steele Is in 20th Year of Turning Out Lavish Revues," *Ebony*, February 1960; Nelson Johnson, *The Northside: African Americans and the Crea-*

tion of Atlantic City (New York: Plexus, 2010); Bryant Simon, Boardwalk of Dreams: Atlantic City and the Fate of Urban America (New York: Oxford University Press, 2004).

3. Preston Lauterbach, The Chitlin' Circuit and the Road to Rock and Roll (New York: Norton, 2002); and Arthur Frank Wertheim, Vaudeville Wars: How the Keith-Albee and Orpheum Circuits Controlled the Big-Time and Its Performers (New York: Palgrave, 2009); "Echoes of the Night," Atlantic City Magazine, September 1998; Press of Atlantic City, July 17, 1994.

4. Simon, Boardwalk of Dreams; Walter David Greason, Suburban Erasure: How the Suburbs Ended the Civil Rights Movement in New Jersey (Madison, N.J.: Fairleigh Dickinson University Press, 2013).

5. Nelson Johnson, Boardwalk Empire: The Birth, High Times, and Corruption of Atlantic City (Medford, N.J.: Ebury Press, 2010); Lizabeth Cohen, A Consumer's Republic: The Politics of Mass Consumption in Postwar America (New York: Vintage, 2003); Thomas H. Hanchett, "U.S. Tax Policy and the Shopping-Center Boom of the 1950s and 1960s," American Historical Review 101, no. 4 (1996): 1082–1110.

6. Atlantic City Tide, May 1936.

7. "The Race All Dressed Up, Nowhere to Go," Baltimore Afro-American, July 20, 1929; "Asbury Park NAACP Wins against Beach Segregation," August 24, 1928, Correspondence of the NAACP, Manuscript Division, Library of Congress, Washington, D.C.

8. "Asbury Park Bathers Annoyed by Jim Crow," Baltimore Afro-American, August 3, 1929.

9. "Pool in Asbury Park Ends Discrimination," Baltimore Afro-American, August 2, 1952; "Segregation on Park Beach Halted," Baltimore Afro-American, September 1, 1952; "Pool Owners to End Jim Crow," Afro-American (Newark, N.J.), January 30, 1954; "Beach Minorities Smeared: White Taxpayers in Asbury Park Ask Commission for Separate Facilities," Afro-American (Newark, N.J.), August 30, 1952.

10. John P. Mulligan, "Perspective On: Civil Rights in New Jersey," NJEA Review, March 1956; Richard Connor, The Process of Constitutional Revision in New Jersey, 1940–1947 (New York: National Municipal League, 1970); Marion Thompson Wright, "Extending Civil Rights in New Jersey through the Division against Discrimination," Journal of Negro History 38, no. 1 (1953). For the most complete treatment on civil rights victories in the post–World War II North, see Thomas Sugrue, Sweet Land of Liberty: The Forgotten Struggle for Civil Rights in the North (New York: Random House, 2008); Simon, Boardwalk of Dreams, 117–19; Daniel Wolff, 4th of July, Asbury Park: A History of the Promised Land (New York: Bloomsbury, 2005), 164–90.

11. Thomas Stanback, Understanding the Service Economy: Employment, Productivity, Location (Baltimore: Johns Hopkins University Press, 1979); Robin G. Sheets, Stephen Nord, and John J. Phelps, The Impact of Service Industries on Underemployment in Metropolitan Economies (Lexington, Mass.: Lexington Books, 1987); and William Julius Wilson, When Work Disappears: The World of the New Urban Poor (New York: Knopf, 1996).

12. "Reclaim by Baltimore Plan," Atlantic City Press, January 23, 1950; "Northside Redevelopment Hearing Slated Tonight," Atlantic City Press, June 23, 1950; "Urban Redevelopment Plans Seen Designed to Decorate the Boulevard," Atlantic City Press,

June 24, 1950. Some of the best works that explore the impact of postwar urban renewal programs on black communities include Arnold R. Hirsch, *Making the Second Ghetto: Race and Housing in Chicago, 1940–1960* (New York: Cambridge University Press, 1983); Beryl Satter, *Family Properties: Race and Real Transformed Chicago and Urban America* (New York: Metropolitan, 2009); Mindy Thompson Fullilove, *Root Shock: How Tearing Up the City Neighborhoods Hurts America, and What We Can Do about It* (New York: Ballantine, 2004); David M. P. Freund, *Colored Property: State Policy and White Racial Politics in Suburban America* (Chicago: University of Chicago Press, 2007); D. Bradford Hunt, *Blueprint for Disaster: The Unraveling of Chicago Public Housing* (Chicago: University of Chicago Press, 2009); Don Parson, "The Decline of Public Housing and the Politics of the Red Scare: The Significance of the Los Angeles Public Housing War," *Journal of Urban History* 33, no. 3 (2007): 400–417; Alexander von Hoffman, "A Study in Contradictions: The Origins and Legacy of the Housing Act of 1949," *Housing Policy Debate* 11, no. 2 (2000): 299–326; Christopher Klemek, *The Transnational Collapse of Urban Renewal: Postwar Urbanism from New York to Berlin* (Chicago: University of Chicago Press, 2011); Samuel Zipp, *Manhattan Projects: The Rise and Fall of Urban Renewal in Cold War New York* (New York: Oxford University Press, 2010); Andrew R. Highsmith, "Demolition Means Progress: Urban Renewal, Local Politics, and State-Sanctioned Ghetto Formation in Flint, Michigan," *Journal of Urban History* 35, no. 3 (2009): 348–68; and Marc Weiss, "The Origins and Legacy of Urban Renewal," in J. Paul Mitchell, ed., *Federal Housing Policy and Programs: Past and Present* (New Brunswick, N.J.: Rutgers University Press, 1995), 253–76.

13. Heather Cox Richardson, *The Death of Reconstruction: Race, Labor, and Politics in the Post–Civil War North, 1865–1901* (Cambridge, Mass.: Harvard University Press, 2001); Eric Foner, *Reconstruction: America's Unfinished Revolution, 1863–1877* (New York: Harper & Row, 1988); and David Quigley, *the Second Founding: New York City, Reconstruction, and the Making of American Democracy* (New York: Hill & Wang, 2004).

14. Michele R. Boyd, *Jim Crow Nostalgia: Reconstructing Race in Brownsville* (Minneapolis: University of Minnesota Press, 2008); William H. Chafe, Raymond Gavins, and Robert Korstad, eds., *Remembering Jim Crow: African Americans Tell about Life in the Segregated South* (New York: New Press, 2001); James Loewen, *How Free Is Free? The Long Death of Jim Crow* (Cambridge, Mass.: Harvard University Press, 2009); Brian J. Norman, *Neo-segregation Narratives: Jim Crow in the Post–Civil Rights American Literature* (Athens: University of Georgia Press, 2010); and Renee C. Romano and Leigh Raiford, eds., *The Civil Rights Movement in American Memory* (Athens: University of Georgia Press, 2006); Henry Louis Gates, Jr., ed., *Race, Writing, and Difference* (Chicago: University of Chicago Press, 1986); George Lipsitz, *How Racism Takes Place* (Philadelphia: Temple University Press, 2011); Paul Gilroy, *Against Race: Imagining Political Culture Beyond the Color Line* (Cambridge, Mass.: Harvard University Press, 2000); Howell S. Baum, *Brown in Baltimore: School Desegregation and the Limits of Liberalism* (Ithaca, N.Y.: Cornell University Press, 2010).

15. Adam Green, *Selling the Race: Culture, Community, and Black Chicago, 1940–1955* (Chicago: University of Chicago Press, 2007); Earl Lewis, *In Their Own Interests: Race, Class, and Power in Twentieth-Century Norfolk, Virginia* (Berkeley: University of Califor-

nia Press, 1993); Andrew Weise, *Places of Their Own: African American Suburbanization in the Twentieth Century* (Chicago: University of Chicago Press, 2004); Michele Mitchell, *Righteous Propagation: African Americans and the Politics of Racial Destiny after Reconstruction* (Chapel Hill: University of North Carolina Press, 2004); Touré Reed, *Not Alms but Opportunity: The Urban League and the Politics of Racial Uplift, 1910–1950* (Chapel Hill: University of North Carolina Press, 2008); Walter Weare, *Black Business in the New South: A Social History of the North Carolina Mutual Life Insurance Company* (Urbana: University of Illinois Press, 1973); Abram L. Harris, *The Negro as Capitalist: A Study of Banking and Business among American Negroes* (Philadelphia: Urban Research, 1936); Leslie Brown, *Upbuilding Black Durham: Gender, Class, and Black Community Development in the Jim Crow South* (Chapel Hill: University of North Carolina Press, 2008); Christopher Silver and John V. Moeser, *The Separate City: Black Communities in the Urban South, 1940–1968* (Lexington: University Press of Kentucky, 1995); J. Douglas Smith, *Managing White Supremacy: Race, Politics, and Citizenship in Jim Crow Virginia* (Chapel Hill: University of North Carolina Press, 2002).

16. Bliven, "American Utopia."

17. Stanback, *Understanding the Service Economy*; Sheets, Nord, and Phelps, *Impact of Service Industries on Underemployment in Metropolitan Economics*; Wilson, *When Work Disappears*; Heather Ann Thompson, *Whose Detroit? Politics, Labor, and Race in a Modern City* (Ithaca, N.Y.: Cornell University Press, 2001); Guian McKee, *The Problem of Jobs: Liberalism, Race, and Deindustrialization in Philadelphia* (Chicago: University of Chicago Press, 2008); Sugrue, *Sweet Land of Liberty*; and Matthew Countryman, *Up South: Civil Rights and Black Power in Philadelphia* (Philadelphia: University of Pennsylvania Press, 2006). Few historians have documented the impact of deindustrialization on postwar northern black employment better than Thomas Sugrue did in *The Origins of the Urban Crisis: Race and Inequality in Postwar Detroit* (Princeton, N.J.: Princeton University Press, 1996). Works that best describe the impact of black radicalism include Robin D. G. Kelley, "'We Are Not What We Seem': Rethinking Black Working-Class History in the Jim Crow South," *Journal of American History* 80, no. 1 (1993): 75–112; Countryman, *Up South*; Robert Korstad and Nelson Lichtenstein, "Opportunities Found and Lost: Labor, Radicals, and the Early Civil Rights Movement," *Journal of American History* 75, no. 3 (1988): 786–811; Brian Purnell, *Fighting Jim Crow in the County of Kings: The Congress of Racial Equality in Brooklyn* (Lexington: University Press of Kentucky, 2013); and Glenda Gilmore, *Defying Dixie: The Radical Roots of Civil Rights, 1919–1950* (New York: Norton, 2008).

Bibliography

Primary Sources

Manuscript Collections

Asbury Park Library (Asbury Park, N.J.)
   "James A. Bradley and Asbury Park: A Biography and History." Published under the
      Auspices of the Bradley Memorial Committee. 1921.
Atlantic City Public Library (Atlantic City, N.J.)
   Camden and Atlantic Railroad. *Annual Report.* 1873.
   Carnesworth (Pseud.). *Atlantic City: Its Early and Modern History.* Philadelphia:
      Wm. C. Harris & Co., 1868.
   A Complete Guide to Atlantic City. Philadelphia: Burk & McFetridge, 1885.
Atlantic County Courthouse, Clerk's Office and Surrogate Office (Mays Landing, N.J.)
   Certificate of Incorporation. Book 5:9. March 7, 1908. "Third Ward Colored
      Organization."
   Certificate of Incorporation. Book 5:9. *Certificate of Incorporation* November 22,
      1909. "Colored Workers' League of the 3rd Ward of Atlantic City."
Heston Collection: African American History in Atlantic City, Atlantic City Free Public
   Library (Atlantic City, N.J.)
   "Atlantic City Board of Trade Convention Bureau." 1936.
   Audrey Hart Photograph Collection of the Black Community in Atlantic City.
   Apex Country Club Photograph Collection.
   Brett, Margaret L. "Atlantic City: A Study in Black and White." *Survey* 28 (September
      1912): 723–26.
   "Charter of the Lighthouse Lodge of the Improved Benevolent Order of the Elks of
      the World (I.B.P.O.E. of W.)." February 12, 1900.
   Heston, Alfred J. *Absegami: Annals of Eyren Haven and Atlantic City, 1609–1904.* 2
      vols. Camden, N.J.: Sinnickson Chew & Co., 1904.
   ———. *Industrial Handbook of Atlantic City, New Jersey.* Atlantic City, N.J.: A. M.
      Heston & Company, 1889.
   "The Negro in New Jersey." Report of a Survey by Interracial Committee of the New
      Jersey Conference of Social Work in Cooperation with the State Department of
      Institutions and Agencies.
   "Survey of Negro Life in New Jersey: Atlantic City." Community Report No. 14.
      July 1932.
   Walls Family Photo Collection.
Library of Congress (Washington, D.C.)
   George Bantham Bain Collection, Prints and Photographs Division, LC-BS-432-8
      "Negroes Swimming, Asbury Park." 1908.

Manuscript Division, Correspondence of the NAACP
  "Asbury Park NAACP Wins against Beach Segregation." August 24, 1928.
Monmouth County Historical Society (Freehold, N.J.)
  James A. Bradley Papers (1830–1921). Processed by Lois A. Herr (1981).
  "Reading the Future in Bradley Beach, N.J." Postcard.
Moorland-Spingarn Research Center, Howard University (Washington, D.C.)
  Directory of Negro Hotels and Guest Houses in the U.S. Washington, D.C.: U.S.
     Department of the Interior–National Park Service, 1939.
  The Hotel Messenger 2, no. 6 (July 1918). Harlem, N.Y.: National Association of
     Headwaiters.
New Jersey Writers' Project, New Jersey Ethnological Survey Records, Box WK-2,
     1940, New Jersey State Archives (Trenton, N.J.)
  Allen, Lola L. "Social Agencies."
  "Atlantic City Industrial Improvement Company."
  "Creative Description of the North Side."
  "Early Hotels in Atlantic City."
  "Education of Negroes in Atlantic City"
  "History of the Negro Church in Atlantic City"
  "The Negro Laborer."
  Palmer, Milton. "Earning a Living in Atlantic City."
  ———. "Economic Shifts and Migratory Influences in Atlantic City."
  ———. "Labor."
  ———. "The Negro in Business."
  "Recreation"
  "The Rise of the Negro Professional Man in Atlantic City."
  "The Rise of the Professional Man in Atlantic City."
New York Public Library Archives and Manuscripts (New York)
  Currier and Ives Darktown Series.
  Howard, Timothy Edward. *Excelsior; or, Essays on Politeness, Education, and the
     Means of Attaining Success in Life, Part I* .Baltimore: Kelly & Piet, 1868.
  *Our Manners at Home and Abroad: A Complete Manual on the Manners, Customs,
     and Social Forms of the Best American Society.* Harrisburg: Pennsylvania Publish-
     ing Company, 1883.

Newspapers/Periodicals

Afro-American (Newark, N.J.)
Appleton's Journal
The Arena
Asbury Park Evening Press
Asbury Park Journal
Asbury Park Press
Atlantic City Daily Press
Atlantic City Daily Union
Atlantic City Evening Union

Atlantic City Gazette
Atlantic City Magazine
Atlantic City Press
Atlantic City Review
Atlantic City Sunday Gazette
Atlantic City Tide
Atlantic Monthly
Atlantic Review
Baltimore Afro-American
Baltimore Sun
Bantu World
Boston Transcript
Camden (N.J.) Courier
Christian Recorder
Cincinnati (Ohio) Daily Gazette
Colored American
The Crisis
Daily Journal
Ebony
Evening World
Frank Leslie's Illustrated Newspaper
Freedom's Journal
Harper's New Monthly Magazine
Hazard's Register of Pennsylvania
Hotel Monthly
Hotel World
Indianapolis Sentinel
Inter Ocean
Kansas City (Mo.) Star
The Liberator
Minnesotan-Herald
Monmouth (N.J.) Democrat
Monmouth (N.J.) Inquirer
New Republic
New York Age
New York Globe
New York Herald
New York Post
New York Recorder
New York Times
New York Tribune
NJEA Review
Pennsylvania Gazette and Democratic Press
Pennsylvania Monthly Magazine
People's Advocate

Philadelphia Bulletin
Philadelphia Call
Philadelphia Evening Bulletin
Philadelphia Inquirer
Philadelphia North American
Philadelphia Public Ledger
Philadelphia Record
Philadelphia Times
Philadelphia Tribune
Pittsburgh (Pa.) Courier
Press of Atlantic City
Red Bank (N.J.) Star
San Francisco Bulletin
Shore Press
The Sun (New York)
Sunday Times (Chicago)
Washington (D.C.) Afro-American
Washington (D.C.) Bee
Washington (D.C.) Post
Washington (D.C.) Times
West Jersey Press

Published Primary Sources

Attwell, Ernest T. "Playgrounds for Colored America." *Park International*. November
     1920.
Buchholz, Margaret Thomas, ed. *Shore Chronicles: Diaries and Travelers' Tales from the
     Jersey Shore, 1764–1955*. Harvey Cedars, N.J.: Down the Shore Publishing, 1999.
Bradley, James. *Three Ways of Telling the History of Asbury Park*. Asbury Park, N.J.:
     M., W., and C. Pennypacker, 1887.
Brett, Margaret L. "Atlantic City: A Study in Black and White." *Survey Magazine* 28
     (1928).
Campbell, Tunis. *Hotel Keepers, Head Waiters, and Housekeepers' Guide*. Boston, 1848.
Connor, Richard. *The Process of Constitutional Revision in New Jersey, 1940–1947*.
     New York: National Municipal League, 1970.
Du Bois, W. E. B. "The Color Problem of Summer." *The Crisis*. July 1929.
———. "The Problem of Amusement." *Southern Workman* 26 (September 1897).
Frost, S. A. *The Laws and By-Laws of American Society*. New York, 1869.
Hartley, Cecil B. *The Gentleman's Book of Etiquette and Manual of Politeness*. Boston,
     1860.
Hervey, George Winfred. *The Principles of Courtesy: With Hints and Observations on
     Manners and Habits*. New York, 1852.
Hoffman, Frederick L. *Race Traits and Tendencies of the American Negro*. New York:
     Macmillan, 1896.

New Jersey State Senate. *Testimony Taken before the Committee on Elections, and Reports of the Committee in the Matter of the Contest for State Senator of Atlantic County, New Jersey between William Riddle, Contestant and Samuel D. Hoffman, Incumbent.* Trenton, N.J, 1893.

Nichols, Frank. "Social Hygiene and the Negro." *Journal of Social Hygiene.* October 1929.

Report of the Proceedings of the Colored National Convention. Rochester, N.Y., 1848.

Rogers, R. Vashon. *The Law of Hotel Life of the Rights and Wrongs of Host and Guest.* San Francisco, 1879.

Tellman, John. *The Practical Hotel Steward.* Chicago, 1900.

Wandell, Samuel H. *The Law of Inns, Hotels, and Boarding Houses: A Treatise upon the Relation of Host and Guest.* Rochester, N.Y., 1888.

Warren, T. Robinson. *Shooting, Boating, and Fishing for Young Sportsmen.* New York, 1871.

Washington, Booker T. *Up from Slavery.* 1901. Reprint, New York: Dover, 1995.

Wood, Horace G. *A Practical Treatise on the Law of Nuisances.* 2nd ed. Albany, N.Y., 1883.

Woods, E. M. *The Negro in Etiquette: A Novelty.* St. Louis, Mo.: Buxton & Skinner, 1899.

Wright, Richard R., Jr. "The Economic Condition of Negroes in the North." *Southern Workman* 40 (May 1911).

Secondary Sources

Abel, Elizabeth. *Signs of the Times: The Visual Politics of Jim Crow.* Berkeley: University of California Press, 2010.

Adams, Jessica. *Wounds of Returning: Race, Memory, and Property on the Postslavery Plantation.* Chapel Hill: University of North Carolina Press, 2007.

Agnevine, Erna. *Roots of the Consumer Movement: A Chronicle of Consumer History in the Twentieth Century.* Washington, D.C.: National Consumers League, 1979.

Allnut, Brian E. "The Negro Excursions: Recreational Outings among Philadelphia African Americans, 1876–1926." *Pennsylvania Magazine of History and Biography* 129 (January 2005): 73–104.

Alsobrook, David E. "The Mobile Boycott of 1902: African American Protest or Capitulation." *Alabama Review* 56, no. 2 (2003): 83–103.

Andreasen, Alan R. *The Disadvantaged Consumer.* New York: Free Press, 1975.

Armstead, Myra B. Young. *"Lord Please Don't Take Me in August": African Americans in Newport and Saratoga Springs, 1870–1930.* Urbana: University of Illinois Press, 1999.

Aron, Cindy. *Working at Play: A History of Vacations in the United States.* New York: Oxford University Press, 1999.

Ashby, William M. *Tales without Hate.* Newark, N.J.: Newark Preservation and Landmarks Committee, 1980.

Ashworth, John. *Slavery, Capitalism, and Politics in the Antebellum Republic, Vol. 1: Commerce and Compromise.* New York: Cambridge University Press, 1995.

Austin, Regina. "'Not Just for the Fun of It!': Governmental Restraints on Black Leisure, Social Inequality, and the Privatization of Public Space." *Southern California Law Review* 71 (May 1998): 667–714.

Ayers, Edward. *The Promise of the New South: Life after Reconstruction*. New York: Oxford University Press, 1992.

Bachin, Robing F. *Building the South Side: Urban Space and Civic Culture in Chicago, 1890–1919*. Chicago: University of Chicago Press, 2004.

Baker, Bruce. *What Reconstruction Meant: Historical Memory in the American South*. Charlottesville: University of Virginia Press, 2007.

Baker, Lee D. *From Savage to Negro: Anthropology and the Construction of Race, 1896–1954*. Berkeley: University of California Press, 1998.

Baum, Howell S. *Brown in Baltimore: School Desegregation and the Limits of Liberalism*. Ithaca, N.Y.: Cornell University Press, 2010.

Bederman, Gail. *Manliness and Civilization: A Cultural History of Gender and Race in the United States, 1880–1917*. Chicago: University of Chicago Press, 1996.

Bernstein, Iver. *The New York City Draft Riots: Their Significance for American Society and Politics in the Age of the Civil War*. New York: Oxford University Press, 1990.

Bethel, Elizabeth Raul. *The Roots of African-American Identity: Memory and History in Free Antebellum Communities*. New York: St. Martin's Press, 1997.

Biondi, Martha. *To Fight and Stand: The Struggle for Civil Rights in Postwar New York City*. New York: Cambridge University Press, 2003.

Bjelopera, Jerome P. *City of Clerks: Office and Sales Workers in Philadelphia, 1870–1920*. Urbana: University of Illinois Press, 2005.

Blackmon, Douglas. *Slavery by Another Name: The Re-enslavement of Black People from the Civil War to World War II*. New York: Doubleday, 2008.

Blackwelder, Julia Kirk. *Styling Jim Crow: African Americans Beauty Training during Segregation*. College Station: Texas A&M University Press, 2003.

Blair, William. *Cities of the Dead: Contesting the Memory of the Civil War in the South, 1865–1914*. Chapel Hill: University of North Carolina Press, 2004.

Blight, David W. *Race and Reunion: The Civil War in American Memory*. Cambridge, Mass.: Harvard University Press, 2001.

Blumin, Stuart M. *The Emergence of the Middle Class: Social Experience in the American City, 1760–1900*. New York: Cambridge University Press, 1989.

Bogen, David S. "Precursors to Rosa Parks: Maryland Transportation Cases between the Civil War and the Beginning of World War I." *Maryland Law Review* 63, no. 4 (2004): 721–51.

Boskin, Thomas. *Sambo: The Rise and Demise of an American Jester*. New York: Oxford University Press, 1998.

Bourdieu, Pierre. *Distinction: A Social Critique of the Judgment of Taste*. Cambridge: Harvard University Press, 1987.

——. *Outlines of a Theory of Practice*. New York: Cambridge University Press, 1977.

Boyd, Michele R. *Jim Crow Nostalgia: Reconstructing Race in Brownsville*. Minneapolis: University of Minnesota Press, 2008.

Breen, T. H. *The Marketplace of Revolution: How Consumer Politics Shaped American Independence*. New York: Oxford University Press, 2004.

Brooks, Daphne. *Bodies in Dissent: Spectacular Performances of Race and Freedom, 1850–1910*. Durham, N.C.: Duke University Press, 2006.

Brown, Dona. *Inventing New England: Regional Tourism in the Nineteenth Century*. Washington, D.C.: Smithsonian Institution Press, 1997.

Brown, Leslie. *Upbuilding Black Durham: Gender, Class, and Black Community Development in the Jim Crow South*. Chapel Hill: University of North Carolina Press, 2008.

Brundage, W. Fitzhugh. *The Southern Past: A Clash of Race and Memory*. Cambridge, Mass.: Harvard University Press, 2005.

Bullard, Robert D. *Dumping in Dixie: Race, Class, and Environmental Quality*. Boulder, Colo.: Westview, 1990.

Bulmer, Martin. *The Chicago School of Sociology: Institutionalization, Diversity, and the Rise of Sociological Research*. Chicago: University of Chicago Press, 1984.

Bundles, A'Leila Perry. *On Her Own Ground: The Life and Times of Madam C. J. Walker*. New York: Scribner, 2001.

Burrows, John H. *The Necessity of Myth: A History of the National Negro Business League, 1900–1945*. Auburn, Ala.: Hickory Hall Press, 1988.

Bushman, Richard L. *The Refinement of America: Persons, Houses, Cities*. New York: Vintage, 1992.

Butsch, Richard. *For Fun and Profit: The Transformation of Leisure into Consumption*. Philadelphia: Temple University Press, 1990.

Cayton, Horace, and St. Clair Drake. *Black Metropolis: A Study of Negro Life in a Northern City*. 2 vols. New York: Harcourt Brace, 1945.

Cell, John W. *The Highest Stage of White Supremacy: The Origins of Segregation in South Africa and the American South*. New York: Cambridge University Press, 1982.

Certeau, Michel de. *The Practice of Everyday Life*. Berkeley: University of California Press, 1984.

Chafe, William H., Raymond Gavins, and Robert Korstad, eds. *Remembering Jim Crow: African Americans Tell about Life in the Segregated South*. New York: New Press, 2001.

Chambers, Thomas. *Drinking the Waters: Creating an American Leisure Class at Nineteenth-Century Mineral Springs*. Washington, D.C.: Smithsonian Institution Press, 2002.

Chandler, Alfred D. *The Visible Hand: The Managerial Revolution in American Business*. Cambridge, Mass.: Harvard University Press, 1977.

Coates, James Roland. "Recreation and Sport in the African-American Community of Baltimore, 1890–1920." Ph.D. diss., University of Maryland, College Park, 1991.

Cockrell, Dale. *Demons of Disorder: Early Blackface Minstrelsy and Their World*. New York: Cambridge University Press, 1997.

Cocks, Catherine. *Doing the Town: The Rise of Urban Tourism in the United States, 1815–1915*. Berkeley: University of California Press, 2001.

Cohen, Joanna. "The Right to Purchase Is as Free as the Right to Sell: Defining Consumers as Citizens in the Auction-House Conflicts of the Early Republic." *Journal of the Early Republic* 30, no. 1 (2010): 25–62.

Cohen, Lizabeth. *A Consumers' Republic: The Politics of Mass Consumption in Postwar America*. New York: Vintage, 2003.

———. *Making a New Deal: Industrial Workers in Chicago, 1919–1930*. New York: Cambridge University Press, 1990.

Cohen, Nancy. *The Reconstruction of American Liberalism, 1865–1914*. Chapel Hill: University of North Carolina Press, 2002.

Connolly, N. D. B. *A World More Concrete: Real Estate and the Remaking of Jim Crow South Florida*. Chicago: University of Chicago Press, 2014.

Cook, James W., Lawrence B. Glickman, and Michael O'Malley, eds. *The Cultural Turn in U.S. History: Past, Present, and Future*. Chicago: University of Chicago Press, 2009.

Countryman, Matthew. *Up South: Civil Rights and Black Power in Philadelphia*. Philadelphia: University of Pennsylvania Press, 2006.

Couvares, Francis. *The Remaking Pittsburgh: Class and Culture in an Industrializing City, 1877–1919*. Albany: State University of New York Press, 1984.

Cromwell, Adelaide M. "The History of Oaks Bluffs as a Popular Resort for Blacks." *Dukes County Intelligencer* 26, no. 1 (1984).

Dailey, Jane. *Before Jim Crow: The Politics of Race in Postemancipation Virginia*. Chapel Hill: University of North Carolina Press, 2000.

———. "Land, Labor, and Politics across the Post-Emancipation South." *Labor History* 44, no. 4 (2003): 509–22.

Danielson, Michael N. *Profits and Politics in Paradise*. Columbia: University of South Carolina Press, 1995.

Davis, Janet M. *The Circus Age: Culture and Society under the American Big Top*. Chapel Hill: University of North Carolina Press, 2002.

Davis, Katherine B. "The Condition of the Negro in Philadelphia." *Journal of Political Economy* 8, no. 2 (1900): 248–60.

Delaney, David. *Race, Place, and the Law, 1836–1948*. Austin: University of Texas Press, 1998.

Diner, Steven J. *A Very Different Age: Americans of the Progressive Era*. New York: Hill & Wang, 1998.

Dunier, Mitchell. *Slim's Table: Race, Respectability, and Masculinity*. Chicago: University of Chicago Press, 1992.

Durr, Kenneth. *Behind the Backlash: White Working-Class Politics in Baltimore, 1940–1980*. Chapel Hill: University of North Carolina Press, 2003.

Edwards, Laura F. *Gendered Strife and Confusion: The Political Culture of Reconstruction*. Urbana: University of Illinois Press, 1997.

———. *The People and Their Peace: Legal Culture, and the Transformation of Inequality in the Post-Revolutionary South*. Chapel Hill: University of North Carolina Press, 2009.

Elliott, Mark. *Color-Blind Justice: Albion Tourgée and the Quest for Racial Equality from the Civil War to Plessy v. Ferguson*. New York: Oxford University Press, 2008.

Enstad, Nan. *Ladies of Love, Girls of Adventure: Working Women, Popular Culture, and Labor Politics at the Turn of the Century*. New York: Columbia University Press, 1999.

Ernest, John. *A Nation within a Nation: Organizing African-American Communities Before the Civil War*. Chicago: Ivan R. Dee, 2011.

Ernst, Daniel R. "Free Labor, the Consumer Interest, and the Law of Industrial Disputes, 1885–1900." *American Journal of Legal History* 36 (January 1992): 19–37.

Ewen, Stuart. *Captains of Consciousness: Advertising and the Social Roots of the Consumer Culture*. New York: Basic, 2001.

Eyerman, Ron. *Cultural Trauma: Slavery, and the Formation of African American Identity*. New York: Cambridge University Press, 2001.

Fabian, Ann. *Card Sharps, Dream Books, Bucket Shops: Gambling in Nineteenth-Century America*. Ithaca, N.Y.: Cornell University Press, 1990.

Fahs, Alice. *The Imagined Civil War: Popular Literature of the North and South, 1861–1865*. Chapel Hill: University of North Carolina Press, 2001.

Fergin, Joe R. *Living with Racism: The Black Middle-Class Experience*. Boston: Beacon Press, 1994.

Field, Phyllis F. *The Politics of Race in New York: The Struggle for Black Suffrage in the Civil War Era*. Ithaca, N.Y.: Cornell University Press, 1982.

Fields, Barbara J. *Slavery and Freedom on the Middle Ground: Maryland during the Nineteenth Century*. New Haven, Conn.: Yale University Press, 1985.

Finnegan, Margaret. *Selling Suffrage: Consumer Culture and Votes for Women*. New York: Columbia University Press, 1999.

Fitzgerald, Michael W. *Urban Emancipation: Popular Politics in Reconstruction Mobile, 1860–1890*. Baton Rouge: Louisiana State University Press, 2002.

Foner, Eric. *Free Soil, Free Labor, Free Men: The Ideology of the Republican Party before the Civil War*. New York: Oxford University Press, 1970.

———. *Reconstruction: America's Unfinished Revolution, 1863–1877*. New York: Harper & Row, 1988.

———. *The Story of American Freedom*. New York: Norton, 1998.

Foner, Philip S., ed. *The Voice of Black America: Major Speeches by Negroes in the United States, 1797–1971*. New York: Simon & Schuster, 1972.

Fortie, Francis M. *San Francisco's Black Community, 1870–1890: Dilemmas in the Struggle for Equality*. San Francisco: R & E Associates, 1973.

Foster, Henry James. "The Urban Experience of Blacks in Atlantic City, New Jersey: 1850–1915." Ph.D. diss., Rutgers University, 1981.

Foster, Mark S. "'In the Face of Jim Crow': Prosperous Blacks and Vacations, Travel, and Outdoor Leisure, 1890–1945." *Journal of Negro History* 84 (Spring 1999): 130–49.

Fox, Richard Wightman, and T. J. Jackson Lears, eds. *The Culture of Consumption: Critical Essays in American History, 1880–1980*. New York: Pantheon, 1983.

Fredrickson, George M. *The Black Image in the White Mind: The Debate on Afro-American Character and Destiny, 1817–1914*. New York: Harper & Row, 1971.

Freund, David M. P. *Colored Property: State Policy and White Racial Politics in Suburban America*. Chicago: University of Chicago Press, 2007.

Fullilove, Mindy Thompson, *Root Shock: How Tearing Up the City Neighborhoods Hurts America, and What We Can Do about It*. New York: Ballantine, 2004.

Funnell, Charles E. *By the Beautiful Sea: The Rise and High Times of That Great American Resort, Atlantic City*. New Brunswick, N.J.: Rutgers University Press, 1975.

Gaines, Kevin. *Uplifting the Race: Black Leadership, Politics, and Culture in the Twentieth Century*. Chapel Hill: University of North Carolina Press, 1996.

Gallagher, Gary. *Causes Won, Lost, and Forgotten: How Hollywood and Popular Art Shape What We Know about the Civil War*. Chapel Hill: University of North Carolina Press, 2008.

Gannon, Barbara. *The Won Cause: White and Black Comradeship in the Grand Army of the Republic*. Chapel Hill: University of North Carolina Press, 2014.

Gates, Henry Louis, Jr., ed. *Race, Writing, and Difference*. Chicago: University of Chicago Press, 1986.

Gatewood, Willard B. *Aristocrats of Color: The Black Elite, 1880–1920*. Fayetteville: University of Arkansas Press, 2000.

Gellman, David, and David Quigley, eds. *Jim Crow New York: A Documentary History of Race and Citizenship, 1777–1877*. New York: New York University Press, 2003.

Geertz, Clifford. *Negara: The Theatre State in Nineteenth Century Bali*. Princeton, N.J.: Princeton University Press, 1980.

Gerstle, Gary. "Race and the Myth of the Liberal Consensus." *Journal of American History* 82, no. 2 (1995): 579–86.

Gienapp, William. *The Origins of the Republican Party, 1852–1856*. New York: Oxford University Press, 1987.

Giesberg, Judith Ann. *Army at Home: Women and the Civil War on the Northern Home Front*. Chapel Hill: University of North Carolina Press, 2009.

Gilfoyle, Timothy J. *City of Eros: New York City, Prostitution, and the Commercialization of Sex, 1790–1920*. New York: Norton, 1994.

———. "White Cities, Linguistic Turns, and Disneylands: The New Paradigms of Urban History." *Reviews in American History* 26 (March 1998): 176–204.

Gillette, Howard, Jr. *Between Justice and Beauty: Race, Planning, and the Failure of Urban Policy in Washington, D.C.* Baltimore: Johns Hopkins University Press, 1995.

Gillette, William. *Retreat from Reconstruction, 1869–1879*. Baton Rouge: Louisiana State University Press, 1979.

Gilmore, Glenda. *Defying Dixie: The Radical Roots of Civil Rights, 1919–1950*. New York: Norton, 2008.

———. *Gender and Jim Crow: Women and the Politics of White Supremacy in North Carolina, 1896–1920*. Chapel Hill: University of North Carolina Press, 1996.

Gilroy, Paul. *Against Race: Imagining Political Culture beyond the Color Line*. Cambridge, Mass.: Harvard University Press, 2000.

Glave, Diane D., and Mark Stoll, eds. *To Love the Wind and the Rain: African Americans and Environmental History*. Pittsburgh: University of Pittsburgh Press, 2006.

Goddard, Richlyn F. "'Three Months to Hurry, Nine Months to Worry': Resort Life for African Americans in Atlantic City, 1854–1940." Ph.D. diss., Howard University, 2001.

Goldberg, David Theo. *Racist Culture: Philosophy and the Politics of Meaning*. Cambridge, Mass.: Blackwell, 1993.

———. *The Threat of Race: Reflections on Racial Neoliberalism*. Cambridge, Mass.: Blackwell, 2009.

Gordon, Linda. "Black and White Visions of Welfare: Women's Welfare Activism, 1890–1945." *Journal of American History* 78, no. 2 (1991): 559–90.

Gordon, Michael. "The Labor Boycott in New York City, 1880–1886." *Labor History* 16 (Spring 1975): 184–229.

Gossett, Thomas F. *Race: The History of an Idea in America*. 1963. Reprint, New York: Oxford University Press, 1997.

Gourevitch, Alex. *From Slavery to the Cooperative Commonwealth: Labor and Republican Liberty in the Nineteenth Century*. New York: Cambridge University Press, 2014.

Glickman, Lawrence. *Buying Power: A History of Consumer Activism in America*. Chicago: University of Chicago Press, 2009.

———. *A Living Wage: American Workers and the Making of Consumer Society*. Ithaca, N.Y.: Cornell University Press, 1997.

Glickman, Lawrence B., ed. *Consumer Society in American History: A Reader*. Ithaca, N.Y.: Cornell University Press, 1999.

Goux, John Joseph. *Symbolic Economies: After Marx and Freud*. Ithaca, N.Y.: Cornell University Press, 1990.

Graham, Lawrence Otis. *Our Kind of People: Inside America's Black Upper Class*. New York: HarperCollins, 1999.

Grave, Diane D., and Mark Stoll. *"To Love the Wind and the Rain": African Americans and Environmental History*. Pittsburgh: University of Pittsburgh Press, 2006.

Greason, Walter D. *The Path to Freedom: Black Families in New Jersey*. Charleston, S.C.: History Press, 2010.

———. *Suburban Erasure: How the Suburbs Ended the Civil Rights Movement in New Jersey*. Madison, N.J.: Fairleigh Dickinson University Press, 2013.

———. "From Village to Suburb: Race Politics and Economics in Monmouth County, N.J., 1890–1900." PhD diss., Temple University, 2004.

Green, Adam. *Selling the Race: Culture, Community, and Black Chicago, 1940–1955*. Chicago: University of Chicago Press, 2007.

Greenberg, Dolores. "Reconstructing Race and Protest: Environmental Justice in New York." *Environmental History* 5 (2000): 223–50.

Greene, Carroll, Jr. "Summertime: In the Highland Beach Tradition." *American Visions* 1 (May–June 1986).

Gross, Ariela. *What Blood Won't Tell: A History of Race on Trial in America*. Cambridge, Mass.: Harvard University Press, 2008.

Gross, Kali N. *Colored Amazons: Crime, Violence, and the Black Women in the City of Brotherly Love, 1880–1910*. Durham, N.C.: Duke University Press, 2006.

Hahn, Stephen. *A Nation under Our Feet: Black Political Struggles in the Rural South from Slavery to the Great Migration*. Cambridge, Mass.: Harvard University Press, 2003.

Hale, Grace Elizabeth. *Making Whiteness: The Culture of Segregation in the South, 1890–1940*. New York: Vintage, 1998.

Halttunen, Karen. *Confidence Men and Painted Women: A Study of Middle-Class Culture in America, 1830–1870*. New Haven, Conn.: Yale University Press, 1982.

Hamilton, Kenneth Marvin. *Black Towns and Profit: Promotion and Development in the Trans-Appalachian West, 1877–1915*. Urbana: University of Illinois Press, 1991.

Hanchett, Thomas H. "U.S. Tax Policy and the Shopping-Center Boom of the 1950s and 1960s." *American Historical Review* 101, no. 4 (1996): 1082–1110.

Harris, Abram L. *The Negro as Capitalist: A Study of Banking and Business among American Negroes*. Philadelphia: Urban Research, 1936.

Harris, Leslie M. *In the Shadow of Slavery: African Americans in New York City, 1626–1863*. Chicago: University of Chicago Press, 2003.

Hartman, Saidiya V. *Scenes of Subjection: Terror, Slavery, and Self-Making in Nineteenth-Century America*. New York: Oxford University Press, 1997.

Hazzard-Gordon, Katrina. *Jookin': The Rise of Dance Formations in African-American Culture*. Philadelphia: Temple University Press, 1990.

Higginbotham, Leon, Jr. *Shades of Freedom: Racial Politics and Presumptions of the American Legal Process*. New York: Oxford University Press, 1996.

Higginbotham, Leon, Jr. *Shades of Freedom: Racial Politics and Presumptions of the American Legal Process*. New York: Oxford University Press, 1996.

Highsmith, Andrew R. "Demolition Means Progress: Urban Renewal, Local Politics, and State-Sanctioned Ghetto Formation in Flint, Michigan." *Journal of Urban History* 35, no. 3 (2009): 348–68.

Hill, Errol G., and James V. Hatch. *A History of African American Theatre*. New York: Cambridge University Press, 2003.

Hirsch, Arnold R. *Making the Second Ghetto: Race and Housing in Chicago, 1940–1960*. New York: Cambridge University Press, 1983.

Hodges, Graham Russell. *Slavery and Freedom in the Rural North: African Americans in Monmouth County, New Jersey, 1665–1865*. Madison, Wis.: Madison House, 1997.

Holt, Sharon Ann. *Making Freedom Pay: North Carolina Freedpeople Working for Themselves, 1865–1900*. Athens: University of Georgia Press, 2000.

Holt, Thomas C. "Racism and the Working Class." *International Labor and Working-Class History* 45 (Spring 1994): 86–95.

Horowitz, Daniel. *The Morality of Spending: Attitudes towards the Consumer in America, 1875–1940*. Chicago: University of Chicago Press, 1992.

Howe, David Walker. *What Hath God Wrought: The Transformation of America, 1815–1848*. New York: Oxford University Press, 2007.

Hoy, Suellen. *Chasing Dirt: The American Pursuit of Cleanliness*. New York: Oxford University Press, 1995.

Hunt, D. Bradford. *Blueprint for Disaster: The Unraveling of Chicago Public Housing*. Chicago: University of Chicago Press, 2009.

Hunter, Tera W. *To 'Joy My Freedom: Southern Black Women's Lives and Labors after the Civil War*. Cambridge, Mass.: Harvard University Press, 1997.

Hurley, Andrew. *Environmental Inequalities: Class, Race, and Industrial Pollution in Gary, Indiana, 1945–1980*. Chapel Hill: University of North Carolina Press, 1995.

Ignatiev, Noel. *How the Irish Became White*. New York: Routledge, 1995.

Isenberg, Andrew, ed. *The Nature of Cities*. Rochester, N.Y.: University of Rochester Press, 2006.

Jacobson, Matthew Frye. *Barbarian Virtues: The United States Encounters Foreign Peoples at Home and Abroad, 1876–1917*. New York: Hill & Wang, 2001.

———. *Whiteness of a Different Color: European Immigrants and the Alchemy of Race*. Cambridge, Mass.: Harvard University Press, 1999.

Janney, Caroline. *Remembering the Civil War: Reunion and the Limits of Reconciliation*. Chapel Hill: University of North Carolina Press, 2013.

Johnson, Nelson. *Boardwalk Empire: The Birth, High Times, and Corruption of Atlantic City*. Medford, N.J.: Ebury Press, 2010.

———. *The Northside: African Americans and the Creation of Atlantic City*. New York: Plexus, 2010.

Jordan, Winthrop. *White over Black: American Attitudes toward the Negro, 1550–1812*. Chapel Hill: University of North Carolina Press, 1968.

Kahrl, Andrew W. *The Land Was Ours: African American Beaches from Jim Crow to the Sunbelt South*. Cambridge, Mass.: Harvard University Press, 2012.

———. "The Political Work of Leisure: Class, Recreation, and African American Commemoration at Harpers Ferry, West Virginia, 1881–1931." *Journal of Social History* 42, no. 1 (2008): 57–77.

———. "'The Slightest Semblance of Unruliness: Steamboat Excursions, Pleasure Resorts, and the Emergence of Segregation Culture on the Potomac River." *Journal of American History* 94, no. 4 (2008): 1108–36.

Kantrowitz, Stephen. "'Intended for the Better Government of Man': The Political History of African American Freemasonry in the Era of Emancipation." *Journal of American History* 96, no. 4 (2010): 1001–26.

Kasson, John F. *Amusing the Millions: Coney Island at the Turn of the Century*. New York: Hill & Wang, 1978.

———. *Rudeness and Civility: Manners in Nineteenth-Century Urban America*. New York: Hill & Wang, 1990.

Kelley, Blair L. M. *Right to Ride: Streetcar Boycotts and African American Citizenship in the Era of Plessy v. Ferguson*. Chapel Hill: University of North Carolina Press, 2010.

Kelley, Robin D. G. *Race Rebels: Culture, Politics, and the Black Working Class*. New York: Free Press, 1994.

———. "'We Are Not What We Seem: Rethinking Black Working-Class History in the Jim Crow South." *Journal of American History* 80, no. 1 (1993): 75–112.

Klarman, Michael J. *From Jim Crow to Civil Rights: The Supreme Court and the Struggle for Racial Equality*. New York: Oxford University Press, 2004.

Klemek, Christopher. *The Transnational Collapse of Urban Renewal: Postwar Urbanism from New York to Berlin*. Chicago: University of Chicago Press, 2011.

Korstad, Robert, and Nelson Lichtenstein. "Opportunities Found and Lost: Labor, Radicals, and the Early Civil Rights Movement." *Journal of American History* 75, no. 3 (1998): 786–811.

Kusmer, Kenneth. *A Ghetto Takes Shape: Black Cleveland, 1870–1930*. Urbana: University of Illinois Press, 1976.

Labbé, Ronald M., and Jonathan Lurie, eds. *The Slaughterhouse Cases: Regulation, Reconstruction, and the Fourteenth Amendment*. Lawrence: University Press of Kansas, 2005.

Laurie, Bruce. *Artisans into Workers: Labor in Nineteenth-Century America*. New York: Hill & Wang, 1989.

Lause, Mark A. *Free Labor: The Civil War and the Making of an American Working Class*. Urbana: University of Illinois Press, 2015.

Lauterbach, Preston. *The Chitlin' Circuit and the Road to Rock and Roll*. New York: Norton, 2002.

Lawson, Melinda. "Imagining Slavery: Representations of the Peculiar Institution on the
    Northern Stage: 1776–1860." *Journal of the Civil War Era* 1, no. 1 (2011): 25–55.
Leach, William. *Land of Desire: Merchants, Power, and the Rise of a New American Cul-
    ture.* New York: Pantheon, 1994.
Lears, T. J. Jackson. *Fables of Abundance: A Cultural History of Advertising in America.*
    New York: Basic, 1994.
———. *No Place of Grace: Antimodernism and the Transformation of American Culture,
    1880–1920.* New York: Pantheon, 1981.
———. *Something for Nothing: Luck in America.* New York: Viking, 2003.
Lee, Ericka. *At America's Gates: Chinese Immigration during the Exclusion Era, 1882–1943.*
    Chapel Hill: University of North Carolina Press, 2003.
Levine, Lawrence W. *Black Culture and Black Consciousness: Afro-American Folk
    Thought from Slavery to Freedom.* New York: Oxford University Press, 1977.
———. *High Brow / Low Brow: The Emergence of Cultural Hierarchy in America.* Cam-
    bridge, Mass.: Harvard University Press, 1988.
Lewis, Earl. *In Their Own Interests: Race, Class, and Power in Twentieth-Century Norfolk,
    Virginia.* Berkeley: University of California Press, 1993.
Lhamon, W. T., Jr. *Raising Cain: Blackface Performance from Jim Crow to Hip Hop.* New
    York: Cambridge University Press, 1998.
Lipsitz, George. *How Racism Takes Place.* Philadelphia: Temple University Press, 2011.
Litwack, Leon T. *Been in the Storm Too Long.* New York: Random House, 1979.
———. *North of Slavery: The Negro in the Free States, 1790–1860.* Chicago: University of
    Chicago Press, 1961.
Loewen, James. *How Free Is Free? The Long Death of Jim Crow.* Cambridge, Mass.: Har-
    vard University Press, 2009.
Lofgren, Charles. *The Plessy Case: A Legal–Historical Interpretation.* New York: Oxford
    University Press, 1988.
Lopez, Ian Haney. *White by Law: The Legal Construction of Race.* Cambridge, Mass.:
    Harvard University Press, 2006.
Lorini, Alessandra. *Rituals of Race: American Public Culture and the Search for Racial
    Democracy.* Charlottesville: University of Virginia Press, 1999.
Lott, Eric. *Love and Theft: Blackface, Minstrelsy, and the American Working Class.* New
    York: Oxford University Press, 1993.
Manning, Chandra. *What This Cruel War Was Over: Soldiers, Slavery, and the Civil War*
    (New York: Vintage, 2007.
Marchand, Roland. *Advertising the American Dream: Making Way for Modernity,
    1920–1940.* Berkeley: University of California Press, 1985.
Martin, Scott C., ed. *Cultural Change and the Market Revolution in America, 1789–1860.*
    Lanham, Md.: Rowman & Littlefield, 2005.
Masur, Kate. *An Example for All the Land: Emancipation and the Struggle over Equality in
    Washington, D.C.* Chapel Hill: University of North Carolina Press, 2010.
———. "'A Rare Phenomenon of Philological Vegetation': The Word 'Contraband' and
    the Meanings of Emancipation in the United States." *Journal of American History* 93,
    no. 4 (2007): 1050–84.

McCoy, Drew. *The Elusive Republic: Political Economy in Jeffersonian America*. Chapel Hill: University of North Carolina Press, 1980.

McGerr, Michael. *A Fierce Discontent: The Rise and Fall of the Progressive Movement in America*. New York: Oxford University Press, 2003.

McKee, Guian. *The Problem of Jobs: Liberalism, Race, and Deindustrialization in Philadelphia*. Chicago: University of Chicago Press, 2008.

Meier, August, and Elliot Rudwick. *Along the Color Line: Explorations in the Black Experience*. Urbana: University of Illinois Press, 1976.

———. "Negro Boycotts of Jim Crow Streetcars in Tennessee." *American Quarterly* 21 (Winter 1969): 755–63.

Melish, Joanne Pope. *Disowning Slavery: Gradual Emancipation and "Race" in New England, 1780–1860*. Ithaca, N.Y.: Cornell University Press, 1998.

Mihm, Stephen. *A Nation of Counterfeiters: Capitalists, Con Men, and the Making of the United States*. Cambridge, Mass.: Harvard University Press, 2007.

Mills, Charles W. *The Racial Contract*. Ithaca, N.Y.: Cornell University Press, 1997.

Mitchell, J. Paul, ed. *Federal Housing Policy and Programs: Past and Present*. New Brunswick, N.J.: Rutgers University Press, 1995.

Mitchell, Michelle. *Righteous Propagation: African Americans and the Politics of Racial Destiny after Reconstruction*. Chapel Hill: University of North Carolina Press, 2004.

Mitchell, Thomas W. "From Reconstruction to Deconstruction: Undermining Black Landownership, Political Independence, and Community through Partition Sales of Tenancies in Common." *Northwestern University Law Review* 95 (Winter 2001): 505–80.

Mjagkij, Nina. *Light in the Darkness: African Americans and the YMCA, 1852–1946*. Lexington: University Press of Kentucky, 1994.

Montgomery, David. *Beyond Equality: Labor and the Radical Republicans, 1862–1872*. New York: Vintage, 1967.

Muhammad, Khalil G. *The Condemnation of Blackness: Ideas about Race and Crime in the Making of Modern Urban America*. Cambridge, Mass.: Harvard University Press, 2010.

Mumford, Kevin. *Interzones: Black/White Sex Districts in Chicago and New York in the Early Twentieth Century*. New York: Columbia University Press, 1997.

Nadell, Martha Jane. *Enter the New Negroes: Images of Race in American Culture*. Cambridge, Mass.: Harvard University Press, 2004.

Nasaw, David. *Going Out: The Rise and Fall of Public Amusements*. Cambridge, Mass.: Harvard University Press, 1999.

Nash, Gary. *Forging Freedom; The Formation of Philadelphia's Black Community, 1720–1840*. Cambridge, Mass.: Harvard University Press, 1988.

Nathans, Heather S. *Slavery and Sentiment on the American Stage, 1787–1861*. New York: Cambridge University Press, 2009.

Neather, Andrew. "'Whiteness' and the Politics of Working-Class History." *Radical History Review* 61 (Winter 1995): 190–96.

Neely, Mark E., Jr. *The Boundaries of American Political Culture in the Civil War Era*. Chapel Hill: University of North Carolina Press, 2005.

Nelson, William E. *The Fourteenth Amendment: From Political Principle to Judicial Doc-trine*. Cambridge, Mass.: Harvard University Press, 1988.

Norman, Brian J. *Neo-segregation Narratives: Jim Crow in the Post–Civil Rights American Literature*. Athens: University of Georgia Press, 2010.

Novak, William. *The People's Welfare: Law and Regulation in Nineteenth-Century America*. Chapel Hill: University of North Carolina Press, 1996.

Ohmann, Richard. *Selling Culture: Magazines, Markets, and Class at the Turn of the Century*. London: Verso, 1999.

Ownby, Ted. *Subduing Satan: Religion, Recreation, and Manhood in the Rural South, 1865–1920*. Chapel Hill: University of North Carolina Press, 1990.

Parson, Don. "The Decline of Public Housing and the Politics of the Red Scare: The Sig-nificance of the Los Angeles Public Housing War." *Journal of Urban History* 33, no. 3 (2007): 400–417.

Pascoe, Peggy. "Miscegenation Law, Court Cases, and Ideologies of Race in Twentieth-Century America." *Journal of American History* 83, no. 1 (1996): 44–69.

Paulsson, Martin. *The Social Anxieties of Progressive Reform: Atlantic City, 1854–1920*. New York: New York University Press, 1994.

Peiss, Kathy. *Cheap Amusements: Working Women and Leisure in Turn-of-the-Century New York*. Philadelphia: Temple University Press, 1986.

Phillips, Kimberly. *Alabama North: African-American Migrants, Community, and Working-Class Activism in Cleveland*. Urbana: University of Illinois Press, 1999.

Philpot, Thomas Lee. *The Slum and the Ghetto: Neighborhood Deterioration and Middle-Class Reform, 1880–1930*. New York: Oxford University Press, 1978.

Pietilo, Antero. *Not In My Neighborhood: How Bigotry Shaped a Great American City*. Chicago: Ivan R. Dee, 2010.

Pike, Helen C. *Asbury Park's Glory Days: The Story of an American Resort*. New Bruns-wick, N.J.: Rutgers University Press, 2005.

Pivar, David J. *Purity Crusade: Sexual Morality and Social Control, 1868–1900*. Westport, Conn.: Greenwood Press, 1973.

Purnell, Brian. *Fighting Jim Crow in the County of Kings: The Congress of Racial Equality in Brooklyn*. Lexington: University Press of Kentucky, 2013.

Quigley, David. *The Second Founding: New York City, Reconstruction, and the Making of American Democracy*. New York: Hill & Wang, 2004.

Rabinowitz, Howard. *Race Relations in the Urban South, 1865–1890*. Athens: University of Georgia Press, 1978.

Rael, Patrick. *Black Identity and Black Protest in the Antebellum North*. Chapel Hill: Uni-versity of North Carolina Press, 2002.

Rael, Patrick, ed. *Pamphlets of Protest: An Anthology of Early African American Protest Literature, 1790–1869*. New York: Routledge, 2001.

Reed, Touré. *Not Alms but Opportunity: The Urban League and the Politics of Racial Uplift, 1910–1950*. Chapel Hill: University of North Carolina Press, 2008.

Reiss, Benjamin. *The Showman and the Slave: Race, Death, and Memory in Barnum's America*. Cambridge, Mass.: Harvard University Press, 2010.

Reiss, Steven. *Touching Base: Professional Baseball and American Culture in the Progres-sive Era*. 1983. Reprint, Urbana: University of Illinois Press, 1999.

Rhodes, Chip. "Writing Up the New Negro: The Constitution of Consumer Desire in the Twenties." *Journal of American Studies* 28, no. 2 (1994): 191–207.

Richardson, Heather Cox. *The Death of Reconstruction: Race, Labor, and Politics in the Post–Civil War North, 1865–1901*. Cambridge, Mass.: Harvard University Press, 2001.

———. *The Greatest Nation of the Earth: Republican Economic Policies during the Civil War*. Cambridge, Mass.: Harvard University Press, 1997.

Rodrigue, John C. *Reconstruction in the Cane Fields: From Slavery to Free Labor in Louisiana's Sugar Parishes, 1862–1880*. Baton Rouge: Louisiana State University Press, 2000.

Roediger, David R. *The Wages of Whiteness: Race and the Making of the American Working Class*. New York: Verso, 1991.

Romano, Renee C., and Leigh Raiford, eds. *The Civil Rights Movement in American Memory*. Athens: University of Georgia Press, 2006.

Rooks, Noliwe. *Hair Raising: Beauty Culture and African American Women*. New Brunswick, N.J.: Rutgers University Press, 1996.

Rosenzweig, Roy. *Eight Hours for What We Will: Workers and Leisure in an Industrial City, 1870–1920*. Cambridge, Mass.: Harvard University Press, 1983.

Rosenzweig, Roy, and Elizabeth Blackmar. *The Park and Its People: A History of Central Park*. Ithaca, N.Y.: Cornell University Press, 1992.

Rothman, Hal. *Devil's Bargain: Tourism in the Twentieth-Century American West*. Lawrence: University Press of Kansas, 2000.

Runcie, John. "'Hunting the Nigs' in Philadelphia: The Race Riot of August 1834." *Pennsylvania History* 29 (April 1972): 187–218.

Ryan, Mary P. *Civic Wars: Democracy and Public Life in the American City during the Nineteenth Century*. Berkeley: University of California Press, 1997.

Rymer, Russ. *American Beach: A Saga of Race, Wealth, and Memory*. New York: HarperCollins, 1998.

Sacks, Marcy S. "'To Show Who Was in Charge': Police Repression of New York City's Black Population at the Turn of the Twentieth Century." *Journal of Urban History* 31 (September 2005): 799–819.

Samson, Peter Edward. "The Emergence of a Consumer Interest in America, 1870–1930." PhD diss., University of Chicago, 1980.

Sandoval-Strauss, A. K. *Hotel: An American History*. New Haven, Conn.: Yale University Press, 2008.

———. "Travelers, Strangers, and Jim Crow: Law, Public Accommodations, and Civil Rights in America." *Law and History Review* 23, no. 1 (2005): 53–94.

Satter, Beryl. *Family Properties: How the Struggle over Race and Real Estate Transformed Chicago and Urban America*. New York: Metropolitan, 2009.

Savage, Kirk. *Standing Soldiers, Kneeling Slaves: Race, War, and Monument in Nineteenth-Century America*. Princeton, N.J.: Princeton University Press, 1997.

Saville, Julie. *The Work of Reconstruction: From Slave Labor to Wage Labor in South Carolina, 1860–1870*. New York: Cambridge University Press, 1994.

Saxton, Alexander. *The Rise and Fall of the White Republic: Class, Politics, and Mass Culture in Nineteenth-Century America*. New York: Verso, 1990.

Schudson, Michael. *Advertising, the Uneasy Persuasion: Its Dubious Impact on American Society*. New York: Basic, 1984.

Schwalm, Leslie A. *Emancipation's Diaspora: Race and Reconstruction in the Upper Mid-west*. Chapel Hill: University of North Carolina Press, 2009.

Scobey, David. Empire City: *The Making and Meaning of the New York City Landscape*. Philadelphia: Temple University Press, 2002.

Scott, James C. *Domination and the Arts of Resistance: Hidden Transcripts*. New Haven, Conn.: Yale University Press, 1992.

Scott, Rebecca J. "Public Rights, Social Equality, and the Conceptual Roots of the *Plessy* Challenge." *Michigan Law Review* 106, no. 777 (2008): 777–804.

Sears, John F. *Sacred Places: American Tourist Attractions in the Nineteenth Century*. New York: Oxford University Press, 1989.

Sellers, Charles. *The Market Revolution: Jacksonian America, 1815–1846*. New York: Oxford University Press, 1994.

Service, Gregory J. *Hotel-Motel Law: A Primer on Innkeeper Liability*. Springfield, Ill.: C. C. Thomas, 1983.

Shaffer, Marguerite S. *See America First: Tourism and National Identity, 1880–1940*. Washington, D.C.: Smithsonian Institution Press, 2001.

Shaw, Stephanie J. *What a Woman Ought to Be and to Do: Black Professional Women Workers during the Jim Crow Era*. Chicago: University of Chicago Press, 1995.

Sheets, Robin G., Stephen Nord, and John J. Phelps. *The Impact of Service Industries on Underemployment in Metropolitan Economies*. Lexington, Mass.: Lexington Books, 1987.

Silber, Nina. *The Romance of Reunion: Northerners and the South, 1865–1900*. Chapel Hill: University of North Carolina Press, 1997.

Silver, Christopher, and John V. Moeser. *The Separate City: Black Communities in the Urban South, 1940–1968*. Lexington: University Press of Kentucky, 1995.

Simon, Bryant T. *Boardwalk of Dreams: Atlantic City and the Fate of Urban America*. New York: Oxford University Press, 2004.

Skotnes, Andor. "'Buy Where You Can Work': Boycotting for Jobs in African American Biltmore, 1933–1944." *Journal of Social History* 27, no. 4 (1994): 735–62.

Slap, Andrew L. *The Doom of Reconstruction: The Liberal Republicans in the Civil War Era*. New York: Fordham University Press, 2006.

Smith, C. Fraser. *Here Lies Jim Crow: Civil Rights in Maryland*. Baltimore: Johns Hopkins University Press, 2008.

Smith, J. Douglas. *Managing White Supremacy: Race, Politics, and Citizenship in Jim Crow Virginia*. Chapel Hill: University of North Carolina Press, 2002.

Smith, Mark M. *How Race Is Made: Slavery, Segregation, and the Senses*. Chapel Hill: University of North Carolina Press, 2006.

Smith, Susan L. *Sick and Tired of Being Sick and Tired: Black Women's Health Activism in America, 1890–1950*. Philadelphia: University of Pennsylvania Press, 1995.

Sterngrass, John. *First Resorts: Pursuing Pleasure at Saratoga Springs, Newport, and Coney Island*. Baltimore: Johns Hopkins University Press, 2001.

Stevenson, Louise. *Victorian Homefront: American Thought and Culture, 1860–1880*. Ithaca, N.Y.: Cornell University Press, 1991.

Spear, Alan. *Black Chicago: The Making of a Negro Ghetto, 1880–1920*. Chicago: University of Chicago Press, 1967.

Sproat, John. *"The Best Men": Liberal Reformers in the Gilded Age*. New York: Oxford University Press, 1968.

Stanback, Thomas. *Understanding the Service Economy: Employment, Productivity, Location*. Baltimore: Johns Hopkins University Press, 1979.

Stanley, Amy Dru. *From Bondage to Contract: Wage Labor, Marriage, and the Market in the Age of Slave Emancipation*. New York: Cambridge University Press, 1998.

Stewart, James Brewer. "The Emergence of Racial Modernity and the Rise of the White North, 1790–1840." *Journal of the Early Republic* 18 (Spring 1998): 181–217.

Stokes, Mason. *The Color of Sex: Whiteness, Heterosexuality, and the Fictions of White Supremacy*. Durham, N.C.: Duke University Press, 2001.

Sugrue, Thomas. *The Origins of the Urban Crisis: Race and Inequality in Postwar Detroit*. Princeton, N.J.: Princeton University Press, 1996.

——. *Sweet Land of Liberty: The Forgotten Struggle for Civil Rights in the North*. New York: Random House, 2008.

Sullivan, Shannon, and Nancy Tuana, eds. *Race and Epistemologies of Ignorance*. Albany: State University of New York Press, 2007.

Szasz, Andrew. *Shopping Our Way to Safety: How We Changed from Protecting the Environment to Protecting Ourselves*. Minneapolis: University of Minnesota Press, 2007.

Sze, Julie. *Noxious New York: The Racial Politics of Urban Health and Environmental Justice*. Cambridge, Mass.: MIT Press, 2007.

Thompson, Heather Ann. *Whose Detroit? Politics, Labor, and Race in a Modern City*. Ithaca, N.Y.: Cornell University Press, 2001.

Toll, Robert C. *Blacking Up: The Minstrel Show in Nineteenth-Century America*. New York: Oxford University Press, 1974.

Trachtenberg, Alan. *The Incorporation of America: Culture and Society in the Gilded Age*. New York: Hill & Wang, 1982.

Tucker, David. *Mugwumps: Public Moralists of the Gilded Age*. Columbia: University of Missouri Press, 1995.

Tucker, William H. *The Science and Politics of Racial Research*. Urbana: University of Illinois Press, 1994.

Van Deburg, William L. *Hoodlums: Black Villains and Social Bandits in American Life*. Chicago: University of Chicago Press, 2004.

Von Hoffman, Alexander. "A Study in Contradictions: The Origins and Legacy of the Housing Act of 1949." *Housing Policy Debate* 11, no. 2 (2000): 299–326.

Walker, Francis A. "The Colored Race in the United States." *Forum* 11 (September 1891): 501–9.

Walker, Juliet E. K. *The History of Black Business in America: Capitalism, Race, Entrepreneurship*. New York: Twayne, 1988.

Walker, Lewis, and Benjamin C. Wilson. *Black Eden: The Idlewild Community*. East Lansing: Michigan State University Press, 2002.

Walton, John. *Histories of Tourism: Representation, Identity, and Conflict*. New York: Multilingual Matters, 2005.

Waters, Hazel. *Racism on the Victorian Stage: Representations of Slavery and the Black Character*. New York: Cambridge University Press, 2007.

Weare, Walter B. *Black Business in the New South: A Social History of the North Carolina Mutual Life Insurance Company*. Urbana: University of Illinois Press, 1973.

Weems, Robert, Jr. *Desegregating the Dollar: African American Consumerism in the Twentieth Century*. New York: New York University Press, 1998.

Weise, Andrew. *Places of Their Own: African American Suburbanization in the Twentieth Century*. Chicago: University of Chicago Press, 2004.

Weiss, Sheila Faith. *Race Hygiene and National Efficiency: The Eugenics of Wilhelm Schallmayer*. Berkeley: University of California Press, 1987.

Weiss, Thomas. "Tourism in America before World War II." *Journal of Economic History* 64, no. 2 (2004): 289–327.

Welke, Barbara. *Law and the Borders of Belonging in the Long Nineteenth Century United States*. New York: Cambridge University Press, 2010.

———. "When All the Women Were White, and All the Blacks Were Men: Gender, Class, Race, and the Road to *Plessy*, 1855–1914." *Law and History Review* 13, no. 2 (1995): 261–316.

Wertheim, Arthur. *Vaudeville Wars: How the Keith-Albee and Orpheum Circuits Controlled the Big-Time and Its Performers*. New York: Palgrave, 2009.

Weyeneth, Robert R. "The Architecture of Racial Segregation: The Challenges of Preserving the Problematic Past." *Public Historian* 27, no. 4 (2005): 11–44.

Wiebe, Robert. *The Search for Order, 1877–1920*. New York: Hill & Wang, 1966.

Wiese, Andrew. *Places of Their Own: African American Suburbanization in the Twentieth Century*. Chicago: University of Chicago Press, 2004.

Wilentz, Sean. *Chants Democratic: New York City and the Rise of the American Working Class, 1788–1850*. New York: Oxford University Press, 1984.

Wilson, Harold F. *The Jersey Shore: A Social and Economic History of the Counties of Atlantic, Cape May, Monmouth, and Ocean*. New York: Lewis Historical Publishing Co., 1953.

———. *The Story of the Jersey Shore*. Princeton, N.J.: D. Van Nostrand, 1964.

Wilson, Kirt H. *The Reconstruction Desegregation Debate: The Politics of Equality and the Rhetoric of Place, 1870–1875*. East Lansing: Michigan State University Press, 2002.

Wilson, William Julius. *When Work Disappears: The World of the New Urban Poor*. New York: Knopf, 1996.

Wiltse, Jeff. *Contested Waters: A Social History of Swimming Pools in America*. Chapel Hill: University of North Carolina Press, 2007.

Wolcott, Victoria W. *Race, Riots, and Rollercoasters: The Struggle over Segregated Recreation in America*. Philadelphia: University of Pennsylvania Press, 2012.

———. *Remaking Respectability: African American Women in Interwar Detroit*. Chapel Hill: University of North Carolina Press, 2001.

Wolff, Daniel. *4th of July, Asbury Park: A History of the Promised Land*. New York: Bloomsbury, 2005.

Woodward, C. Vann. *The Strange Career of Jim Crow*. New York: Oxford University Press, 1955.

Wright, Marion Thompson. "Extending Civil Rights in New Jersey through the Division against Discrimination." *Journal of Negro History* 38, no. 1 (1953).

Zipp, Samuel. *Manhattan Projects: The Rise and Fall of Urban Renewal in Cold War New York*. New York: Oxford University Press, 2010.

Index

advice literature, 25, 28, 58, 60, 62, 76;
cultural laws, 31, 42, 50, 59, 72, 81, 129;
Progressive era moral reformers, 98,
102–3, 106
African Methodist Episcopal Church, 40,
51, 81
Albion Hotel, 53, 87
Altman, Joseph, 121
amusement venues: in the Antebellum
North, 19–20, 28; in Asbury Park,
22–23, 29, 31, 38, 121, 124; in Atlantic
City, 25–26, 85–86, 101, 103–5, 121, 123;
in Cape May, 16–17; in Gloucester City,
32, 45; in Lakeside Park, 32; in Philadelphia, 19–20; in Red Bank, 49 . *See also*
black-owned facilities; consumption;
service economy
annexation, 109–19, 121, 128
antebellum resorts, 1, 6, 16–17, 23, 46
Apex Hair and News Company, 94–97
Asbury Park: black community life in
the West End, 27, 121; black workers'
challenging segregation in, 38, 41–42,
44, 47–50, 52–54, 110–11, 115–16, 118,
123–24; James Bradley's attempts to
regulate consumption in, 23–24, 29;
James Bradley's attempt to segregate
black northerners in, 36–37, 56, 58–59,
69; early history, 18, 22–23; racial violence in, 38; white tourists' initial calls
for segregation in, 31–32
Asbury Park Black Progressive Party, 124
Atkins, Charles, 117–18
Atlantic City: black community in the
Northside, 85–87, 89–91, 93–97, 101, 105,
121–22, 126; black tourists in, 60–61, 79;
black workers in, 27, 29–30, 34; black

workers' challenging segregation in, 45,
50, 52–53, 60, 88; early history, 23–26;
on local Democratic officials, 105–8;
on local Republican rule, 105–8; white
business owners defend segregation
in, 63–64, 69–70; white tourists call for
segregation in, 13, 35, 63
Atlantic City Board of Trade, 129
Atlantic City Chamber of Commerce, 122
Atlantic City Progressive Club, 108

Baker, John A., 22
Baltimore, Maryland, 27, 124
beauty culture, 94, 96. *See also* Apex Hair
and News Company; Washington, Sara
Spencer
Berry, William A., 115
Bishop, William, 25
Bishop's Law, 103
black-owned facilities: amusement venues,
85, 121–22; bathhouse, 85–86; beauty
school, 94–97; hotels, 89–92; staffing
agency, 93; vice raids on, 101, 103–5. *See
also* Apex Hair and News Company;
Club Harlem; Fitzgerald, B. G.; Maggie
Ridley; Walls, George; Washington,
Sara Spencer; Young Women's Christian Association
black workers: in Atlantic City, 45–50;
black elite's critiques of, 77–78, 80–83;
calls for a free consumer society, 7–8,
39, 51–54; consumer protests in Asbury
Park, 38, 43, 45, 48–49; labor strike, 88;
in Red Bank, 49; seasonal living conditions, 92–94, 110–11; violent clashes
with white tourists, 38; "wade-ins,"
48–49

Hans L. Trefousse, *Impeachment of a President: Andrew Johnson, the Blacks, and Reconstruction.*

Richard Paul Fuke, *Imperfect Equality: African Americans and the Confines of White Ideology in Post-Emancipation Maryland.*

Ruth Currie-McDaniel, *Carpetbagger of Conscience: A Biography of John Emory Bryant.*

Paul A. Cimbala and Randall M. Miller, eds., *The Freedmen's Bureau and Reconstruction: Reconsiderations.*

Herman Belz, *A New Birth of Freedom: The Republican Party and Freedmen's Rights, 1861 to 1866.*

Robert Michael Goldman, *"A Free Ballot and a Fair Count": The Department of Justice and the Enforcement of Voting Rights in the South, 1877–1893.*

Ruth Douglas Currie, ed., *Emma Spaulding Bryant: Civil War Bride, Carpetbagger's Wife, Ardent Feminist—Letters, 1860–1900.*

Robert Francis Engs, *Freedom's First Generation: Black Hampton, Virginia, 1861–1890.*

Robert F. Kaczorowski, *The Politics of Judicial Interpretation: The Federal Courts, Department of Justice, and Civil Rights, 1866–1876.*

John Syrett, *The Civil War Confiscation Acts: Failing to Reconstruct the South.*

Michael Les Benedict, *Preserving the Constitution: Essays on Politics and the Constitution in the Reconstruction Era.*

Andrew L. Slap, *The Doom of Reconstruction: The Liberal Republicans in the Civil War Era.*

Edmund L. Drago, *Confederate Phoenix: Rebel Children and Their Families in South Carolina.*

Mary Farmer-Kaiser, *Freedwomen and the Freedmen's Bureau: Race, Gender, and Public Policy in the Age of Emancipation.*

Paul A. Cimbala and Randall Miller, eds., *The Great Task Remaining Before Us: Reconstruction as America's Continuing Civil War.*

John A. Casey Jr., *New Men: Reconstructing the Image of the Veteran in Late-Nineteenth-Century American Literature and Culture.*

Hilary Green, *Educational Reconstruction: African American Schools in the Urban South, 1865–1890.*

Christopher B. Bean, *Too Great a Burden to Bear: The Struggle and Failure of the Freedmen's Bureau in Texas.*

David E. Goldberg, *The Retreats of Reconstruction: Race, Leisure, and the Politics of Segregation at the New Jersey Shore, 1865–1920.*